Developing a Better Health Care System for Children

HARVARD CHILD HEALTH PROJECT

VOLUME III

This is the third volume of a three-volume series. Under the direction of David S. Mundel, Associate Professor of Public Policy at Harvard University, a team of researchers studied the current state of children's health care under a grant to the Harvard Graduate School of Education by the Robert Wood Johnson Foundation. In volume I, *Toward a Primary Medical Care System Responsive to Children's Needs*, the Harvard Child Health Project Task Force summarizes the project's findings and conclusions. Both this volume and volume II, *Children's Medical Care Needs and Treatments*, contain the background reports of the project researchers, from which the summary was derived. All three volumes are published by Ballinger.

Developing a Better Health Care System for Children

Report of the Harvard Child Health Project Task Force

Ballinger Publishing Company • **Cambridge, Massachusetts**
A Subsidiary of J.B. Lippincott Company

This book is printed on recycled paper.

International Standard Book Number: 0-88410-509-1

Library of Congress Catalog Card Number: 77-3367

Printed in the United States of America

Library of Congress Cataloging in Publication Data
Harvard Child Health Project.
    Developing a better health care system for children.

    (Its Harvard Child Health Project ; v. 3)
    1. Child health services—United States. 2. Medical policy—United
States. I. Title. [DNLM: 1. Child health services—United States.
2. Child care. 3. Primary health care—In infancy and childhood.
WA320 H339h]
RJ102.H37a   vol. 3   362.7'8'0973s   [362.7'8'0973]
ISBN 0-88410-509-1   77-3367

Contents

List of Figures   ix

List of Tables   xi

List of Advisory Committee   xv

Part I   Delivery of Primary Care for Children   1

Chapter 1
Issues of Organization and Financing
of Delivery Systems
—William Capron   3

Financing Health Care for Children   4
Organization of Children's Health Care Services   5
The Rights and Special Needs of Children   7

Chapter 2
Policy for Primary Medical Care for Children:
A Framework of Basic Choices
—David S. Mundel   9

Summary   21

Part II   Issues in the System of Health Care for Children   25

Chapter 3
Current Structure of the Health Care Delivery
System for Children
—John A. Butler and *Elaine D. Baxter*   27

Children's Health Care Utilization   27
Regular Sources of Care   40
Summary   49

Chapter 4
Determinants of Utilization of Children's
Health Services
—Diane L. Beauchesne and *David S. Mundel*   55

Final Outcomes—Improved Health and Satisfaction   56
Immediate Outcomes   57
Independent Variables   61
Resulting Directions of Policy Change   72

Chapter 5
Providing Primary Care Practitioners
for Children
—Judy Baumann and *David Calkins, M.D.*   77

Who Delivers Care?   78
How Many Physicians are Enough?   85
What Alternatives Exist for Increasing the Supply?   86
What are the Effects of PNP Utilization?   88
How Can We Encourage Utilization of PNPs?   91
Summary   95

Chapter 6
Financing Children's Health Care
—John A. Butler   99

Private and Public Child Health Expenditures   99
The Medicaid Experience   104
Prepayment and Children's Care: Research Findings   117
The "Children's HMO"   130

Chapter 7
Children and National Health Insurance
—*Theodore R. Marmor*   135

National Health Insurance and American Politics   135
What Would National Health Insurance Mean for Children?   153
Organizational Issues   172
Programs for Children through NHI   176
Discussion   185

Part III   *Influencing Decisionmaking in the Health Sector*   191

Chapter 8
Children's Advocacy and Primary Health Care
—*Richard F. Tompkins*   193

Children's Health Status   194
Characteristics of the Health Sector   195
The Advocate: Tactics and Organization   202
Issues for Children's Advocates   211
Fostering Children's Advocacy in the Health Sector   220

Chapter 9
Allocation of Child Medical Care
Decisionmaking Authority
—*Robert Bennett*   231

Decisionmaking Authority: Legal Elements   232
The State as Decisionmaker   238
Decisionmaking Authority Reconsidered: An Interest
    Analysis   244
A Prescription for the Law of Child Medical Care
    Decisionmaking   256

List of Figures

4–1   Utilization Rates vs. Family Income for Children Under Fourteen from 1964 to 1969   59

4–2   Travel Time to Physicians by Income for Children Under Fourteen   64

4–3   Waiting Time in Office of Clinic by Income for Children Under Fourteen   67

5–1   Active Physicians per 100,000 Population, 1931 and 1973, Primary and Nonprimary Care Providers   80

5–2   Active Physicians (MD and DO) per 100,000 Population by Geographic Region: 1973   83

7–1   Decline in Acute Illness with Advancing Age   154

List of Tables

2-1   A Policy Framework for Primary Medical Care for
       Children   22
3-1   Indicators of Health Care Utilization for Children
       Under Six Years of Age, by Family Income: 1972   28
3-2   Indicators of Health Care Utilization for Children Six
       through Sixteen Years of Age, by Family Income:
       1972   28
3-3   Indicators of Health Care Utilization for Children
       Under Six Years of Age, by Type of Place of Residence:
       1972   29
3-4   Indicators of Health Care Utilization for Children Six
       through Sixteen Years of Age, by Type of Place of
       Residence: 1972   29
3-5   Physician Visits per Capita by Age and Family Income
       Group, Fiscal Years 1964, 1967, and Calendar Years
       1969, 1971   30
3-6   Estimated Annual Visits to Private and Public Ambula-
       tory Services, Early 1970s   32
3-7   Active Registered Nurses Reporting Pediatrics as Area
       of Clinical Practice by Field of Employment vs. Active
       Physicians Reporting Pediatrics as their Primary
       Specialty by Base of Practice   35
3-8   Sources of Regular Medical Care for Children by Age,
       Family Income, and Other Characteristics: 1970   42
3-9   Source of Regular Medical Care by Age, Family
       Income, and Residence: 1970   43

3-10 CHAS/NORC 1970 Survey of Health Care Utilization and Expenditures Access Factors by Source of Care: Children Under Fifteen 45

4-1 Symptoms-Response Ratio by Poverty Level, by Race, by Age 62

5-1 Full Time Equivalent Child Health Physician Data, 1973 82

5-2 Primary Care Residency Programs and Number of Full Time Equivalent Child Health Physicians in Training: 1974 82

5-3 Comparison of Cost of Three Alternative Strategies to Increase Number of Full Time Equivalent Child Health Physicians 88

6-1 Percent Distribution of Persons Under Seventeen Years of Age by Intervals of Total Annual Out-of-Pocket Expense (Including Insurance Premiums), Average Expense for Persons with Expense, and per Capita Expense by Family Income: United States: 1970 101

6-2 Mean Expenditure for All Personal Health Services per Person by Source of Payment, by Age, by Family Income, by Residence: 1970 102

6-3 Percentage Increases in Nonfree Expenditures for Selected Age Groups: 1953 to 1963 and 1963 to 1970, Adjusted for Inflation 104

6-4 Estimated Personal Health Care Expenditures Under Public Programs, by Program and Source of Funds, for Children Under Nineteen and All Ages: 1975 105

6-5 Medicaid Rates for High-Risk, Medium-Risk, and Low-Risk States 108

6-6 Medicaid Payments for All Medical Services per Recipient, by Race, Age, Region, and Residence, 1969 110

6-7 Percent of Expenditures for All Personal Health Services Paid by Medicaid or Free Care among Low-Income Families, by Age Group: 1970 111

6-8 Percent Physician Visits to Selected Kinds of Physicians, by Income: 1969 114

6-9 Annual Utilization Rates per Member for the Four Plans 124

6-10 Annual Out-of-Plan Utilization by HIP Medicaid Enrollees at Fee-for-Service Providers: 1973 126

7-1 The Growth of Personal Health Care Expenditures by Source of Payment 140

7−2   Federal Outlays per Medicaid Recipient in Constant
        Dollars, Fiscal Years 1968−1974   141
7−3   AMA "Medicredit" Plan (Fulton-Broyhill-Hartke
        Bill)   143
7−4   Long-Ribicoff-Wagonner, Catastrophic Protection   145
7−5   Kennedy-Corman Bill   146
7−6   Comprehensive Health Insurance Plan (CHIP): Ford
        Administration Proposal   148
7−7   Kennedy-Mills Bill   150
7−8   Total Expenditures for Health Services as a Percentage
        of the Gross National Product, Seven Countries,
        Selected Periods, 1961−69   152
7−9   U.S. Hospital Discharges by Age Group, 1972   157
7−10   CHIP Bill: Selected Benefit Provisions   158
7−11   Kennedy-Mills Bill: Selected Benefit Provisions   159
7−12   Kennedy-Corman Bill: Selected Benefit Provisions   160
7−13   Redistributive Effects of Medicare Measured by
        Average Annual Visits to a Physician by Income
        Group Before and After Medicare, 1969−72   161
7−14   Allocation of Costs by Age Group, Province of
        Quebec, 1971−73   162
7−15   Long-Ribicoff Bill, Medical Assistance Plan: Selected
        Benefit Provisions   163
7−16   Long-Ribicoff Bill, Catastrophic Plan: Selected Benefit
        Provisions   164
7−17   1970 Family Expenditure for Medical Care by Family
        Income   166
7−18   Kennedy-Corman Bill: Coverage of Preventive Services   167
7−19   Long-Ribicoff Bill: Coverage of Preventive Services   168
7−20   Comprehensive Health Insurance for Preschoolers and
        Pregnant Women   178
7−21   Tax Credits Under the Marmor Plan and Tax Savings
        Under Current Personal Income Tax Medical
        Deductions   181

Harvard Child Health Project
Advisory Committee

William M. Capron

Associate Dean
John F. Kennedy School of Government
Harvard University
Cambridge, Massachusetts

Robert J. Blendon

Vice President
The Robert Wood Johnson Foundation
Princeton, New Jersey

Marian Wright Edelman

Children's Defense Fund
Cambridge, Massachusetts

Peter Edelman

Director
New York State Division for Use
Albany, New York

Leon Eisenberg, M.D.

Maude and Lillian Presley Professor; and
Chairman of the Executive Committee of
the Department of Psychiatry
Harvard Medical School
and
Senior Associate in Psychiatry
Children's Hospital Medical Center
Boston, Massachusetts

Howard Hiatt, M.D.

Dean
Harvard School of Public Health
Cambridge, Massachusetts

Gilbert Steiner

The Brookings Institution
Washington, D.C.

Homer Wadsworth

The Cleveland Foundation
Greater Cleveland Associated Foundation
Cleveland, Ohio

Kerr White, M.D.

School of Hygiene and Public Health
Johns Hopkins University
Baltimore, Maryland

Paul N. Ylvisaker

Dean
Harvard Graduate School of Education
Cambridge, Massachusetts

✻ *Part I*

Delivery of Primary
Care for Children

Chapter 1

Issues of Organization and Financing of Delivery Systems

William Capron

For years issues involving health care have been very high on the agenda of public and political discussion. Particularly since the adoption of Medicare and Medicaid in the mid-1960s, policymakers have continuously debated how and to what extent the federal government should organize and fund a system to defray the costs of health care for all Americans.

Despite all the attention paid by political leaders, the media, and the public to health-related issues, relatively little attention has been focused on children's health needs. When these needs are considered, one of the most striking observations is the difference in the health care needs of children and adults. Briefly, children are sick a lot, but their sicknesses are overwhelmingly of short duration and self-curing. They catch colds and have upset tummies, but they tend to recover fast. Preventive care practices, particularly immunizations, are especially important for children; good health care in childhood, it is believed, will lead to healthy adulthood.

Of course, there are serious diseases that affect a small number of children, and a growing number of children with chronic or handicapping conditions require management. Further, accidents among children resulting in serious fractures and other complications require attention. In the past, however, when children's health needs have been addressed, the emphasis has been on the serious and crippling illnesses. One example is the March of Dimes, which since the 1930s has called attention to one of the most serious illnesses striking children: infantile paralysis. This focus on the dramatic health needs of children is in line with society's attention to the serious health problems of adults, such as cancer or heart transplants. In this volume, however, we focus on the *primary* health care needs of children, that first-contact, comprehensive, and continuing medical care which serves as the point of entry into the health care system for the individual.

It is worth emphasizing that sensible consideration of ways to improve the primary care delivery system for children requires one to examine simultaneously both financing mechanisms and organizational issues. The interaction between financing and organization, at least in some alternative designs, is so strong that one cannot sensibly consider one without paying attention to the other. The recent introduction of nurse practitioners and other types of physician's assistants to the health team has given rise to a current example of such interaction. In Chapter 5, Judy Baumann and David Calkins point out that physician-extenders can significantly increase the productivity of the children's physician. They warn, however, that unless current restrictions on third-party reimbursement for services performed by physician-extenders are relaxed, the economic incentive for physicians to hire them will be small, and their potential usefulness will not be achieved.

FINANCING HEALTH CARE
FOR CHILDREN

At one extreme, one can argue that the federal government should leave any organizational modifications to the states, localities, and the private sector, confining its own role to improving access—or at least the potential of access—via the provision of a form of national health insurance designed to do away with financial barriers to health care. From this view, the most glaring defect in the health care system is that children from poorer families face a major financial barrier to adequate primary care. When the various national health insurance proposals now before Congress are examined, however, it appears that few of them will have an impact on reducing the financial barriers to children's primary health care. All the plans are designed primarily to mitigate the disastrous financial effects of long hospitalization and expensive treatments.

As Theodore Marmor indicates (Chapter 7), some specific modifications in presently considered national health insurance proposals might go a long way toward improving the availability of reasonably adequate primary care for children. For example, a national insurance program might provide for children's primary care with no cost-sharing up to some limit (a capitation grant for each child of $100 to $200), together with catastrophic coverage for serious, long-term ailments suffered by children. This might be combined with the proposals widely associated with the name of Professor Martin Feldstein which involve cost-sharing for adults with free care (up to a limit) for all children, or alternatively with a sliding scale based on family income. A proposition along these lines is supported by the argument that the most important function of primary care for children is preventive and that families in the lower-income and middle-income brackets need this kind of positive encouragement to seek such care for their youngsters. It is even argued that effective primary care for children can actually reduce the average lifetime medical costs the individual would incur. Early detection and treatment of some ailments that begin in childhood may forestall the development of much more serious conditions which can develop as children grow into adulthood.

Another proposal that presumably would be more acceptable and easier to adopt than certain of the above possibilities is to "federalize" the existing Medicaid program. This would make it possible to bring the kind and level of services currently supported across the nation up to the level of those few states that currently have the most comprehensive and generous provisions.

ORGANIZATION OF CHILDREN'S HEALTH CARE SERVICES

Today we have no one system to meet children's health needs. Rather, we find a whole set of largely uncoordinated "subsystems" and marked variations in who is served by these subsystems. Our fragmented health care delivery system is described by Elaine Baxter and John Butler (Chapter 3). As suggested earlier, the best quality care appears to be available to those children whose families can afford the regular services of a private pediatrician. Poor children living in the central city, on the other hand, get much of their care in hospital emergency rooms and outpatient clinics. Some preventive health needs of large numbers of children are met through school health departments and state and municipal public health departments.

In spite of the differences in the health care needs of children and adults, there are strong arguments, in my view, against any attempt to develop a "children only" health subsystem. A dual system, one for children and one for adults, would lead to significant inefficiencies in the use and management of our health resources. Beyond the strict efficiency considerations, persuasive arguments point to recognizing the *family* as the primary unit when addressing questions of health care organization and financing. For example, Diane Beauchesne and David Mundel report that whether or not children receive preventive care is related to whether their mothers receive care (Chapter 4). With this caveat in mind, it is useful to think about the characteristics of an effective system of health care focused on children, since this will help us identify the components of a comprehensive health care system that must be included if children are to be well served.

Because it is questionable whether most forms of health insurance currently under consideration would do much, if anything, to improve the provision of primary care for children, some argue that such programs need to be supplemented by federally mandated categorical programs, especially for those living in geographic areas with a scarcity of health practitioners.

Another option is to sharply increase the flow of funds into the existing primary care infrastructure. Thus, one could imagine a substantial allocation of federal funds to school health programs and health departments in order to expand the capacity of these delivery units to attend to children's primary care needs. Serious doubts are naturally raised about relying on these existing institutions in a major way, because of the major inadequacies that most knowledgeable observers find in the programs presently operated by these institutions. To be sure, it seems worth while for the federal government to make a serious effort, almost certainly involving some additional funding, to encourage the redirection and restrengthening of these existing institutions; but because of the wide variation in the capacity of existing subsystems of this sort among the various states and localities, a strong federal role will be required if any significant improvement is to be expected.

A basic question underlying the specific route the federal government takes to improve children's health care in the United States is the extent to which federal dollars can be directed to improve the interaction of existing systems at the local level. Our present system of health care delivery is fragmented, which has serious negative consequences in the areas of problem recognition and follow-up. Experience in other program areas in which the federal government has attempted, via the provision of funds, to improve coordination at the state and local level does not make one very sanguine that we can expect from such an attempt. It is partly because of skepticism regarding the efficacy of this approach that some argue strongly for direct federal involvement in the delivery of primary care to children via the development of specific categorical programs.

The health care cycle, from problem recognition through diagnosis, treatment and follow-up, seems well served by the type of care offered through Health Maintenance Organizations (e.g., Kaiser, Group Health) but thus far a small fraction of the total population has access to HMOs. Neighborhood Health Centers, demonstration projects initially supported by the Office of Economic Opportunity, now are supported at a sharply reduced level by the Department of Health, Education and Welfare. The impact of national health insurance and other financing schemes on the development of more HMOs and NHCs needs to be studied.

THE RIGHTS AND SPECIAL NEEDS OF CHILDREN

Children, of course, cannot vote and are limited in their ability to articulate their needs. This limitation decreases as the age of the child increases. Two chapters in this volume look at the issue of children's rights and interests of children. Robert Bennett (Chapter 9) looks at the legal problems inherent in medical care decisionmaking with a view toward the interests involved: the child, the parents, the medical practitioner and the state. Richard Tompkins (Chapter 8), on the other hand, looks at the inability of children to articulate their own interests in the political arena and describes some areas where children's advocates, acting for children, can be effective in directing the attention of policymakers to children's health care needs.

The principal theme developed in this volume is straightforward: at the national level we are moving ahead to reaching some significant and far-reaching decisions under the general rubric of "national health insurance." We must recognize that decisions in this vital policy area will vitally affect the manner and effectiveness with which we meet legitimate child health care needs in the United States. In 1980, those under fourteen will represent 25 percent of our population. The health needs of this significant part of our population must be carefully weighed as we examine alternative comprehensive measures to better serve the total health requirements of the American people.

Children have a legitimate interest in seeing improvement in the way their health needs are met. Moreover, society as a whole has an interest in improving the health status of all its children, rich and poor. Healthy children are more likely to grow into healthy adults, and consequently to make fewer demands as adults on the health care system. If we want to improve the total health care picture, can we afford to ignore our children's needs?

Chapter 2

Policy for Primary Medical Care for Children: A Framework of Basic Choices

David S. Mundel[a]

All too often policy for children is made without careful consideration of its effect. Many reasons exist for this flaw in the policy process. First, children are relatively uninvolved in decisionmaking in both public and private arenas; thus, the potential beneficiaries—or victims—of alternative actions cannot vocalize their needs.[b] Second, children, like apple pie and motherhood, are often viewed as mythological "goods" within the American society; the desirability of actions taken in their behalf is seldom questioned.[c] Third, in spite of the quantity of research conducted on children's programs, little is known about the effects of policy or programmatic alternatives. Consequently, policy processes and inputs—for instance, staff:child ratios in day-care settings—are often treated as goals rather than as means for achieving ends (Lajoie et al., 1975).

The debates regarding policy for primary medical care for children suffer from these same failures and omissions. The Harvard Child Health Project, conducted at the Graduate School of Education under the support of the Robert Wood Johnson Foundation, was an

[a] An earlier version of the paper was prepared for the Sun Valley Health Forum, Sun Valley, Idaho—August 1975.

[b] The noninvolvement of children in politics is discussed in D.S. Mundel, "Some more thoughts on the direction of children's policy," in N.B. Talbot, M.D. (ed.), *Raising Children in Modern America*, 1976. Child Advocacy groups may be an important articulator of children's needs and their role is discussed in R. Tompkins, "Children's Advocacy and Primary Health Care," this volume.

[c] Some recent studies have begun to question whether, in fact, America is a child-loving society.

effort to ameliorate the effect of these deficits. The basic approach of the project was to review existing research reports and summarize their findings within a framework that would stress both policy implications and the remaining need for policy-relevant knowledge.

The basic concerns of policymaking are choices: choices among goals, choices among alternative instruments to achieve them, and choices among alternative commitments of resources. The choices involved in developing policy for primary medical care for children can be summarized within a framework of six basic questions:

1. Should society increase the utilization of primary medical care by children instead of using resources for other services, such as, education, or for other levels of the medical care system?
2. Should the society use limited resources for primary medical care for children as opposed to using these resources for the care of other population groups, for instance, the elderly?
3. Should society devote its attention and resources for primary medical care differentially among groups of children?
4. Which modes and systems of care should be used in delivering primary medical care to children?
5. Which treatments should be provided within children's primary medical care?
6. What kind of a financing system—modes and sources of support— should be utilized to provide resources and incentives within the system delivering primary medical care for children?

The answers to these questions are obviously interrelated. Questions 1 and 2 cannot be answered without answers to 3, 4, 5, and 6, both with respect to primary medical care for children and the provision of other services for children and adults. Consequently, we took as our task the development of answers to the questions that relate specifically to primary medical care for children—3 through 6. Our findings thus provide implications for policy change *within* this narrowly defined sector. They do not, however, provide implications for the allocation of social support and attention between children and other population segments or between primary medical care and other services for children.

Should Society Devote Its Attention and Resources for Primary Medical Care Differentially Among Groups of Children? Several factors affect the answer to this question. First, are there groups of children with more need for medical services than other groups? Second, are there groups of children who are receiving fewer medical services than they apparently need? Third, are there groups of children who would utilize additional medical services in response to either a decrease in cost or increase in availability that would result from an expansion of government support? Fourth, are there politically legitimate ways to discriminate among groups of children that will not decrease the over-all effectiveness of the medical delivery system to the extent that the benefits resulting from discrimination (i.e., targeting of resources) are outweighed by the induced losses or costs?

Although the evidence on the efficacy of medical care in either preventing or curing health problems is limited, the clearest indicator of need for care is poor health. This does not mean that all conditions of poor health indicate a need for medical care, but simply that on average individuals with poor health need more medical care than those with better health. In general, children do not suffer from severe disabling conditions, although they are often ill with relatively minor conditions. The fraction reported to be in "fair or poor health" is low.

Children from disadvantaged backgrounds—lower-income (under $5000) and father-absent families—are between three and four times more likely to have limitations in their activity due to chronic conditions than children from more advantaged families. Data on restricted activity days, days of confinement to bed, and missed school days show somewhat similar patterns of unequal health status. These factors are a less clear signal of need for medical care, because their incidence may depend on medical care utilization and medical advice rather than simply on poor health. Other data derived from medical screening and diagnostic tests show that lower-income children have poorer health status than children from higher-income families (Chapter 3).

There are two ways of determining whether or not there are groups of children receiving less medical care than they need. First, we can compare the frequencies with which different kinds of children utilize care. This approach implicitly assumes that one group's (presumably the highest users) utilization rate provides a norm toward which policy should seek to move the rates of all groups. Second, we can compare the utilization pattern of population segments with the rates that medical professionals estimate to be appropriate for their reported symptoms. This approach implicitly assumes the accuracy of the reported symptoms and the practitioner-estimated needs for care.

Comparisons of utilization rates show that children from lower-status families see physicians and dentists and utilize hospitals less frequently than children from more advantaged families. Approximately 80 percent of younger children (ages 0−6) from lower-income families visited a physician during 1972 while over 90 percent of younger children from higher-income families did. The comparable utilization rates of six-to-sixteen-year-olds were 53 and 72 percent, respectively (Chapter 4).

Another index of utilization rates is the average number of physician visits per year. Throughout the 1960s, children from families in the lower quarter of the income distribution had three or fewer physician visits per year, on average, while the average for those in the top quarter was more than four visits per year (Chapter 4).

Studies of medical care utilization in response to health status show similar patterns of inequality among groups of children. Lower-income and minority group children are not brought to medical attention as early as other children with similar symptoms; consequently, they arrive for care with more severe conditions than children from higher-income and majority families. This same research has shown that children as a whole are extensive overutilizers of care in that they are more frequently brought to medical attention than they need to be, as assessed by medical personnel (Taylor et al., 1974). Reanalysis of this data shows that lower-income children, especially nonwhites, use care much less frequently in response to symptoms. These groups may actually be underutilizers in that they use medical care less often than their symptoms would appear to necessitate.

The third factor in assessing whether or not public resources should be unevenly distributed is the responsiveness of different population groups to changes in medical care prices or availabilities. If subsidy-induced price reductions do not result in utilization increases, the net effect of government assistance is simply an income supplement to current medical care users. Although evidence on the impact of price reductions on the utilization of primary health care by children is limited, the price of care—especially in relation to income—appears to be a salient aspect of utilization for some segments of the population. The increases in utilization by the poor when Medicaid reduced or eliminated the prices they faced demonstrate that cost of care is a barrier to utilization (Davis, 1975). This barrier may still exist for those whose annual health care costs consume a disproportionate amount of their income or who remained uncovered by Medicaid programs in certain states.

Although the price of care has a relatively small impact on aggregate levels of health service use, its impact on use by the low-income population is substantial. After the introduction of national health insurance in Canada, the proportion of nonusers of medical services in different income groups became more equal over time. However, the use of physical examinations, the basic service of primary care, became only slightly more equal (Beck, 1973). In the United States, utilization rates have become more equal across income categories following the introduction of Medicare and Medicaid, but the trend toward equality of utilization rates has been slower for children than for adults (Bice et al., 1972). Aday (1971) and Cauffman (1967) report that the removal of out-of-pocket expenses by insurance coverage resulted in increased utilization by children. Aday found that when such costs were removed, poor children equaled or exceeded high-income children in utilization. Consequently, it is evident that price subsidies affect use of health services by poor children. The effect on children's utilization may be substantially less than on adult utilization rates.

The fourth issue that influences an assessment of the desirability of a system with uneven resource distributions is its political feasibility and legitimacy and technical performance. Programs that provide assistance to families and individuals on the basis of low income or need receive substantial support from federal and state governments. Among the more sizable programs are Aid to Families with Dependent Children (AFDC), Medicaid, Public Assistance, and Food Stamps. Although these programs are not without critics and detractors, it is clearly a mistake to assume that the criticism they receive indicates that other income-related or need-conditioned programs would not receive substantial support. On the other hand, programs that support individuals on the basis of their race are clearly thought illegitimate and those that condition support on the basis of urban residence do not appear to receive high levels of support.

Thus, both the technical efficiency criteria and political assessments point toward a children's primary health care policy in which government resources are provided disproportionately for the care of children from lower-income families.

In response to this suggestion many advocates observe that "programs for poor people inevitably become poor programs." This inevitability should, however, be in doubt. First, policies that provide resources disproportionately for children from lower-income families do *not* have to provide resources solely for those from low-income families. A sliding scale of subsidies designed to provide support, although in lesser amounts, to moderate and below-middle-income families could spread the orientation of the policy. It would, however, also spread available resources more thinly. Second, a policy that provides resources disproportionately to lower-income children does not have to restrict their utilization of care to sites used solely by subsidized consumers. The lessons derivable from comparisons of the performance of the food stamp and the public housing programs should be familiar to the designers of primary health care policy. In the food stamp program the food purchase site is not restricted to subsidized individuals; in public housing programs the subsidies are restricted to particular housing units. In general, policies that provide resources disproportionately to disadvantaged population groups should encourage utilization in sites with heterogenous clientele and should allow consumer choice among potential suppliers.

Which Modes and Systems of Care Should be Used in Delivering Primary Medical Care to Children? As with the question of the distribution of public resources among different groups of children, the choice of an appropriate primary care delivery system depends on several factors. Chief among these are: cost, efficacy and effectiveness, and the impact of the delivery system on utilization.

The principal costs of primary—as opposed to secondary and tertiary—medical care are personnel costs. Similarly, the principal constraint on the expansion of the supply of primary medical care is the availability of personnel. For example, the delivery units in which physician-extenders such as pediatric nurse practitioners (PNPs) work in combination with or under the supervision of physicians have been found to be the least costly modes of delivering primary health care. In an analysis of the shortages of children's primary care practitioners, Baumann and Calkins report that an increased role for physician-extenders would be the least expensive strategy for increasing the supply of primary medical care services. The quality of services should be as important a criterion in the choice among delivery modes as cost. The effectiveness of physicians and physician-extenders in delivering primary care appears equal in most studies of test performance, patient records, and patient-reported satisfaction (Chapter 5). Bernick found that most screening tests could be done effectively by nonphysicians (Bernick, "Issues in Pediatric Screening," volume II).

The second major component of primary care cost is the cost of the technological devices found in many sites, especially large-scale delivery units such as those in some outpatient clinics of hospitals. In general, most primary care involves little technical assistance, although a clear exception is the availability or accessibility of diagnostic laboratory services. Thus, the presence of high-technology devices and their required support and operating staffs within a primary care site contributes more to cost than performance. Thus, both cost and quality factors point toward the desirability of a primary medical care system that makes extensive use of nonphysician medical personnel and limited use of technological apparatus.

The issues of efficacy and effectiveness relate to the delivery system's capacity and orientation for the nontechnical components of primary care and provision of the full range of activities involved in primary care. Most studies that have sought to compare the technical efficacy of alternative delivery modes have found little, if any, differences among the modes (Weber, 1975).

Comparisons of the nontechnical components of primary care—those that relate to the "caring function" (Haggerty, 1975)—have, however, found some differences. Brooks (1973) found patient satisfaction (or dissatisfaction) equal at large centralized clinics and small neighborhood clinics. However, the grounds for reported satisfaction were different. Satisfaction in the large clinics was a function of their medical services, while dissatisfaction was a function of bureaucratic complexities. The role of the factors was reversed for small sites.

Okada et al. (1971) report a modest patient preference for private over public sources of care. Olendzki et al. (1972) studied the care-seeking patterns of Medicaid recipients in New York City. This study found that although some patients who continued to receive their care from a comprehensive hospital clinic expressed a preference for private care, others felt the best care and more qualified doctors were available in the hospital clinics. Consumer preferences for private care may be based on attitudes towards the nonmedical aspects of health care provision which current private practice arrangements appear to satisfy more fully than public practice arrangements. Consumer satisfaction with children's primary care arrangements is probably more affected by these nonmedical or caring aspects of the delivery unit than the medical or technical curing aspects.

The comprehensiveness of a primary care site relates to its capacity to provide the range of services involved in primary care and to actively connect the patient successfully with other levels of medical care if their efforts become necessary. Comprehensiveness of a primary care site does *not* relate either to its capacity to deliver all types of services or to its proximity to institutions that can. Primary medical care includes recognition, diagnosis, treatment, compliance, and follow-up. The appropriate delivery system and its constituent modes should provide or encourage this full range of services (Starfield, "Health Needs of Children," volume II). There is little empirical evidence of the relative degrees of comprehensiveness achievable by different delivery modes or within different delivery systems.

The effect of primary care delivery modes and systems on utilization is equally difficult to specify. If consumer satisfaction is a contribution to increased utilization and if the "caring function" rather than the technical nature of medical services is a determinant of consumer satisfaction with primary care, then the existence of smaller, less bureaucratically oriented, and lower technology sites should expand utilization. Although no hard empirical evidence exists to support these contentions, some observers' reports seem to support the validity of this argument.[d]

Another factor by which the delivery system affects utilization is distance between patient and provider (Chapter 4). A delivery system made up of smaller units can be located, on average, closer to potential health care consumers. The magnitude of effect of distance on primary care utilization is uncertain. Studies of the effects of distance on utilization suggest the need to locate children's primary care facilities closer to their potential users than adult care facilities are placed to their users. A good, thorough study of the role distance plays in children's health care utilization is needed. Nevertheless, given the existing evidence and the desirability of decentralizing children's primary care to small, nonhospital-based sites delivering low-technology care, a policy that increased the proximity of delivery units to children appears appropriate.

Which Treatments Should be Provided Within Children's Primary Medical Care? A major assumption within most analyses and policy debates regarding medical care is that such care is effective in preventing or ameliorating the effects of poor health. As a result of this assumption, policies that expand and equalize the utilization of care are viewed favorably. In most instances this assumption is left implicit and unexamined. Thus, little effort is devoted toward choosing which services delivery units should provide and which services public financing should support and encourage.

Several factors should be considered in making these choices:

1. What are the incidence/prevalence rates of particular health conditions among children?
2. What are the consequences of these conditions?
3. What are the consequences of *not* administering medical or clinical procedures to children with these poor health conditions?
4. What is the variety of medical/clinical procedures that can be administered to children with poor health conditions?
5. What are the effects of these alternative procedures?

[d]This view is expressed by Dr. Phil Porter, who runs the Cambridge, Mass., PNP-based health delivery program.

6. What are the costs of these different procedures?
7. What are the effects of using different personnel to perform similar procedures?
8. What are the ranges of procedure quality that would result in actual, as opposed to experimental, delivery units?

The general finding resulting from our review of the literature on medical treatments is that the efficacy and effectiveness of primary care processes have been largely unexamined. Our review was limited to a subset of all conditions and thus should not be taken as providing the final word on the validity of this assumption. Starfield found that of the five processes involved in primary care—recognition, diagnosis, treatment, compliance, and follow-up—diagnosis, compliance and follow-up were rarely investigated in clinical studies that did investigate these parts of the primary care process; diagnosis and follow-up were found to be the weaker links of therapy.

Studies that compare, or examine, the efficacy and effectiveness of particular procedures are even more inconclusive. Starfield found that although extensive research had been devoted to examining the effect of different treatments of measured iron-deficiency anemia, little had been devoted to examining the effect of iron deficiencies on poor health. Without this information the importance of the condition in determining poor health and the resulting desirability of targeting resources or delivery units toward reducing anemia cannot be assessed. The review of the literature on otitis media resulted in somewhat opposite findings, but they still leave the primary care system designer in some quandary. Although repeated ear infections result in substantial hearing loss and poor hearing is strongly associated with poor school performance, little research has been devoted to examining the effectiveness of alternative therapies in reducing the harmful effects of ear infections. Wennberg and Kimm's review of hospital procedures indicated that although for many conditions ambulatory and hospital services appear interchangeable, there is little research on the comparative efficacy and effectiveness of treatments delivered in different settings (Wennberg and Kimm, "Common Uses of Hospitals: A Look at Vermont," volume II).

Our reviews of the literature on screening instruments and programs and on learning disabilities (primarily reading problems) were even more inconclusive and disturbing. Bernick found that most screening activities had not been evaluated in either clinical or field trials. Although the criteria for choice among screening services appear to be straightforward—cost, accuracy, etc.—little evidence exists on the actual performance of screening tests (Bernick, "Issues in Pediatric Screening," volume II). The area of learning disabilities is one in which primary medical care professionals are becoming increasingly interested and involved. Some observers have seen it as the next major growth area in the medical sector. Regrettably, little information exists on the efficacy or effectiveness of screening, diagnostic, and treatment procedures within this area of "new morbidity" (Longfellow and Freeman, "Reading Disability," volume II).

In summary, a review of the research relating to the efficacy and effectiveness of medical therapy does not provide one with much of an answer to the question "Which treatments should be provided within children's primary medical care?" This inconclusiveness does not mean that care should not be provided until better information exists, because primary care may well provide important medical and psychological benefits to patients and their families. It does mean, however, that we should design flexibility into any financing or delivery system in order that it may adjust the supply and utilization of services in response to new information. We should also seek to expand the follow-up functions of primary care delivery units in order that they may produce information of value to themselves and others on the effects of their services (Starfield, "Health Needs of Children," volume II). The final policy direction resulting from this research review is that more research with respect to efficacy and effectiveness of screening, diagnostic, and treatment procedures is needed, not merely research into where and to whom health care is delivered.

What Kind of Financing System—Modes and Sources of Support— Should be Utilized to Provide Resources and Incentives Within the System Delivering Primary Medical Care for Children? The choice of an appropriate and effective financing system for children's primary medical care depends on several factors. Appropriateness and effectiveness are a function of the design or character of the financing system and the flows or resources and incentives which that system creates. Much of the debate surrounding the choice of a medical care financing system has implicitly presumed that insurance schemes, capitation grants, and fee-for-service systems are inherently desirable or undesirable. In fact, their desirability should be assessed on the basis of whether or not they would allow careful targeting of resources; whether or not they would help to stimulate the development of an effective delivery system; and whether or not they would encourage the delivery of the kinds of care that are medically effective. The impact of a financing system on role of individuals (including children), institutions, professionals, and government agencies in defining the character of the primary care sector should also be considered.

If the desired distribution of resources is uneven among families on the basis of income, it seems most appropriate to choose a financing system that allows carefully targeted and discriminatory subsidization and which minimizes the simple replacement of private sources of support with public resources. A financing system that provides resources to the consumer side as opposed to the institutional side of the marketplace could probably be more finely targeted. A system of support for consumers would also be more likely to stimulate utilization in sites serving heterogeneous populations as opposed to utilization in more segregated facilities. This would avoid further development of a class-based system of medical care or at least would minimize the government's further inducement of such a system.

It is of course possible to design a supplier-oriented financing scheme that would provide differential subsidies to institutions on the basis of the populations they serve. One way would be to provide grants based on the economic characteristics of a delivery unit's catchment area, but this would tend to encourage segregated utilization. A subsidization scheme based on economic characteristics would also ignore the fact that individuals in a particular neighborhood may consume primary care at several different sites. A second method for providing subsidies to suppliers on the basis of the economic characteristics of their consumers is to require suppliers to maintain records of user characteristics; subsidies would then be based on the number of people served in particular income classes. Alternatively, the society could reimburse suppliers for services delivered to particular consumers based on the consumers' incomes. The flow of subsidies among the population groups and supply units resulting from these last two could be made similar to the flow resulting from a consumer-oriented targeting scheme. Consequently, the choice between carefully targeted consumer and supplier subsidization schemes should be based on the incentives for utilization and appropriate supply which they would create and upon the technical costs and likely abuses resulting from the operations of the alternative systems. There does not appear to be empirical evidence on which these assessments can be based, and the development of such evidence should be an important focus of further research and experimentation.[e]

The second major purpose of the financing system should be the encouragement of development of an effective delivery system. As

[e] One such experiment is already underway with the federally supported National Health Insurance experiment conducted by the RAND Corporation.

noted previously, the most appropriate delivery system for children's primary medical care is one with small, dispersed, low-technology delivery units that make extensive use of physician extenders. Three parts of the financing structure can contribute to this encouragement. First, the reimbursement scheme should allow for the payment of nonphysician medical personnel. The reimbursement rate for services should be a function of the least-cost method of delivery as opposed to either a function of physician charges or the costs of particular care-providers. Cost reimbursement schemes that are not constrained will neither encourage the utilization of low-cost modes nor create incentives for suppliers to deliver care in the most efficient manner.

The second way in which the financing structure creates incentives for delivery system change is related to the complexity of the process of reimbursement and payment. Financing structures that require extensive proposal writing efforts or that have long delays between service provision and reimbursement create needs for large overhead units which can only be supported by large delivery units—e.g., hospitals. Larger delivery units also have more extensive access to loan funds (including internal borrowing) which enable them to maintain cash flows during periods of repayment delay.

The third mechanism by which the financing mechanism can stimulate development of an appropriate delivery system is by providing resources for provider development. Loan funds and grants may be effective in stimulating the development of small delivery units and expanding the supply of physician-extenders. The need for and efficacy of these capacity-development incentives remains largely unexamined.

The financing structure also affects the kinds of treatments delivered within the delivery system. Because of the absence of research comparing the efficacy and effectiveness of alternative treatments, there is little evidence on which to base a system of allowable and unallowable charges. There does, however, appear to be a necessity to increase the financing and thus the provision of problem recognition, diagnostic, and follow-up procedures within children's primary health care. Although it is not now possible to decide on the inclusion or exclusion of certain services from reimbursement, the financing structure should be designed so that as information on therapy efficacy and effectiveness comes into being, services can be either encouraged or discouraged by changes in reimbursable or billable services.

The fourth role of the financing structure is to create a system of control within the primary medical care process. If we wish to increase the role of individuals, both parents and children, in the process of deciding on care utilization, we should increase their direct influence over the flow of resources and reimbursements (Chapter 9). If, on the other hand, we wish to create incentives for aggregate cost control and therefore strengthen the role of the government in the flow of resources, a financing system or structure that provides resources directly from government units to suppliers and includes explicit cost or budget constraints would be more effective (Chapter 7). Alternatively, we could provide resources directly to supplying institutions and allow those groups of professionals and institutions that dominate the medical care sector to control the allocation of funds and the distribution of services.

On balance, the most appropriate financing structure for the stimulus of an improved children's primary medical care system appears to be one in which a major share of the resources are controlled directly by potential consumers. The use of the resources should be monitored and restricted by government regulations that encourage the use of least-cost strategies of care. To some extent the government should probably support the development both of new small and low-cost delivery units and new nonphysician delivery personnel.

SUMMARY

Answers to four of the six questions that form a framework for developing policy for primary medical care for children are summarized in Table 2–1.

Table 2–1. overleaf. . .

Table 2–1. A Policy Framework for Primary Medical Care for Children

Question	Direction of Policy Guidance	Adequacy of Research Evidence
Should society devote its attention and resources for primary medical care differentially among groups of children?	Government support should be provided disproportionately to children from low- and moderate-income families.	On the whole, the research evidence is adequate, but better information on the impact of alternative policies on utilization is needed.
Which modes and systems of care should be used in delivering primary medical care to children?	Small dispersed delivery units that utilize nonphysician care providers should be encouraged.	Capacity of these units to deliver comprehensive range of primary care services needs to be assessed.
Which treatments should be provided within children's primary medical care?	The delivery and financing systems should be flexible enough to adjust to new information on the efficacy and effectiveness of therapies.	Evidence on the efficacy and effectiveness of a wide range of primary medical care services is virtually nonexistent.
What kind of financing system should be utilized to provide resources and incentives within the system delivering primary medical care for children?	Least cost vs. physician cost should be the standard for reimbursement. New delivery units and nonphysician care providers may require financial assistance to develop.	The incentive effects of targeted consumer and supplier subsidies should be evaluated.

REFERENCES

·Aday, L.A. *Dimensions of Family's Social Status and Their Relationships to Children's Utilization of Health Services*, unpublished. Baltimore, M.D.: Johns Hopkins University Department of Medical Care and Hospitals, 1971.

Aday, L.A. *The Utilization of Health Services: Indices and Correlates, A Research Bibliography 1972*. DHEW Pub. No. (HSM) 73–3003. Washington, D.C.: National Center for Health Services Research and Development, 1972.

Beck, R.G. "Economic class and access to physician services under public medical care insurance," *Intl J Health Serv* 3 (1973): 341–55.

Brooks, C.H. "Associations among distance, patient satisfaction and utilization of two types of inner-city clinics," *Med Care* 11 (1973): 201.

Cauffman, J.G., et al. "The impact of health insurance coverage on health care of school children," *Pub Health Rep* 82 (1967): 323–28.

Davis, K. "A decade of policy developments in providing health care for low-income families," (draft for *A Decade of Federal Anti-Poverty Policy: Achievements, Failures and Lessons*, edited by R. Haveman. Madison: University of Wisconsin Institute for Research on Poverty, 1977), xerox, 1975.

Haggerty, R.J., et al. *Child Health and the Community*. New York: John Wiley and Sons, Inc., 1975.

Lajoie, S.N., et al. *A Study of Research and Development Needs for the Making of Social Policy Toward Young Children: Executive Summary*, unpublished. Cambridge, Mass.: Harvard University, 1975.

National Center for Health Statistics. *Statistical Data Prepared for the Child Health Task Force*, unpublished. Washington, D.C.: NCHS, 1974.

Okada, L., et al. *Differential Patterns of Poverty and Health Care Utilization in Eight Urban Areas*. Paper presented at the Meeting of the American Association for Public Opinion Research, Pasadena, California, 22 May 1971.

Olendzki, M., et al. "The impact of medicaid on private care for the poor," *Med Care* 10 (1972): 201–06.

Taylor, D.G., et al. "A social indicator of access to medical care," *J Health and Soc Behav* 16 (1975): 38.

U.S. Department of Health, Education and Welfare, National Center for Health Statistics. *Volume of Physician Visits by Place of Visit and Type of Service, United States—July 1963–June 1964*. Public Health Service Pub. No. 1000, Series 10, No. 18. Washington, D.C.: Government Printing Office, 1965.

U.S. Department of Health, Education and Welfare, National Center for Health Statistics. *Volume of Physician Visits, United States—July 1966–June 1967*. Public Health Service Pub. No. 1000, Series 10, No. 49. Washington, D.C.: Government Printing Office, 1968.

U.S. Department of Health, Education and Welfare, National Center for Health Statistics. *Physician Visits, Volume and Interval Since Last Visit, United States—1969*. DHEW Pub. No. (HSM) 72–1064, Vital and Health Statistics Series 10, No. 75. Washington, D.C.: Government Printing Office, 1972a.

U.S. Department of Health, Education and Welfare. *Preliminary Findings of the First Health and Nutrition Examination Survey, 1971–72*. Washington, D.C.: PHS, HRA, 1972b.

Weber, G.T. *An Evaluation of an Expanded Public Role in the Financing of Health Care Services for Children*, unpublished draft. San Francisco: University of California, 1975.

Weiss, J.E., and Greenlick, M.R. "Determinants of medical care utilization: the effect of social class and distance on contacts with the medical care system," *Med Care* 8 (1970): 456—62.

✳ *Part II*

Issues in the System of Health Care for Children

Chapter 3

Current Structure of the Health Care Delivery System for Children

John A. Butler
Elaine D. Baxter

This chapter describes patterns of medical care use among children, with special emphasis on where children receive primary care and who provides it. We first examine volume of ambulatory care visits and the characteristics of different sources of care, including their number and location. Second, we review data on factors affecting children's patterns of utilization and the likelihood that a child will have a regular source of care.

CHILDREN'S HEALTH CARE UTILIZATION

On the average, American children under seventeen visit a physician somewhat more than four times each year (NCHS, 1975). Averages for subgroups vary greatly, however, according to age, family income, race, and place of residence. Andersen et al. (1972) report that in the aggregate, children under six visit a doctor almost twice as often as children six to seventeen. Children from affluent white families have almost twice the physician visits of children who are poor and nonwhite. Roughly the same gap exists between children from large SMSAs and children from the rural South (Davis, 1975).

A somewhat different, although highly correlated, indicator of variation among child subgroups is the percent of children with one or more physician visits each year. Tables 3–1 and 3–2 show this indicator for doctor and dentist visits, by family income.

For the most part, differences based on the age of the child can be attributed to a higher level of prescribed preventive care and somewhat higher level of morbidity for younger children. For dental visits,

Table 3–1. Indicators of Health Care Utilization for Children Under Six Years of Age, by Family Income: 1972

| | | Family Income | | | |
| | | | $5000 — 9999 | $10,000 — 14,999 | |
Indicators	Total	Under $5000			$15,000 or More
Children under six: Total (000s)	20,733[a]	3,953	7,172	5,687	2,925
Indicators of Health Services Received:					
Percent with one or more doctor visits	86.3	79.9	85.9	89.2	91.3
Percent with one or more dentist visits	17.5	9.5	13.8	22.3	29.9

[a]Includes children with family income unknown.

Source: Tables 3–1 through 3–4 have been prepared from data presented in "Current Estimates from the Health Interview Survey, United States 1974," DHEW Publication Number (HRA) 76–1527, September 1975.

Table 3–2. Indicators of Health Care Utilization for Children Six through Sixteen Years of Age, by Family Income: 1972

| | | Family Income | | | |
| | | | $5,000 — 9,999 | $10,000 — 14,999 | |
Indicators	Total	Under $5000			$15,000 or More
Children six to sixteen: Total (000s)	44,132[a]	6,518	12,446	12,590	9,857
Indicators of Health Services Received:					
Percent with one or more doctor visits	63.7	52.8	60.0	66.9	72.3
Percent with one or more dentist visits	60.8	37.9	52.5	66.9	79.2

[a]Includes children with family income unknown.

age differences reflect the fact that parents usually seek little restorative work for their children until the children have their permanent teeth. Income-related differences are harder to justify. Affluent children are more likely to experience a doctor visit each year, and far more likely to see a dentist. This pattern persists for both the younger and older age groups. Disparities also can be seen according to

Table 3–3. **Indicators of Health Care Utilization for Children Under Six Years of Age, by Type of Place of Residence: 1972**

		SMSA[a]		*Non-SMSA*[a]	
			Outside		
		Central	*Central*		
Indicators	*Total*	*City*	*City*	*Nonfarm*	*Farm*
Children Under Six Years of Age: Total (000's)	20,733	5,778	7,360	6,917	678
Indicators of Health Services Received:					
Percent with one or more doctor visits	86.3	87.6	88.8	83.2	79.2
Percent with one or more dentist visits	17.5	16.1	21.0	14.8	19.1

Place of Residence

[a] Standard Metropolitan Statistical Area.
Source: National Center for Health Statistics/Health Interview Survey.

Table 3–4. **Indicators of Health Care Utilization for Children Six through Sixteen Years of Age, by Type of Place of Residence: 1972**

		SMSA[a]		*Non-SMSA*[a]	
			Outside		
		Central	*Central*		
Indicators	*Total*	*City*	*City*	*Nonfarm*	*Farm*
Children Six to Sixteen Years of Age (Total (000's)	44,132	11,023	16,694	14,488	1,928
Indicators of Health Services Received:					
Percent with one or more doctor visits	63.7	63.8	67.2	61.0	52.4
Percent with one or more dentist visits	60.8	56.6	67.3	56.9	57.2

Place of Residence

[a] Standard Metropolitan Statistical Area.
Source: National Center for Health Statistics/Health Interview Survey.

place of residence (Tables 3–3 and 3–4). Children from central cities and those living outside SMSAs are less apt to visit a physician each year.

Despite continuing differences of use by children of various income groups and residential areas, trends in use over the past fifteen years show that this gap is not as great as it was before and during the 1960s. Income differences in utilization rates have been reduced somewhat, with greatest gains in visits among young central city children. Among children in the age group one to five, gains for poor children can be contrasted with the pattern for middle-income and high-income groups, who actually show reduced numbers of physician visits in 1970 as compared to 1963 (Andersen et al., 1972).

Table 3–5 presents trend data enabling comparisons of use rates among children of different income groups, adults of different income groups, and between children and adults. Increases in use among the poor of all ages presumably can be traced in large part to the effects of Medicaid, which has significantly reduced financial barriers for eligible families.

The data support two further generalizations. First, by 1971 poor

Table 3–5. Physician Visits per Capita by Age and Family Income Group, Fiscal Years 1964, 1967, and Calendar Years 1969, 1971

Age and Income Group	*1964*	*1967*	*1969*	*1971*
All Ages	4.5	4.3	4.3	5.0
low income	4.3	4.3	4.6	5.6
middle income	4.5	4.2	4.0	4.7
high income	5.1	4.6	4.3	4.9
ratio, high income to low income	1.2	1.1	0.9	0.9
Under Fifteen Years				
low income	2.7	2.8	2.8	4.0
middle income	2.8	3.9	3.6	4.1
high income	4.5	4.4	4.3	4.8
ratio, high to low income	1.7	1.6	1.5	1.2
Fifteen to Sixty-Four Years				
low income	4.4	4.6	4.8	5.8
middle income	4.7	4.1	4.1	4.9
high income	4.9	4.6	4.2	4.8
ratio, high to low income	1.1	1.0	0.9	0.8
Sixty-Four and Older				
low income	6.3	5.8	6.1	6.7
middle income	7.0	6.7	5.8	6.4
high income	7.3	6.5	7.5	7.5
ratio, high to low income	1.2	1.1	1.2	1.1

Source: Adapted from Andreopoulos, 1974, p. 163, and Davis, 1975.

children still used somewhat less care than their more advantaged peers. By 1971, on the other hand, poor adults were visiting physicians more than affluent adults; there had been a shift in use rates sufficient to reverse the earlier pattern of lower use for the poor. Unfortunately, we have no good baseline for equity comparisons between child use and adult use adjusted for need. But it is clear that equal levels of use, even among the same age groups, do not indicate equality of access. Some groups, notably the poor and nonwhite, are more likely to be sick than others. Andersen et al. (1972) argue that in order to demonstrate "equality" of use among rich and poor children, use for poor families may have to exceed that of higher-income groups to compensate for higher levels of illness and disability, more closely approximating current levels of use among poor and affluent adults.[a]

Second, even though in 1971 poor children were still lower users than affluent children, the utilization difference between poor and affluent children had been dramatically reduced in the previous two years, and during this two-year interval redistributive effects were more powerful for children than adults. Davis (1976) has pointed out that this disproportionate increase in use rates among children can be attributed to the great increase in numbers of AFDC-enrolled families, with more children than adults represented in such families. Children's use rates clearly are price sensitive, although it remains to be specified how price reductions affect children's patterns of use as compared to adult patterns.

Distribution of Use Across Provider Settings

A rough estimate of the distribution of use across modes of care is presented in Table 3–6, adapted from Roemer (1970). The table shows numbers of visits for the general population during the early 1970s to various types of ambulatory services, comparing volume of visits at different sites. It also shows estimates of the number and percent of services for children provided at each site. The table thus gives not only an idea of the over-all pattern of use, but the differences between patterns of use for the total population and for children. It must be remembered that public health clinic and school health visits are mostly for health supervision and preventive care.

[a]Preliminary analysis of data subsequent to 1971 suggests that trend lines for both adults and children have leveled off somewhat, and the gap between poor and nonpoor children is further reduced. But by 1975 poor children still showed lower use rates than more affluent children, and poor adults still showed higher use rates than other adults.

Table 3–6.   Estimated Annual Visits to Private and Public Ambulatory Services, Early 1970s

	Total Population		Children Under Fifteen		
Type of Service	Millions of Visits	Percent of Total	Millions of Visits	Percent of Total	Percent Omitting Schools and Public Health Clinics From Total
Private practice					
Solo	545	49.5	138.7	49.2	60.3
Group	185	16.8	44.5	15.8	19.3
	730	66.3	183.2	65.0	79.6
Hospital outpatient departments	200	18.2	32.9[a]	11.7	14.3
School and college health services	55	5.0	36.7	13.0	
Industrial health units	40	3.6			
Public health clinics	30	2.7	15.0	5.3	
Special government programs	25	2.3	8.9	3.2	3.9
Special voluntary agencies	20	1.8	5.0	1.8	2.2
Total	1100	99.9[b]	281.7	100.0	100.0

[a] Includes emergency room visits.
[b] Total of percentages is 99.9 because of rounding.
Source: Adapted from Roemer, 1975.

Two sets of percentages are therefore given, one including and one excluding these two modes of service delivery.[b]

Private Practice Arrangements. It is clear from Table 3—6 that for both children and adults, private medical practitioners are visited most often. In 1969, about 65 percent of all child visits were to physicians in private office-based practice. The total is close to 80 percent when we exclude health department and school visits from the total. Rosenbloom and Ongley (1974) report that for children up to fifteen years in 1971, contacts with office-based physicians were divided almost evenly among pediatricians and GPs, with a small proportion of care (about 5 percent) provided by osteopaths and others.

In 1973, there were approximately 11,600 pediatricians and 57,900 general and family practitioners in office-based practice. Recent data from the National Ambulatory Care Survey provide an estimate of the time these physician groups spend on children under fifteen (NACS, 1974). Office-based pediatricians spend about 94 percent of their time on children, general and family practitioners about 19 percent. This suggests that in full-time equivalencies there are 10,943 pediatricians and 9103 general and family practitioners in private, office-based children's practice.

The AAP (1970) reports that while in 1949 about 80 percent of private pediatricians were in solo practice and 17 percent in some form of group practice, by the late 1960s only 45 percent remained in solo practice, with 17 percent in two-person partnerships, 25 percent in single specialty groups, and 17 percent in multispecialty groups.

Most pediatric group practices have only three to five physicians. But there is currently a perceptible trend toward increased numbers of pediatricians in larger multispecialty practice. Such a trend is not surprising, given the new preference for practice arrangements in or close to large urban hospital complexes, medical schools, and suburban medical parks. Part of the incentive to join group practice arrangements comes from their convenience for those wishing to practice part time in office-based primary care and part time in the hospital setting.

The AAP survey also reported that about half the private practitioners had one or more diploma nurses working for them. The percentages were somewhat lower for solo practitioners (39 percent) than two-person partnerships (47 percent) or groups (60 percent).

[b] In commenting on an earlier draft of this paper, Miller (personal communication, February 1976) has noted that there are strong regional differences in the services provided by local health departments, with departments in the South Atlantic and Pacific states more likely than others to offer comprehensive ambulatory services.

Hospital Outpatient Departments and Emergency Rooms. There were close to 33 million outpatient department and emergency room visits per year among children in the past several years, indicating the magnitude of hospital use. This proportion has increased greatly — about 300 percent — from 1954 to 1973 (AHA, 1972). The trend is most pronounced for emergency room visits, which have increased to almost six times 1954 levels, and less pronounced for organized outpatient clinic visits, which nonetheless have increased to twice this 1954 level. Increases in utilization have at times been much greater for teaching hospitals and medical schools than community hospitals. Heagarty et al. (1970) report that "in the decade from 1957 to 1967, emergency clinic visits at the Children's Hospital Medical Center in Boston increased from 4500 per year to 50,000 per year" (p. 596).

The most frequent users of hospital outpatient services are poor children, minority children, and those living in the central cities. For the general child population, only 12.3 percent of outpatient visits were to hospital-based facilities. For the child population in central cities about 18 percent visited these sources, and among poor children in central cities, the percentage was as high as 36 percent (Wilson, 1974). Those who use the hospital tend to live close by. Weinerman (1965) reports that over half of all clinic visits to the Yale–New Haven ambulatory care clinics are made by patients from the relatively depressed central city area around the hospital.

Making the broad assumption that average length of a primary care visit in the hospital setting is roughly equivalent to those in private settings, and that nonphysician personnel are no more often seen by children in the hospital than in other care settings, we may estimate that nationally as many as 3600 full-time equivalent physicians are currently employed in hospital-based primary care for children.[c] This is equal to about 20 percent of the office-based physician supply. Because care in the hospital setting is provided by the part-time efforts of pediatricians, along with residents, interns, and specialists in non-child-related fields, children's primary care is increasingly the occasional activity of many physicians rather than the exclusive specialty of some.

Disproportionate numbers of pediatric nurses (almost two-thirds of the RNs) work in hospital settings. Among active registered nurses reporting pediatrics as an area of clinical practice, there are more than eight times as many nurses in hospitals as in doctors' offices (Table 3–7). Yankauer, Connelly and Feldman (1969) interpret this

---

[c]This estimate is rough. It is calculated as the ratio of private to hospital-based child health visits divided into the total of full-time equivalent children's primary care physicians in private practice.

Table 3–7. Active Registered Nurses Reporting Pediatrics as Area of Clinical Practice by Field of Employment vs. Active Physicians Reporting Pediatrics as their Primary Specialty by Base of Practice

Field of Employment or Base of Practice	Pediatrician	Pediatric Nurses	Nurse:Physician Ratio
Hospital	4,739	27,910	5:9
Doctor Office	10,089	3,481	0:3

Source: Yankauer et al., 1973. Reprinted with permission.

as a commentary on the history of the nursing profession, which has been identified with the institutional needs of hospitals. "Even if all the school nurses and all the public health nurses in the country are considered 'pediatric' nurses, the ratio is substantially lower than the hospital pediatric nurse:physician ratio" (p. 1114). It should be added, however, that not all pediatric nurses in hospital settings are providing primary care, nor is children's primary care in the hospital provided by pediatric nurses to the exclusion of other RNs.

Federally Initiated Demonstration Projects. Federally initiated demonstration projects in comprehensive care to the poor and near-poor are found for the most part in central cities, with some also located in rural areas of provider scarcity. Programs involving direct provision of services include the Neighborhood Health Centers launched by the Office of Economic Opportunity, the Title V Children and Youth projects (C and Y) and Maternity and Infant Care projects (MIC), Wallace, Goldstein, and Oglesby (1975) illustrate the limited impact of these demonstration programs to date by comparing the actual groups of children served by each with the potential target population represented by the number of children in the lowest 20 percent of the family income distribution. By this comparison, Neighborhood Health Centers include about 4 percent of potential target children, the C and Y projects about 4 percent, and the MIC projects about 7 percent of infants. The Headstart program, which contracts for medical services with local providers, serves about 50 percent of a much more circumscribed target group of four- and five-year-olds from poor families. There is substantial overlap between the child populations benefiting from all of these programs, further limiting their combined impact.

Children under fifteen total 37 percent of the Neighborhood Health Center registrant group, considerably more than their proportions in the general population (DHEW, 1974). Total numbers of children registered in the centers are about 471,500. Centers vary greatly in size and staffing patterns, but the median number of physicians per center is 6.5, with 1.8 midlevel practitioners, 8.0 nurses, and 4.5 others. If one-third of physician time is spent on children, and there are a total of 101 projects, we may estimate that there are a total of about 219 full-time equivalent children's physicians in the programs. If we further assume that one-third of the time of nurses and midlevel practitioners also is spent on children, and that there are about ten such health professionals per center (combining nurses with other midlevel practitioners), we estimate a total of 337 full-time equivalents. This is equivalent to only 1 percent of the total supply of pediatric nurses (Yankauer, 1973).

C and Y projects, a form of age-specific neighborhood health centers, offer comprehensive care to about half a million school-aged children. Along with complete medical services, some projects also dispense prescription drugs, give parent counseling, and provide supplemental food for child participants. Many of the projects also have an extensive dental care component. As with the OEO centers, size of the program varies widely, from a project with only 1000 children to one with 40,000. Median project size is 4500 registrants. Weckworth estimates that physicians in the projects total roughly 296 full-time MDs, 347 part-time MDs, and 124 unpaid part-time MDs. In addition, the projects employ over 500 nurses and over 60 nurse practitioners (Weckworth, personal communication, 1975).

MIC projects, with a client population of about 141,000 women, were originally initiated to combat infant mortality in high-risk areas, notably areas of urban poverty, and offer comprehensive medical, nutritional, and dental services to mothers, also using active outreach to draw eligible women into the program early in pregnancy. It is difficult to estimate full-time equivalent primary care physicians for children in this program because the hospital component of care is such a major factor. In one sense this is not a primary care program for children at all, but in another sense it may be the most important of primary care programs.

C and Y and MIC projects are for the most part concentrated in large urban areas, especially in the central cities of the fifty largest SMSAs. Davis and Carney (1975) point out that over 90 percent of the registrants of C and Y projects are in these large cities, with over 90 percent of program expenditures devoted to them and over three-quarters of the centers themselves in large cities.

Health Departments. Health department clinics show about four times the number of encounters with children that the federally sponsored demonstration projects show, and about half the total for visits to outpatient departments and emergency rooms. Even though health department visits are apt to be only for well-baby and well-child supervision, they clearly represent a major component of the care delivered to children. County and city health departments, because of their limited mandate, low budgets, and long history of questionable effectiveness, tend to be ignored in discussions of the organization of primary care services. It must be realized, however, that in the realm of preventive care and case recognition health department services are universally available and more capable of reaching children in some areas than any other type of primary care arrangement.

Myers et al. (1968) discovered in a national survey of health departments that about 82 percent of the departments provided well-child supervision through their own staff or facility, and almost all districts provided these services in some way. About 50 percent had physicians on their own staff, about 82 percent of the departments provided well-child supervision through their own staff or facility, and almost all districts provided these services in some way.

Palumbo et al. (1969), who sampled fourteen health departments of various sizes, computed a rough percentage estimate of the average hours of work divided by a "typical" department among various health programs. These researchers estimate that crippled children, school-aged child health, maternal health, and family planning involve a total of about 36 percent of total department time. Child health and school-aged child health alone account for an estimated 23 percent. Thus, a sizable proportion of total health department effort is spent on programs for mothers and children.

The Myers et al. survey also suggests, however, that per capita expenditures of the health departments are by and large minimal, with 60 percent of the districts in 1966 reporting outlays of less than 2 dollars per capita. There was a trend toward somewhat higher expenditures in the largest and smallest districts, probably as a reflection of matching Title V funds being channeled to central cities and rural areas.

Nationally, it can be estimated that health departments control at least 13 percent of the Neighborhood Health Centers, nearly 30 percent of the Children and Youth projects, and three-fourths of the Maternity and Infant Care projects. In a survey of the health officers in the twenty-five largest U.S. cities, over half indicated an interest in converting more facilities to comprehensive care units. But three principal barriers to conversion were cited: insufficient space, financial limitations, and personnel shortages. At the time of the survey, about one-third of the cities contacted had traditional preventive care programs with no comprehensive care facilities of any kind, and only four had made a major commitment to comprehensive care facilities.

Estimates of numbers of full-time equivalent children's physicians and other health personnel currently offering children's services in health departments are somewhat impressionistic. We know from Miller (1975) that the "average" department—a statistical entity—employs one full-time physician equivalent, about twelve nurses, and two or three outreach workers. If we assume that services for mothers and children occupy about one-third of the time of this group, based on figures offered by Palumbo et al. (1969), then the total number of full-time equivalent children's physicians in the nation's 2300 departments is on the order of 770. This is less than 5 percent of the total of children's physicians in office-based practice, but it is still not an insubstantial number. More impressive is the total for full-time equivalent nurses—9200—which is about a third as large as the total number of pediatric nurses cited by Yankauer (1973).

Schools. The number of school-based preventive care encounters, based on estimated numbers of students in schools with health personnel present, total over 36 million. School health encounters must be understood as a type of service qualitatively different from that offered in most other sites, but these numbers are nonetheless impressive. A large proportion of children get at least some component of preventive care from the school. As many as 80 percent of school systems offer some free medical services, and almost 90 percent of schools report a doctor or nurse available (National Center for Educational Statistics, 1968).

States usually express their interest in preventive medicine in part by legal guidelines for school entry and school health programs. Twenty-five states and the District of Columbia by law require some form of immunization as a prerequisite for school entry, and another quarter of the states delegate immunization authority to boards of education and health. Forty-two states allow for some kind of screening or examination of school children. Eleven of these states require only limited screening procedures, usually vision and hearing tests, but most of the rest require in addition a general physical examination at least once during elementary schooling. Services are either purchased directly by school authorities or contracted out to health departments.

The issue of who administers school health services is clarified somewhat by National Education Association (NEA) surveys of 1966 and 1971. These data suggest that school systems are more likely to control them. In the six-year interval between surveys there was a mild trend toward increased school system control and proportionately decreased health department control. This trend was most evident in smaller districts. Looking only at the 1971 statistics, we may assume that school administrators retain substantial or complete budgetary and administrative responsibility for school health services in almost half the school districts in the country. If we include those programs for which joint control was assigned with the health department, the total comes to more than 75 percent.

It is difficult to get a detailed picture of patterns of preventive care in schools. Just as with local health department programs, data collected in school-based programs are sparse and often not comparable from state to state and district to district. In many states physical exams still are the greatest expenditure item. In California, atypically but perhaps a precedent for the future, the budget is much more evenly allocated across diverse activities, many of them relating to psychosocial and emotional problems of school children, learning difficulties, and other quasi-medical concerns (Hazell et al., 1972). Total national expenditures for the school health programs in fiscal year 1974 were estimated to be as much as 320 million dollars.

School health efforts have been augmented by the expenditure of some proportion of ESEA Title I funds and Follow Through project funds on the health of low-income students. These funds have gone toward food programs, intensive screening, and follow-up.

How many physicians and nurses currently work in school programs? Among the nation's public primary and secondary schools, almost 90 percent report the availability of a physician. The National Center for Educational Statistics (1968) estimates that there are about 1400 full-time equivalent physicians working in the public elementary and secondary schools, or about 7 percent of all office-based full-time equivalent children's physicians. It is hard to know the overlap between this personnel pool and the health department pool.

Physicians were more than half again as likely to be available in schools located in SMSAs than in areas outside large metropolitan areas. Among the schools where physicians were available, about one-third responded that physicians were "resident in the school," presumably meaning that they were the employee of a single school; the remaining two-thirds responded that they were on demand to the school with some waiting time required for services. A low proportion of schools report the availability of dentists and dental hygienists, only 28 and 16 percent, respectively.

The ratio of physicians to nurses is lower in school than in most other primary care settings. Silver (1971) has reported that there are about 16,000 school nurses in the United States. The total for 1970–71 listed by the NCES is closer to 18,000, with the differences probably explained by part-time public health nurses. Either estimate is about half as large as the total of pediatric nurses working in private practice offices and hospitals (Yankauer, 1973). Thus, school nurses are a major component of the personnel working in children's primary care. Nurses are also much more apt to be "resident" in the schools than physicians: 88 percent of schools reported the availability of a school nurse, and 63 percent of schools indicated they had access to a nurse employed by the schools (NCES, 1968). Additional evidence from an HEW questionnaire to school systems with 12,000 or more enrollment suggests that among elementary schools the typical pattern is for nurses to work across more than one school, with 62 percent of schools reporting a full-time nurse in each school. This pattern of divided service across schools was less evident at the high school level because of the larger average size of these schools.

REGULAR SOURCES OF CARE

We have looked briefly at patterns of use and personnel deployment as they are distributed across various sites of care. Next, what can be said about the ways individual families use the system of care? In particular, it is interesting to know how many families say that they have a single site where their children's care is for the most part provided.

There is a sizable body of evidence suggesting the importance of having a regular source of care (Aday, 1972).[d] Those who say they do have such a source make greater use of physician's services, even when controls are introduced for various socioeconomic background variables (Bice et al., 1972). They also are more apt to use preventive care services (Andersen and Bentham, 1970). Most important, Taylor,

---

[d]It is worth noting that when respondents profess to have a regular source of medical care this often may indicate only a higher understanding or level of familiarity with medical care alternatives. We know, for instance, that when study subjects in the California Medical Copayment Experiment without a regular source of care were asked their reasons for not having one, over half gave as their reason, "new in area." Transience is apt to be somewhat higher in California than elsewhere, but we may suspect this is a common reason everywhere. In addition, for some a "regular" source of care may simply mean an accessible source. Most of those without a regular source in the California experiment who did not list "new in area" suggested instead that they had a transportation problem, a language problem, or a fear or dislike of doctors (Brian and Gibbens, 1974).

Aday, and Andersen (1975) report that people who claim a regular source of care are more apt to show appropriate use patterns than others. This conclusion was reached in an analysis of utilization rates employing a composite outcome variable that the authors call a symptom/response ratio, which is corrected for the respondent's level of medical care need according to epidemiological evidence on morbidity for his sociocultural and age group. Similar conclusions emerged from research employing a use/disability index (Aday, 1974).

The authors discovered, however, that among those with a regular source of care, appropriate use was not uniformly great. Whites and affluent families were much more apt than nonwhites and the poor to see a doctor when they should, according to the assumptions of the symptoms/response index. This suggests that those who indicate a regular source of care do not all have equal access to that source or benefit equally from it.

Seven percent of American children apparently have no regular care source (Table 3—8). There is a somewhat lower probability of a regular source among older children, a clear trend in the South and West not to have such a source, and strong differences by income, race, family size, and residential area. Children in low-income families are almost eight times as likely to have no regular source than those in affluent families, nonwhites more than three times as likely as whites, children in largest families three times as likely as those in smallest families, and those living in central cities two to three times as likely as those in suburbs.

Table 3—9 enables us to look at the effect of low income and living in the inner city as they relate to the likelihood a child will have a physician as a regular source of care.[e] In this regard family income is a better predictor for children than for adults, especially in central cities. Another fact of central city care is that there appears to be a

[e]There is reason to believe that the CHAS/NORC estimates of numbers of children without a regular source of care may be conservative. First-quarter data from the 1974 Health Interview Survey were analyzed provisionally by Wilson (1974) in an attempt to determine the "usual" place of care for American children. It was reported that 86 percent of children have parents who answered that they have "one particular doctor or place they usually go when they are sick or need advice about their health." (Variation was from 78 percent among families with incomes less than $5000 to 90 percent among families with incomes above $15,000.) This is a somewhat different conception of regular care source than that reported by Andersen, yielding an estimate of children with no usual source of care almost twice as great as the CHAS/NORC estimate.

Differences may stem in part from different samples, sampling procedures, and phrasing of the question, but most likely are a reflection of the fact that the CHAS/NORC team probed with two questions in sequence while the Health Interview Survey team did not.

Table 3-8.   Sources of Regular Medical Care for Children by Age, Family Income, and Other Characteristics: 1970 *(percent)*

| | *Source* | | | |
	Physician	*Clinic*	*Osteopath or Other*	*No Regular Source*
All	67	21	5	7
Age				
0-4	71	19	4	6
5-9	65	24	4	7
10-14	66	19	7	7
Family Income				
$0-5999	44	37	5	15
6000-10,999	69	17	6	8
11,000-45,000	75	18	5	2
Race				
White	71	18	6	5
Nonwhite	45	38	2	16
Residence				
SMSA-central city	56	31	4	9
SMSA-other	75	14	5	6
Urban-nonSMSA	71	24	2	3
Rural	70	17	7	6
Region				
Northeast	81	8	6	5
North Central	58	32	5	5
South	70	17	5	8
West	53	32	5	10

Source: Harvard Child Health Project analysis of data provided by the Center for Health Administration Studies from the 1970 Survey of Health Care Utilization and Expenditures.

major split between low-income and middle-income families in the likelihood that they will have a private physician as source of care, but no comparable split between middle-income and high-income families. Middle-income and affluent children look a good deal alike in the probability that they will use a private physician, but both can be contrasted with the poor. There is no similar pattern for other age groups. High-income children are the most likely of any age group to have a private physician as regular source of care, regardless of residential area. Low-income children, on the other hand, are the

Table 3–9.   Source of Regular Medical Care by Age, Family Income, and Residence: 1970

| | | Source of Regular Care (12)[a] | | | | | | | | |
| | | Percent M.D. | | | Percent Clinic | | | Percent No Regular Care | | |
Age (1)	Family Income (7)	SMSA Central City	Other Urban	Rural	SMSA Central City	Other Urban	Rural	SMSA Central City	Other Urban	Rural
0–17[b]	Low	26	57	64	56	27	22	18	16	14
	Middle	64	78	74	22	16	18	14	6	8
	High	77	82	81	20	17	17	3	1	2
18–64	Low	41	65	68	35	18	17	24	18	15
	Middle	62	75	72	19	15	19	18	10	9
	High	73	75	75	12	14	13	15	11	12
All ages	Low	41	67	68	39	18	18	21	15	14
	Middle	64	76	73	20	15	18	15	8	8
	High	74	78	78	15	15	15	10	7	8
All ages	Total	61	75	73	24	16	17	15	9	10

[a] In this table percentages are computed so that in any row the sum across a particular residence category equals 100, subject to rounding error. For example, in the first row for SMSA, central city: 26 + 56 + 18 = 100.
[b] Includes infants under one year of age.
Source: Andersen et al., 1972, p. 6.

least apt to. The penalty of being poor, nonwhite, from a large family, or in a central city is greater for the younger age group.[f]

More also can be said about the strong differences in levels of access to a regular source of care. Table 3–10 reports the results of analysis performed for the subset of children one to fourteen relating regular source of care to the following questions:

1. What kind of transportation is usually used to take (person) to (regular source of care)?
2. How long does it usually take to get there?
3. Does (person) usually have to make an appointment ahead of time when (he/she) goes to (place) or not?
4. How long does (person) usually have to wait before seeing the doctor for a routine visit after (doctor) is called for an appointment?
5. How long does (person) usually have to wait to see the *doctor*, once (he/she) gets there?
6. In the past two weeks, did (person) talk to a doctor about (his/her) health?
7. How long ago did (person) last have a physical exam or checkup?
8. Did (person) ever see a physician in 1970?

Clear differences of access emerge between private physicians and clinics. First, those going by family car rather than some other means of transportation are more apt to be going to a private physician, a reflection of income and residential patterns. But for those who took less than fifteen minutes to reach the regular source of care, a disproportionate number were users of private physicians; clearly, those who must travel for longer times tend to be the institutional care users, even though distances traveled may not be greater.

Predictably, those who make appointments are much more likely

---

[f]It seems likely that "clinic" for lower-income respondents refers more often to outpatient clinics or emergency rooms of hospitals, perhaps also well-child clinics and neighborhood health centers, while for higher income respondents the same category is apt to refer to a group practice arrangement, prepaid or otherwise.

Among those who said they used a clinic as a regular source of care, the further question was asked, within the service did they usually see the same doctor. This data enables some inferences about the kind of care arrangements that were meant by "clinic," since some arrangements were much more likely to result in seeing the same doctor over time than others (e.g., group practice arrangements as against hospital emergency rooms). The other use of this information is to infer questions of continuity of care; one form of continuity is contact with the same medical personnel over time. Children over-all are similar to young and middle adults, but not the aging, in the aggregate proportions seeing a particular doctor. Low-income children, blacks, and persons in urban areas, however, were in general much less likely to enjoy this form of continuity of care.

Table 3–10. CHAS/NORC 1970 Survey of Health Care Utilization and Expenditures Access Factors by Source of Care: Children Under Fifteen

	M.D.	*Clinic*	*Osteo/Other*	*None*
Totals	72.0	22.6	5.4	6.7
Transportation to Regular Source				
goes in family car	75.7	18.6	5.7	—
other	53.9	42.0	4.1	—
Time to Reach Regular Source				
1–15 mins.	77.4	17.6	5.0	—
15–30 mins.	68.8	25.5	5.7	—
over 30 mins.	56.9	39.8	3.2	—
Appointment or Walk in				
appointment	75.1	20.2	4.6	—
walk in	61.2	30.7	8.1	—
Appointment Waiting Time				
same day	77.3	15.1	7.6	—
1–2 days	75.9	20.3	3.8	—
3–4 days	68.0	26.9	5.1	—
5–7 days	76.4	19.6	4.0	—
1–2 weeks	64.0	36.0	—	—
2–4 weeks	74.5	25.5	—	—
over month	84.3	15.7	—	—
Office Waiting Time				
immediate	75.8	18.8	5.3	—
1–15 mins.	74.0	19.4	6.7	—
15–30 mins.	75.0	17.0	8.0	—
30 mins. –1 hr.	71.5	24.4	4.1	—
1–2 hrs.	69.7	28.9	1.3	—
2–4 hrs.	58.6	37.9	3.5	—
Talk With Doctor in Past Two Weeks				
yes	75.8	12.4	4.6	7.7
no	66.6	21.5	5.2	6.8
Last Physical				
up to 6 mos. ago	74.6	17.0	4.3	4.2
more than 6 mos. ago	64.4	22.7	5.4	7.5
missing data	57.4	23.7	1.3	17.6
See Doctor in 1970				
yes	71.2	21.0	4.9	2.8
no	58.9	21.4	5.3	14.4

Source: Harvard Child Health Project analysis of data provided by the Center for Health Administration Studies from the 1970 Survey of Health Care Utilization and Expenditures.

to be users of private physicians. Office waiting time differentials are not great, but the trend is in the expected direction, toward longer waits among those in the clinic setting. If rural residents are removed from the analysis, differences are much more dramatic. Among those seen with no office waiting time in central city and suburban settings, for instance, about 90 percent are private physician users and only 10 percent clinic users.

In the responses relating to how recently a physician was seen, there also is evidence that those who have been to the physician more and have complied with routine physical examination schedules are more likely to use private physicians than clinics.

This general picture of care suggests that among children one to fourteen, those using doctors' offices have somewhat higher access and use their care source somewhat more regularly than others. These tend to be the higher-income families.

Starfield et al. (1973) have drawn upon the Baltimore SMSA data from the World Health Organization household interview survey of medical care utilization to give a somewhat more detailed discussion of the relationship between the types of physicians serving as the regular source of care for children and the extent to which these sources are actually perceived by parents as accessible. Their findings correspond rather closely with those of the CHAS/NORC survey in regard to numbers of children without a regular source of care, about 6 percent of the sample. Thirteen percent identified an institutional setting as a regular source, with 75 percent identifying an individual physician, higher than the national average but in keeping with patterns for the Northeast region. The study discovered that for more than 50 percent of the sample, regular sources of care were located less than fifteen minutes away.

Starfield et al. also contribute to our understanding of the pyramidal income-related structure of access to various sources of care, and the relative importance of financial barriers to care compared with other barriers. They discovered the predictable income-related split in types of regular source of care, with about 75 percent of the children whose families reported an institutional setting as a regular source being poor and only about a third of children reporting a physician being poor. They also discovered, however, that income-related trends are found *within* the group of children using a private physician as source of care: the affluent are far more apt to use a pediatrician and the poor more likely to see a general practitioner or nonpediatric specialist.

The few office-based pediatricians in Baltimore (only about 1.67 per 10,000 children under fifteen) tend to serve the most affluent families, and pediatricians tend to charge 15 to 20 percent more than GPs. Although they are less accessible from the standpoint of distance, more likely to require appointments, and have more formal office procedures, office-based pediatricians are in greater demand and are somewhat more likely than other physicians to be available at odd hours and on weekends. The study showed that those children with a pediatrician as regular source of care make visits more frequently and systematically, while those with a GP as regular source were apt to have allowed more time to elapse since their last physician visit. The Starfield et al. data also enable us to conclude that access to a regular source of care, and perhaps even quality of routine health supervision, can vary greatly among the middle-income and higher-income groups even though these two groups appear in other data to be quite similar in numbers of families reporting an office-based physician as regular care source.

Multiple Sources of Care

The notions of "site of physician visit" and "regular source of care" do not give a complete picture of the pattern of utilization actually seen in most families. People often use more than one source of care, and families differ in the number of different sources of care they use, as well as the dispersion of such sources across various organizational modes and the redundancy of services provided in the various settings. Very little evidence is currently available on utilization patterns of individual children and families across provider arrangements, but we at least have examples of two kinds of studies which bear upon the question and deserve more emphasis in the future.

The first line of research, using consumer interview techniques, makes a distinction between *central* source of care and *volume* source of care (Solon, 1967). Central source is the one in which the consumer places greatest trust and reliance; volume source is the one most often used. These can differ notably. Another distinction surrounds *compactness* and *cohesiveness* of medical care utilization patterns. Compactness of medical care pattern is defined by Solon according to the number and type of care sources. Families can use a single source of care, a single type of source (e.g., several outpatient departments), or a variety of types of source (e.g., private practitioner and outpatient department). In one study involving a low-income Pittsburgh community sample (50 percent under age fifteen, with a two-to-one white:nonwhite ratio) Solon discovered that prior to the installation of a neighborhood health center there was a compactness pattern in which fewer than 50 percent of families used only a single source of care. We may take these data as a reasonable prior estimate of national urban levels, mindful that they may not be reflected in areas where comprehensive care programs have consolidated utilization patterns.

Another line of research relating to utilization of services across modes of care involves selecting a representative sample of users from the rolls of a particular provider arrangement and exploring either prospectively or retrospectively their use of other modes of care. Much of the information we have on "multiple" users of hospital services is of this type. Alpert et al. (1969) have been led by their study of an emergency room user population in Boston to hypothesize that there are two types of users: those families who rely on their own physician except for referrals and emergencies, and those who only occasionally go to a private physician. Of families without a personal physician, some are referred by a physician and others come directly to the hospital. Alpert et al. report that 57 percent of the families using the emergency room as a source of routine medical care in their 1964 sample had no usual physician for their children, and only 24 percent could be said to have a stable relationship with a physician for children's medical care. Most of the families used the clinic on an ad hoc basis, seldom seeing the same physician more than once. Weinerman (1965) has also suggested that "the inability of low income families to maintain ongoing relations with a private physician is the major factor in the pattern of using emergency facilities for nonurgent problems" (p. 949).

Another study which attempted to understand the over-all patterns of medical care use among patients of two hospital emergency rooms, one in a central city and the other in a suburb, indicated substantially different patterns for the populations using the two different emergency rooms (Solon and Rigg, 1972). As a rule, suburban patients used the emergency room only under unusual circumstances, while in the central city the outpatient department and emergency room accounted for about 8 percent of the regular care sources cited by members of the study sample, and another 6 percent cited the emergency room as a routine supplement to private care. The authors point out: "Significantly more of the Inner City emergency patients seemed to make continuing and important use of the emergency unit as part of their regular medical care pattern (14 percent as compared to Suburban's 7 percent)" (p. 68). Equally important, the use of a single source of care for virtually all utilization ("compactness" of medical care pattern) was characteristic for over half of the suburban patients and only about a third of the central city patients.

The authors also inquired about cohesiveness of patterning of care, to find out if there were substantial duplications of utilization rather than complementary patterns of utilization. In general, the study's conclusions were that the large majority of those patients had legitimate complementary sources. This was not what many would have hypothesized. At least one study currently being undertaken by Levy and her associates at Boston's Children's Hospital should add new findings in this area.

Wingert, Friedman, and Larson (1968) go a step further, arguing that emergency room users are not a hapless clientele seeking a caresource-of-last-resort, but rather a clientele that has sought advice about available alternatives and used the emergency room as a preferred source of care. These investigators studied the determinants of utilization among over 3000 users of the pediatric emergency room of a large Los Angeles County hospital. Their study was especially valuable in illuminating the informal and formal network of counseling and referral that resulted in a child being brought to the emergency room. They inquired about who most often gave the family medical advice, who referred the child to the hospital, and whom the parents spoke to before deciding to bring the child to the hospital. As a source of general medical advice, only about half of the parents before coming to the hospital had made any contact with a private physician, although public health centers were a source of occasional advice for over two-thirds and grandparents a source for about one-third. School nurses, druggists, and other relatives and friends all were cited by about a quarter of the families as significant sources of advice. Specific sources of referral were in most cases friends or relatives, or else self-referral. Physicians were cited in only 12 percent of the cases. The same was true of those consulted prior to deciding to bring the child to the hospital. These were far more apt to be relatives and friends than a physician or other health worker.

Clearly those who use the hospital have varying expectations about its role as a source of occasional care, supplementary care, or regular care.

SUMMARY

1. Differences in physician use rates among income groups have been reduced considerably in the past fifteen years. Presumably this trend comes largely as the result of the initiation of Medicaid and various federal categorical grant programs. Poor children in central cities, especially young children, have benefited more during this interim than rural children.

2. Data on physician care reveal reduced but persisting differences between subgroups of children in levels of primary care use.

Income-related inequities are particularly troublesome; statistics on morbidity would suggest that poor children should use more care; in fact, they use less. This is especially true in underserved central cities and rural farm areas. The same pattern does not exist for adults; among them the poor now use more care than the affluent.

3. The distribution of use across various provider arrangements still shows private practice as the largest component of children's care. If we exclude those sites where only preventive care is offered, individual practice offices explain about 60 percent of all visits, and group practice explains about another 19 percent. Percentages are much lower, however, for poverty populations.

4. Hospital-based primary care, in outpatient departments and emergency rooms, has become an increasingly important component of children's care. Almost 15 percent of children's care is provided now in hospitals, making them much more important in the volume of visits they handle than special government programs or voluntary programs. The percentage of visits in hospital settings is much higher for poor central city children, for whom more than one-third of all visits are to the outpatient department or emergency room.

5. Comprehensive care programs for the poor, usually relying on federal categorical funding, have received much publicity and been extensively evaluated, but thus far they serve only a small fraction of the nation's children. Neighborhood Health Centers and Children and Youth projects remain demonstration programs, as yet reaching less than 5 percent of all children.

6. If we include health department and school-based preventive care programs as part of the full set of primary care arrangements for children, these programs account for as much as 18 percent of the total encounters with the primary care system. About 13 percent are accounted for by the schools alone. This is a sizable proportion of the total interaction between health care personnel and children and must be seen as a major commitment of physician and nursing time, even though the nature of care in health department and school programs is more circumscribed than in other settings.

7. A minimum of 7 percent of all children have no regular source of medical care. Low-income children are eight times more likely than high-income children to have no regular care source. The percentages of children without a regular source are also greater for children in nonwhite families, larger families, and those in the central city. Among those who report a usual source of care, two-thirds of white children receive this care at a physician's office, while only 40 percent of nonwhites do. In one large SMSA, as many as 70 percent

of children whose families report an institutional site of care as a regular source are poor.

8. Regular sources of care are less accessible if they are clinics than private physicians. Clinics require more time to get to and have somewhat longer waiting times. This is much more true for clinics available to poor families than others. Moreover, "regular" care is less frequent at clinics, according to measures of most recent physician visit and physical examination. Within the group reporting private physicians as regular care source, there are differences between those using pediatricians and those using general practitioners and other specialists. Pediatricians tend to charge more for services and be less accessible geographically than GPs, with the result that they are used much less by low-income children.

9. We may estimate that fewer than 50 percent of families use only a single source of care for all family primary care. The role of the private physician as a "central" source of care for central city families is difficult to estimate, with differing professional opinion on the matter among researchers, but there is reason to believe that parents increasingly are using hospital-based services directly, with no intermediation by office-based physicians. Some central city parents routinely use both office-based physicians and hospital services.

In conclusion, the data support the notion that American children use a widely dispersed system of care, with a substantial split between the private and public sectors and between preventive and acute care providers. The primary care system for the poor remains largely separate from the system for the affluent, with the poor more apt to use public and clinic-based care while the affluent tend to use private, office-based and pediatrician care. It is further apparent that there is a greater fragmentation of preventive and acute care for the poor, who tend to seek occasional care at hospitals and GP offices but are less likely to have a regular source of care and must rely for preventive care on public agency services based in health departments and schools. By contrast, for affluent and suburban children, one private pediatrician often provides all basic services except in cases of emergency.

REFERENCES

Aday, L.A. *The Utilization of Health Services. Indices and Correlates. A Research Bibliography, 1972.* DHEW Pub. No. (HSM) 73–3003. Washington, D.C.: National Center for Health Services Research and Development, Department of Health, Education and Welfare, 1972.

Aday, L.A. "Economic and non-economic barriers to the use of needed medical services." *Med Care* 3 (1975): 447.

Alpert, J.J., et al. "The types of families that use an emergency clinic," *Med Care* 7 (1969): 55.

American Academy of Pediatrics. *Lengthening Shadows.* Evanston, Ill.: author, 1971.

American Hospital Association. *Hospital Statistics 1972.* Chicago: author, 1972.

Andersen, R., and Bentham, L. "Factors affecting the relationship between family income and medical care consumption," in *Empirical Studies in Health Economics*, edited by H. Klaman. Baltimore: Johns Hopkins Press, 1970.

Andersen, R., et al. *Health Service Use: National Trends and Variations.* DHEW Pub. No. (HSM) 73–3004. Washington, D.C.: National Center for Health Services Research and Development, Department of Health, Education and Welfare, 1972.

Andreopoulos, S., et al. *Primary Care; Where Medicine Fails.* New York: John Wiley and Sons, 1974.

Bartholomew, N. *Data on School Health Personnel.* Washington, D.C.: National Education Association, Education Research Service, 1966.

Bice, T.W., et al. "Socioeconomic status and use of physicians' services: a reconsideration," *Med Care* 12 (1972): 261.

Brian, E., and Gibbens, S. "California's Medi-Cal copayment experiment," *Med Care Supp* 12 (1974): 1.

Davis, K. "Medicaid payments and utilization of medical services by the poor," *Inquiry* 13 (1976): 122.

Davis, K. "A decade of policy developments in providing health care for low-income families," (draft for *A Decade of Federal Anti-Poverty Policy: Achievements, Failures and Lessons*, edited by R. Haveman. Madison: University of Wisconsin Institute for Research on Poverty, 1977), xerox, 1975.

Davis, K., and Carney, M.K. *Medical Care for Mothers and Children: The Title V Maternal and Child Health Program.* Washington, D.C.: Brookings (xerox) preliminary draft, December, 1974.

Hazell, J.W., et al. "Intermediate benefit analysis—Spencer's Dilemma and school health services," *Am J Public Health* 62 (1972): 560–65.

Heagarty, M., et al. "Some comparative costs in comprehensive versus pediatric care," *Pediatrics* 46 (1970): 596.

Miller, C.A. Data analyzed for the Harvard Child Health Project from the 1974 National Survey of Public Health Officers, conducted by the University of North Carolina School of Public Health, 1975.

Myers, B.A., et al. "The medical care activities of local health units," *Public Health Rep* 83 (1968): 757.

National Ambulatory Medical Care Survey: *Background and Methodology.* DHEW Pub. No. (HRA) 74–1335. Washington, D.C.: Government Printing Office, 1974.

National Center for Educational Statistics. *Summary Data on Percent of Public Schools Reporting Pupil Personnel Specialists Available, by Level and*

Location of School: 48 contiguous states and D.C., Fall 1968. Washington, D.C.: author, 1968.

National Center for Health Statistics. *Current Estimates From the Health Interview Survey: United States 1974.* DHEW Pub. No. (HRA) 76–1527. Washington, D.C.: Department of Health, Education and Welfare, 1975.

Palumbo, D., et al. "A systems analysis of local public health departments," *Am J Public Health* 59 (1969): 673–79.

Renthal, A.G. "Comprehensive health centers in large U.S. cities," *Am J Public Health* 61 (1971): 324.

Roemer, M. "From poor beginnings: the growth of primary care," *Hospitals* 49 (1975): 38.

Rosenbloom, A., and Ongley, J. "Who provides what services to children in private medical practice?" *Am J Dis Child* 127 (1974): 357.

Silver, H.K. "The school nurse practitioner program," *JAMA* 216 (1971): 1332–34.

Solon, J. "Changing patterns of obtaining medical care in a public housing community: impact of a service program," *Am J Public Health* 57 (1967): 772.

Solon, J., and Rigg, R. "Patterns of medical care among users of hospital emergency units," *Med Care* 10 (1972): 60.

Starfield, B., et al. "How 'regular' is the 'regular source of medical care'?" *Pediatrics* 51 (1973): 822.

Taylor, D., et al. "A social indicator of access to medical care," *J Health Soc Behav* 16 (1975): 38.

Wallace, H., et al. "Child health care in the United States: expenditures and extent of coverage with selected comprehensive services," *Pediatrics* 55 (1975): 76.

Weinerman, E. "Outpatient-clinic services in the teaching hospital. *N Engl J Med* 72 (1965): 18.

Wilson, R. *Statistical Data Prepared for the Child Health Task Force.* Washington, D.C.: Division of Analysis, National Center for Health Statistics, (mimeo), 1974.

Wingert, W., et al. "The demographical and ecological characteristics of a large urban pediatric outpatient population and implications for improving community pediatric care," *Am J Public Health* 58 (1968): 859.

Yankauer, A. "Child health supervision—is it worth it?" *Pediatrics* 52 (1973): 208.

Yankauer, A., et al. "Task performance and task delegation in pediatric office practice," *Am J Public Health* 59 (1969): 1104.

✳ *Chapter 4*

Determinants of Utilization of Children's Health Services

Diane L. Beauchesne
David S. Mundel

Efforts to improve child health by providing adequate services cannot succeed if services are not used.[a] Utilization of health services cannot be equated with demand for them. Utilization depends on the interaction of demand with the services available. Many characteristics of the medical care system and potential consumers affect use of medical services. Some variables, such as population shifts, are beyond the scope of policy control. Information on the relationship of such variables to utilization is needed to design delivery systems to meet changing needs. This chapter, however, focuses on variables that can be altered by the adoption of policy recommendations, for instance, by changing the price or the location of medical services.

A review of the relationships of such variables and utilization may indicate how to alter variables to increase use of existing services, or how to alter services to encourage use. In addition, data on utilization trends may be helpful in predicting and planning for shifts in utilization patterns. Such predictions are of great importance in the medical care market, where a large number of providers are known to respond slowly or not at all to consumer demand for needed services.[b] In sectors where needs are less immediate, market forces

---

[a] Although various health care services and the manner in which they are used differ in effect on health status, all uses will be assumed effective in this chapter.

[b] Judy Baumann and David Calkins, (Chapter 5), cite the failure of some physicians to introduce physician-extenders in spite of profitability as evidence of the lack of responsiveness of the medical care supply system. Zeckhauser and Eliastam ("The productivity potential of the physician assistant," *J Human Ressources* 9 [1973]: 95) also refer to the inefficiency of current office arrange-

might be left to respond at their own pace. In the health care market, where failure to provide needed care can have an immediate and profound effect on the health status of the consumer, policy intervention is needed to shorten the gap in time between the demand for needed services and the development of the capacity to deliver them. Studying utilization patterns may also point the way toward reallocating present services to reduce wasteful misuse of health care resources.

FINAL OUTCOMES—IMPROVED HEALTH AND SATISFACTION

The results of utilization, for instance, health status or immunization status, are final outcome variables and these final outcomes can be both physical and psychological. In physical terms, the desired final outcome is improved health status; in psychological terms it is consumer satisfaction, that is, the consumer's perception that his health is good and that the health care available and received is close to what is desired. The relationship between different types of utilization (preventive care use, illness-related use) and these desired final outcomes indicates which elements of medical care utilization should be encouraged or, perhaps, discouraged.

Physical Outcomes

Although much research has been addressed to the effect of utilization on health status, only preliminary evidence exists. The effectiveness and efficacy of treatments for a number of children's health conditions are discussed in volume II of this series: tonsillectomy and adenoidectomy, treatments for iron-deficiency anemia, lead poisoning, and streptococcal pharyngitis, to name a few. These reviews indicate that a positive relationship between medical interventions and improved health status exists, but that often utilization does not result in the provision of a potentially efficacious cycle of care.

Consumer Satisfaction

Other investigators have addressed the levels of consumer satisfaction with medical care. Baumann and Calkins (Chapter 5) cite studies that indicate consumers are equally satisfied with care by physicians or by physician-extenders. Dodge et al. (1970) report that members

---

ments. Most nonsolo practice institutions are public or not-for-profit, while those physicians in private, for-profit practice continue to enjoy a monopoly position. Consequently, insulation from market forces is characteristic of the medical care system.

of various ethnic, income, educational, and socioeconomic status groups rate the importance of various health measures such as immunizations and screening tests equally, although some had thought such attitudes varied among these groups. Brooks (1973) found patient satisfaction equal at large centralized clinics and small neighborhood clinics.

Okada et al. (1971) report a modest patient preference for private over public sources of care. Olendzki et al. (1972) studied the care-seeking patterns of Medicaid recipients in New York City. This study found that although some patients who continued to receive their care from a comprehensive hospital clinic expressed a preference for private care, others felt the best care and more qualified doctors were available in the hospital clinics. Consumer preferences for private care may be based upon attitudes toward the nonmedical aspects of health care provision which current private practice arrangements appear to satisfy more fully than public practitioners. Such nonmedical attributes are probably more important to the healthier patient. Children as a class have higher rates of illness than adults under sixty-five, but over all their illnesses are less severe and more self-limiting. If children are "healthier," nonmedical aspects of care may play a greater role in consumer satisfaction with children's health care services than with those received by adults.

INTERMEDIATE OUTCOMES

In the absence of adequate research on the health improvements and satisfaction resulting from utilization, a variety of intermediate outcomes may serve as indicators of appropriate and effective utilization. The quality of the care available to various consumer groups and the rates of utilization by these groups are two such indicators.

Quality as an Intermediate Indicator

The quality of care available to consumers may indicate their standing on final outcomes. There is little evidence from quality reviews on whether the care received by children of different income or socioeconomic status levels differs in quality (Greene, 1976). Kessner et al. (1974) studied the care provided for three common childhood disorders (otitis media, anemia, and vision defects) and found the health status of groups of children using various public and private providers to be substantially the same. The nonrandom nature of the Kessner sample, however, makes it impossible to derive conclusions about the relative quality of care given by different providers.

Okada et al. (1971) found that low-income people shifted from public to private practitioners when private care became available and low in price. This may indicate that consumers perceive private delivery modes to be of higher quality than public modes, but it is not clear that quality of medical care considerations alone accounted for the shift. Consumers may have been expressing a preference for certain nonmedical (or "caring" rather than "curing") features of private care.

Patterns of Utilization

If utilization of health services is assumed effective, the rates of utilization by various groups should be related to the relative health status of the groups. That is, utilization rates may serve as intermediate indicators of final outcome status. Feldstein and Carr (1964) found strong positive relationships between income and utilization of health services (measured by expenditures for medical care) during 1950 and 1960. Over past decades, the use of medical services has become more equal across income groups. This trend has been especially marked since the introduction of Medicare and Medicaid (Davis, 1975). Bice et al. (1972) cite data collected from three national surveys during the sixties in which the positive relationship between income and physician visits per person per year which existed in 1963–64 no longer held for adults and was reduced for children by 1969. Beck (1973) reports a similar trend in Canada after the introduction of that country's national health insurance, although some negative correlation between nonuse and income persisted.

Children's Utilization Rates. Equalization of utilization rates across income levels has been less marked for children than for adults. Utilization rates for poor children changed relatively little in relation to rates for nonpoor children between 1963 and 1969, while poor adults have matched or nearly matched the utilization of nonpoor adults (Bice et al., 1972). The 1969 physician visit rate of children with family income under $4000 was 0.65 times the rate of children with family income above $10,000. In 1963 the poor children made 0.53 times the visits of the more well-to-do. The poorest adults under sixty-five made 0.84 to 0.98 times the physician visits of the richest adults in 1963–64, and 1.05 to 1.28 times the visits in 1969. Although the relationship between utilization and income has become less strong over time, it still exists for children.

In summary, in spite of either subsidies through national health insurance (in Canada) or through reimbursement (in the United

Figure 4–1. Utilization Rates vs. Family Income for Children *(Under Fourteen)* from 1964 to 1969

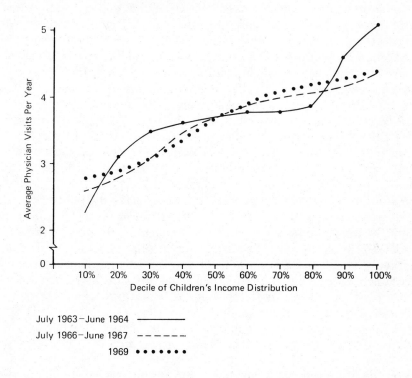

July 1963 – June 1964 ——————

July 1966 – June 1967 — — — — —

1969 • • • • • •

Source: Calculated from U.S. Department of Health Education and Welfare, *Volume of Physician Visits by Place of Visit and Type of Service,* United States, July 1963–June 1964, Public Health Service, Pub. No. 1000, Series 10, No. 18; July 1966–June 1967, PHS Pub. No. 1000, Series 10, No. 49; and U.S. Department of Health, Education and Welfare, *Physician Visits, Volume and Interval Since Last Visit,* United States – 1969, DHEW Pub. No. HSM 72–1064, Series 10, No. 75.

States through Medicaid), health services remain unequally utilized by children of different income groups.

Preventive Care. The inequalities in children's utilization may not be distributed equally across all types of medical services. Richardson (1969) found that preventive care visits composed 10.8 percent of physician visits for families whose incomes were below $2000 and 17.5 percent of visits by families whose incomes exceeded $10,000 in 1963–64. Only 15.7 percent of children under seventeen in the first group had a routine physical exam during the year; 53.9 percent of children in the latter group did. Berginer and Yerby (1968) found the number of immunizations received by children to be positively related to income.

In another study, Richardson (1970) found that income-related differences in health services utilization were less pronounced for serious than for nonserious illness. The more serious an illness is, the more the utilization behavior of the poor resembles that of the non-poor. Consequently, financing and provision of preventive services in particular appear more important for low-income populations, since it is this sort of care they are most likely to underutilize.

Bice et al. (1972) consider it likely that the persistent relationship they found between income and utilization among children resulted from differential use of preventive care, since children use most of such care, and it is among children that utilization differences by income remained greatest. In a study of children's utilization in Monroe County, New York, Medicaid enrollees made 40 percent fewer preventive care visits, but only 20 percent fewer visits for illness in 1969 than did children with Blue Cross coverage (Roghmann, 1975). Beck (1973) shows that health insurance financing in Canada had markedly less effect on the nonuse of physical examinations (a service much utilized by children) than it had on nonuse of services as a whole. This relative ineffectiveness of health insurance in altering nonuse of physical exams lends support to the hypothesis that the remaining differences in children's care utilization are largely the result of differences in their use of preventive care.

Care in Response to Symptoms. Utilization rates most adequately indicate health status outcomes when they are considered in relation to symptoms and disabilities. Information on symptoms and disability days permits the estimation of "appropriate" utilization rates.

Alpert et al. (1971) found that low-income families obtained medical care in only 14.3 percent of cases when medical attention was the appropriate response to symptoms. Moreover, children's symptoms were somewhat less likely to receive medical care than adults' symptoms (Alpert et al., 1967). Aday (1975) found that although utilization rates for the poor and the nonpoor have become more equal under Medicaid, the poor still use fewer services per disability day than the nonpoor. (Figures for children's utilization and disability days were not reported separately.)

Taylor et al. (1975) found that nonwhites and the poor used less care than appropriate in response to symptoms, as judged by medical experts. Children and adolescents were likely to use more care than required in response to their symptoms. Nonwhite children above and below the poverty level, however, tend to use services at or below the rate warranted by their symptoms. Poor white children use services at rates significantly below those of their nonpoor counterparts (Table 4—1).

To summarize, although aggregate care utilization has become more equal across income levels, use in relation to need remains lower for poor and disadvantaged individuals. This pattern is not as clear among children, however, since children as a group appear to use more care than necessary when "symptomatic appropriateness" is considered. The continuing gap in utilization between poor and nonpoor children suggests that excessive utilization by poor children, if it exists, is probably less than that of the nonpoor.

INDEPENDENT VARIABLES

A review of existing utilization rates reveals that children's use of health services remains uneven, especially in relation to their need for care. Price, distance, travel time, waiting time, regular source of care, parental perception of need, and outreach are variables that affect these utilization patterns. The following discussion examines the relationships that have been found between these variables and utilization, and the implications of changes in these variables for changing utilization.

Price and Income
Price of care in relation to income is a salient aspect of availability. Although the price of care has a relatively small impact on aggregate levels of health service use, its impact on use by the low-income population is substantial. After the introduction of national health insurance in Canada, the proportion of nonusers of medical services in different income groups became more equal over time (Beck, 1973). In the United States, the increase in utilization by the poor when Medicaid reduced or eliminated the prices they faced demonstrates that cost of care is a real barrier to utilization (Davis, 1975). Aday (1971) and Cauffman et al. (1967) report that removal of out-of-pocket expenses by insurance coverage resulted in increased utilization by children. Aday found that when such costs were removed, poor children equalled or exceeded high-income children in utilization.

Although utilization rates have become more equal among income groups following the introduction of Medicare and Medicaid, the trend toward equality of utilization has been slower for children than

Table 4–1.   Symptoms-Response Ratio by Poverty Level, by Race, by Age

Poverty Level	Race	Age	Actual Number of Visits for Symptoms (A)	Estimated Number of Visits for Symptoms (E)	Discrepancy between Actual and Estimated Number of Visits (A−E)	Symptoms-Response Ratio $\frac{A-E}{E}$ (100)
Above	White	0–5	2706.2	1907.4	798.8	41.9
		6–14	4308.7	3576.0	732.7	20.5
	Nonwhite	0–5	46.5	78.5	−32.0	−40.8
		6–14	235.6	207.0	28.6	13.8
Below	White	0–5	441.0	349.7	91.3	26.1
		6–14	879.2	843.0	36.2	4.3
	Nonwhite	0–5	218.5	229.8	−11.3	−4.9
		6–14	467.1	726.9	−259.8	−35.9

Source: This table received in a personal communication from Lu Ann Aday, based on data developed at the Center for Health Administration Studies at the University of Chicago.

for adults (Bice et al., 1972). Therefore, the price barrier may still exist for those whose annual health care costs consume a disproportionate amount of their income.

In summary, it is evident that price subsidies affect use of health services by poor children. Persistent inequalities in children's utilization indicate that despite Medicaid, some children may still face a price barrier that could be eliminated or reduced by subsidy. In some states, Medicaid eligibility criteria and reimbursement policies have limited the medical care price reductions to only a segment of the lower income population.

Distance and Travel Time

Distance from providers and the time needed to reach them are other aspects of accessibility of care. In Baltimore, Bice (1971) found that poor families were slightly more likely to live in areas of low physician density. Data from the 1969 Health Interview Survey reveal that poor people tend to travel somewhat longer to reach their source of care, though the range of difference is not great. Visits made by children from higher-income families are more likely to require only a one-to-fifteen-minute trip to the site of care; while visits by poor children are more likely to require fifteen to thirty minutes of travel (Figure 4−2).

In general, the early literature describing the effect of distance upon utilization consisted of studies in rural settings where distances traveled to receive health care were relatively great (Jehlik and Mc-Namara, 1952). Urban distances vary over a smaller range; consequently their effects on utilization may be less. Aday (1972) reviewed the literature on utilization and found that distance does not affect whether or not care is sought, but does affect where care is sought.

Nevertheless, the aggregate impact of distance upon utilization is still uncertain. Bice et al. (1972) report on a Cleveland study in which most individuals did not regularly seek care from the nearest doctor. The tendency not to use the nearest physician was evident in all income groups. However, Weiss et al. (1971) examined the utilization patterns of enrollees in a Portland, Oregon, health maintenance organization (HMO) and found that patients made most of their physician visits at the HMO facility nearest their home. In another study of HMO members, Weiss and Greenlick (1970) reported that distance influenced the manner in which care was sought. Middle-class enrollees living at greater distance from the HMO clinics used the telephone more often and scheduled appointments less often than middle-class members living nearer to clinics. For working-class

Figure 4–2. Travel Time to Physician by Income for Children Under Fourteen

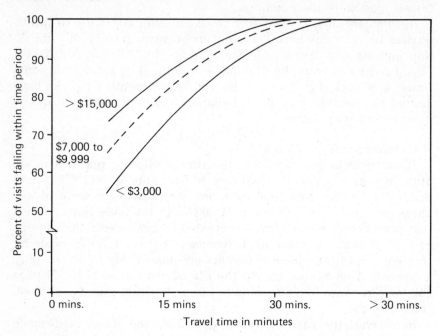

Source: Based on 1969 Health Interview Survey data tapes from the National Center for Health Statistics.

enrollees, use of scheduled appointments decreased and unscheduled visits apparently increased at greater distances.

Aday (1975) examined use related to need (disability days) and found that the insured poor and the uninsured nonpoor made fewer physician visits when their regular source of care was more than thirty minutes away. Travel time had little impact on use by the uninsured poor (who reported greater need, i.e., more disability days), and longer travel times were related to greater use by the insured nonpoor. Acton (1973) found that the urban poor are sensitive to travel time (especially for public sources of care) and cost in their choice of care site and in their decisions whether or not to utilize care.

In summary, distance has not been clearly shown to affect whether or not care is used, but it may affect where and how care is sought. Travel time may be more directly related to utilization than simple distance.

Children's Utilization and Distance. Most distance studies have examined only adult utilization or have not disaggregated their findings by client age. The few studies that have looked at children's utilization specifically have found that distance plays a greater role in determining children's medical care utilization than adult's.

Weiss et al. (1971) reported that distance influenced the choice of site (among HMO clinics) more for pediatric visits than for visits by enrollees over eighteen years of age. It is not clear, however, whether distance to the site of care matters more for children's visits, or whether parents believe the quality of children's care varies less among sites than does the quality of adult care. In addition, Morris et al. (1966) report that transportation difficulties are often cited as the reason well-child appointments are missed.

These studies suggest the need to locate children's primary care facilities close to their potential users. A good, thorough study of the role distance plays in children's health care utilization is needed. Nevertheless, given the existing evidence cited above (and the parallel desirability of decentralizing children's primary care to smaller, non-hospital-based sites) a policy of increasing proximity of delivery units to children appears desirable.

Waiting Time

Appointment Waiting Time. Waiting time is an important aspect of availability. Where there is little or no out-of-pocket cost for care, as in prepaid group practices, the queue serves as a major rationing device. If waiting times for appointments are substantially longer for some classes of children than others, their access to care is less.

Aday (1975) found that when income and insurance status were controlled, appointment waiting times of more than a week reduced the number of physician visits per 100 disability days for all groups but the uninsured poor. Since this group made the fewest physician visits in relation to need (disability days), Aday hypothesizes that the seriousness of their condition when care is sought may account for the lack of impact of appointment waiting time on their care-seeking.

There are no apparent data on whether there are significant differences in appointment waiting times among children, or on the effect possible differences might have upon utilization by children in particular.

Office Waiting Time. Another type of waiting time is that spent in office or clinic waiting rooms before seeing a physician or physician extender. For those whose time costs are great or who have difficulty arranging child care, long waits may limit access. Data on children under fourteen from the 1969 Health Interview Survey indicate that low income children are slightly more likely to have office or clinic waiting times in excess of one hour; the longest waiting times, however, are more common among upper-income children (see Figure 4−3).

Aday (1975) found that the uninsured (both poor and nonpoor) with waiting times of over one half hour at their regular source of care made fewer physician visits in relation to need (disability days) than did the uninsured poor and nonpoor with waiting times of one half hour or less. (The insured nonpoor made slightly fewer visits per 100 disability days when waiting times were longer, but the insured poor had a higher visit/disability day ratio at waiting times over one half hour.) Again, data on the effect waiting time has on utilization by children in particular are lacking.

Regular Source of Care

Taylor et al. (1975) found that individuals with a regular source of care have rates of medical care utilization more appropriate to their symptoms than those without such a regular provider. Aday (1975) found that in general those without a regular source of care made fewer physician visits in relation to need (as represented by disability days) than did those with a regular source of care. This was especially true of the uninsured poor, but untrue of the insured nonpoor.

In a summary study of utilization research, Aday (1972) reported other evidence that having a regular source of care tends to increase use of services. This evidence, although scant, supports the argument that appropriate utilization can be encouraged by delivering all of a child's health care at one site, which serves as "regular source of care," rather than delivering various services at a number of sites. Regularity of utilization would be increased if all primary care services required by the entire family were provided at the same site, but there is little evidence that family primary health facilities encourage more appropriate utilization than do children's primary health facilities.

Parental Perception of Need

Under most circumstances children's use of health services is determined by their parents rather than by the children themselves (Chapter 9). Thus, parental perception of the need for care is an important variable influencing utilization patterns. In most instances mothers make the decisions about obtaining health care for children

Figure 4–3. Waiting Time in Office of Clinic by Income for Children Under Fourteen

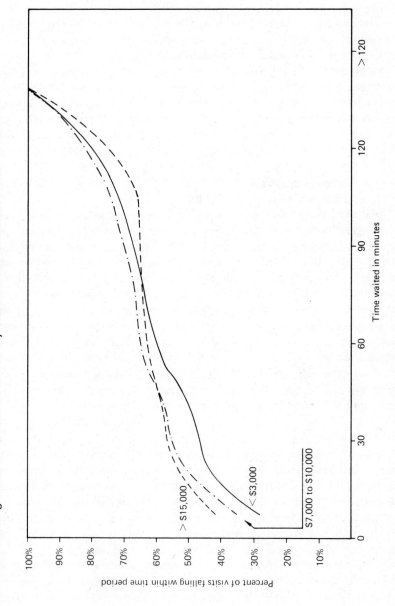

Source: Based on 1969 Health Interview Survey data tapes from the National Center for Health Statistics.

(Alpert et al., 1967). Aday (1971) found mothers' attitudes toward health care useful in explaining differences in preventive care utilization among children. The behavior of mothers in seeking care for themselves was also related to preventive care use by their children. Children whose mothers had not had a physical in the past year and were skeptical of the value of care were less likely to have received a physical exam themselves in the previous year.

Dodge et al. (1970) found that mothers' beliefs about the relative importance of a number of preventive health measures for their children were not significantly related to ethnic, socioeconomic, income, or educational status. The actual performance of the mothers, as indicated by use of tuberculosis skin tests and measles vaccine by their children, accorded with their opinions about care. Morris et al. (1966) found that the greater the feelings of alienation, powerlessness, and social isolation on the part of the mother, the fewer the immunizations received by her child.

To summarize, these studies indicate that the attitudes and medical care behavior of mothers are related to the utilization of preventive medical care by children. Consequently, one might want to promote adequate child use of preventive services by parent training programs. Broad public education programs would be needed to reach parents with little or no contact with the health care system. Other programs could be targeted at improving the utilization of children already in the system; for example, a paraprofessional might instruct parents on appropriate utilization (both preventive and in response to symptoms) while a child was being seen by a physician or nurse practitioner. Delivering physical examinations and other primary care to parents—especially mothers—and children at the same time also might stimulate greater use of preventive care.

Outreach

Outreach services designed to establish familiarity with available health care resources and encourage their use have often been proposed as a means of increasing utilization.[c] An outreach program has many other, more specific goals. These include: promoting community participation in running the health facility; giving various types of counseling; matching individuals with other available social agencies or resources; and providing general health education. An Abt Associates report (unpublished) lists, among other potential benefits, assisting patients in becoming eligible for Medicaid, clarifying physician instructions, promoting early action before the patient's illness

[c]This section on outreach was written by Peter M. Barkin.

becomes serious, lowering utilization of hospitals through more care in the home, and lowering the number of walk-ins by urging patients to make appointments and keep them. Also, often the outreach worker can help a person speaking another language to overcome his fear. The worker often comes from the same neighborhood and, if he doesn't understand the patient's language, can often refer him to someone who does.

Measures of Success. There are several possible ways to measure the success of an outreach program. The most straightforward is simply to measure increased utilization. Or one might assess success by looking at increased follow-up or compliance with prescribed regimens. Other important measures include increased enrollment, fewer broken appointments, increased case finding, and a high number of encounters.

One would like to measure the effect of outreach on appropriate utilization. It is impossible to know whether an increase in utilization actually represents improvement without considering whether use is appropriate. A utilization measure can be tied to a health status index, such as that of Aday and Andersen (1974) or Fanshel and Bush (1970). One can attempt to measure the effect of outreach on health status directly by choosing some marker condition as a health status indicator, as Gordis (1973) did with rheumatic fever. The Abt Associates report (unpublished) ascribes to outreach part of the decrease in rheumatic fever reported in Gordis's study.

It is difficult to imagine the logistics of indexing the health status of nonusers as well as users of a facility in order to link outreach with appropriate utilization. A much simpler concept would also be useful. One might measure straightforward utilization rates (such as the number of visits per time period). The health provider could classify each user he sees as having made either an appropriate or inappropriate visit. As long as the percentage of inappropriate visits does not increase significantly, the relative success of the outreach program could be measured simply by the utilization rates.

Effect of Outreach. One of the most widely quoted studies on outreach was conducted in Idaho for the Early and Periodic Screening, Diagnosis and Treatment program (EPSDT). Three methods of recruitment were evaluated. When families were mailed a brochure describing the screening services and asking the families to set up their own appointments, only 10 to 15 percent of those contacted used the service. When the mailing was followed by a visit from a social worker who arranged for appointments, 50 percent of the families contacted used the service. When the social worker also described the EPSDT program before making the screening appointment, 80 percent of those visited used the service (USDHEW, 1973).

Most of the available evidence about outreach has been accumulated through the experience of neighborhood health centers and other types of health centers. Of the several outreach reports that health centers have generated, virtually all have recorded at least some measure of success. However, few of the studies have been statistically rigorous. Furthermore, since the outreach programs described usually have characteristics specific to the particular project, making generalizations is difficult.

The Columbia Point Health Center, for example, has used outreach workers to help combat patterns of intermittent, crisis-oriented care-seeking. After two years of the program, the proportion of residents reporting that they or someone in their family had postponed medical care in the preceding six months dropped from 23 percent to 10 percent (Bellin and Geiger, 1972). These results are difficult to interpret because it is hard to know how much of the program's success can be attributed to outreach, because users of the health center are almost all residents of a single housing project complex where the center is located.

Luckham and Swift (1969) report the successful use of health aides in two studies: an immunization campaign and a follow-up on "closed cases." Twenty-five percent of families contacted by aides appeared at the next scheduled immunization clinic. Twenty-six out of thirty "closed cases" responded positively in some way when visited by an aide. The absence of a control group in both studies makes it impossible to determine how much of the reported success may be attributed to the aides.

Three studies that approach good experimental design have obtained differing results on the effect of outreach. Baran and Mudge-Lisk (1973) studied two groups of AFDC recipients who received nearly identical health coverage benefits at the Puget Sound Group Health Cooperative. They did not find a significant difference in utilization rates, although one group received considerable outreach and transportation services and the other group had minimal contact with outreach workers. A low-income, non-AFDC control group scored similarly to the two experimental groups in most respects. Unfortunately, the subjects were not randomly assigned to the three groups. Also, utilization of medical services outside the health center was not measured.

The Kaiser Foundation at Portland, Oregon, conducted a study in which Neighborhood Health Center Project enrollees were randomly assigned to experimental (outreach) and control (without outreach) groups (Freeborn et al., undated). Preliminary results indicated significantly greater outpatient utilization of the project's services by individuals with outreach coordinators than by those without (an annual average of 6.3 and 5.6 contacts per person, respectively). But although those enrollees with coordinators averaged more outpatient contacts, the experimental and control groups had similar proportions of nonusers (enrollees who made no use of the project's outpatient services during the study period). However, there were serious problems in the study design: some control group families had previously received coordinator services for up to two years; also, coordinators sometimes continued to help these control group members after the study began; and new enrollees were added to the control group during the study.

The Health Care Outreach Project in Contra Costa County, California, has conducted a more rigorous outreach study (Contra Costa County Human Resources Agency, 1973). Randomly selected families were assigned to an experimental or a control group. Members of the experimental group received five continuous stages of outreach. Members of the control group received an initial evaluation visit followed by a six-week delay before receiving the remaining four stages. The percentages of clients in the experimental and control groups who obtained needed care in five treatment areas were compared at two points: at the end of the six-week delay and after the control group received the complete outreach series. At the end of six weeks, no significant difference was found between the two groups in three areas: sickle-cell testing, acute dental care, and TB testing. The experimental group was significantly better than the control group in obtaining needed acute medical care; a significantly greater percentage of clients in the control group received needed immunizations. After the control group received the remaining four stages of outreach, it scored significantly better than the experimental group in obtaining care in all areas except acute dental care, which showed no significant difference. The study showed outreach to be effective in improving clients' use of needed preventive and acute medical care services. The results also suggest that the outreach, referral, and follow-up process is more effective when it is discontinuous. The addition of a second control group, receiving no outreach throughout the study, would have improved the research.

In summary, the growing literature on outreach is still inconclusive. Research studies demonstrating beneficial effects of outreach have often been poorly designed, and studies of outreach programs with special characteristics are often ungeneralizable. In the most rigorous study (Contra Costa County Human Resources Agency, 1973) outreach was successful for patients needing certain treatments and was most successful when used discontinuously. Outreach may prove more effective in increasing the appropriateness of utilization than in reducing nonuse (i.e., increasing penetration) of care.

The immediate need is for well-designed, well-executed research. Reports should contain clear and complete descriptions of the outreach activities being studied and their intended goals. Costs of the program and of alternatives should be explicitly reported. It is impossible to assess alternatives without cost data. The research should be based on randomized, controlled trials. Evaluations of outreach should incorporate a utilization measure sophisticated enough to include appropriateness of use.

RESULTING DIRECTIONS OF POLICY CHANGE

Investigate Effectiveness of Care

We have assumed that all utilization is effective utilization. In fact, only a small proportion of medical procedures and treatments have yet demonstrated benefits in controlled experimental circumstances. The adoption of policy measures to increase utilization should be accompanied by research to determine which components of care affect health status positively. Policy should then be targeted to encourage those forms of utilization. Two major questions must be addressed: What constitutes appropriate care in various acute situations (e.g., upper respiratory infections), and what preventive care measures are useful in promoting improved health? There is little question of the effectiveness of immunizations in reducing the incidence of many diseases. The benefits of preventive physical examinations, however, remain undemonstrated. Whether such exams produce reasonable health returns when given at currently recommended frequencies is especially questionable.

Improve Organization and Financing

Children's health care services should be decentralized to bring the sites nearer to the users. The suitability of low-technology sites for most children's primary care and the lower overhead cost at such sites strengthen the case for decentralization. Since utilization is greater and more appropriate for those with a regular source of care, primary and preventive care should be delivered at a single site for each child, not in numerous places. Because mothers' own care-seeking behavior is related to their behavior in seeking care for their children, providing health services to mothers or both parents at the same site where children's services are delivered may encourage greater utilization by children. Utilization by children in low-income families will be increased if policy measures are taken to reduce the out-of-pocket cost of their health care to their families.

Investigate Organizational Alternatives

The distribution of existing children's primary care delivery sites in metropolitan areas should be studied to determine whether more are needed to bring providers conveniently close to the child population. The impact of price and distance on children's use of primary and preventive services should be investigated. Evidence should be obtained on how the provision of services to mothers or to both parents at the same site their children use would affect utilization by children. Well-controlled studies of the effect of outreach activities on appropriate utilization by children should be undertaken.

REFERENCES

Abt Associates, Inc. *An Analysis of Benefits and Costs of Ambulatory Care Services Offered by the Bureau of Community Health Services but not Covered by National Health Insurance*, unpublished draft. Cambridge, Mass.: 28 March 1975.

Acton, J.P. *Demand for Health Care Among the Urban Poor, with Special Emphasis on the Role of Time*. Report R—1151—OEO/NYC. New York: The New York City Rand Institute, 1973.

Aday, L.A. *Dimensions of Family's Social Status and Their Relationships to Children's Utilization of Health Services*, unpublished manuscript. Baltimore, Md.: Department of Medical Care and Hospitals, Johns Hopkins University, 1971.

Aday, L.A. *The Utilization of Health Services. Indices and Correlates. A Research Bibliography, 1972*. DHEW Pub. No. (HSM) 73—3003. Washington, D.C.: National Center for Health Services Research and Development, 1972.

Aday, L.A. "Economic and non-economic barriers to the use of needed medical services," *Med Care* 3 (1975): 447.

Aday, L.A., and Andersen, R. "A framework for the study of access to medical care," *Health Serv Res* 9 (1974): 203.

Alpert, J.J., et al. "Medical help and maternal nursing care in the life of low-income families," *Pediatrics* 39 (1967): 749.

Alpert, J.J., et al. "A month of illness and health care among low-income families," *Public Health Rep* 82 (1971): 705.

Baran, S., and Mudge-Lisk, B. *Evaluation of Neighborhood Health Center Outreach Programs: Measures of Input and Output*. Paper presented at the 101st Annual Meeting of the American Public Health Association, San Francisco, Calif., November 1973.

Beck, R.G. "Economic class and access to physician services under public medical care insurance," *Intl J Health Serv* 3 (1973): 341.

Bellin, S.S., and Geiger, H.J. "The impact of a neighborhood health center on patients' behavior and attitudes relating to health care: a study of a low income housing project," *Med Care* 10 (1972): 224.

Bergner, L., and Yerby, A. "Low income and barriers to use of health services," *N Engl J Med* 278 (1968): 541.

Bice, T.W. *Medical Care for the Disadvantaged: Report on a Survey of Use of Medical Services in the Baltimore Standard Metropolitan Statistical Area 1968–1969.* Final report of research conducted under Contract Number HSM 110 69 203, NCHSRD. Washington, D.C.: National Center for Health Services Research and Development, Department of Health, Education and Welfare, 1971.

Bice, T.W., et al. "Socioeconomic status and use of physicians' services: a reconsideration," *Med Care* 12 (1972): 261.

Brooks, C.H. "Associations among distance, patient satisfaction and utilization of two types of inner-city clinics," *Med Care* 11 (1973): 373.

Cauffman, J.G., et al. "The impact of health insurance coverage on health care of school children," *Public Health Rep* 82 (1967): 323.

Contra Costa County Human Resources Agency. *Final Evaluation Report, Health Care Outreach Project.* Title XI, Section 1115 Research and Demonstration Project, Grant Number 11–P–57098/9–01. Contra Costa County, Calif.: 1973.

Davis, K. "A decade of policy developments in providing health care for low-income families," (draft for *A Decade of Federal Anti-Poverty Policy: Achievements, Failures and Lessons,* edited by R. Haveman. Madison: University of Wisconsin Institute for Research on Poverty, 1977), xerox, 1975.

Dodge, W.F., et al. "Patterns of maternal desires for child health care," *Am J Public Health* 60 (1970): 1421.

Fanshel, S., and Bush, J.W. "A health-status index and its application to health service outcomes," *Operations Research* 18 (1970): 1021.

Feldstein, P.J., and Carr, J.W. "The effect of income on medical care spending," *Proceedings of the Social Statistics Section, American Statistical Association* (1964): 93.

Freeborn, D.K., et al. *Evaluating the Effect of Outreach Workers on Medical Care Utilization in the Kaiser-Permanente Neighborhood Health Center Project,* Xeroxed. Portland, Oregon: Health Services Research Center, Kaiser Foundation Hospitals, undated.

Gordis, L. "Effectiveness of comprehensive care programs in preventing rheumatic fever," *N Eng J Med* 289 (1973): 331.

Greene, R. *Assuring Quality in Medical Care: The State of the Art.* Cambridge, Mass.: Ballinger Publishing Company, 1976.

Jehlik, P.J., and McNamara, R.L. "The relation of distance to the differential use of certain health personnel and facilities and the extent of bad illness," *Rural Sociology* 17 (1952): 261.

Kessner, D.M., et al. *Assessment of Medical Care for Children.* Washington, D.C.: Institute of Medicine, National Academy of Sciences, 1974.

Lewis, C.E., and Keairnes, H.W. "Controlling costs of medical care by expanding insurance coverage," *N Engl J Med* 282 (1970): 1405.

Luckham, J., and Swift, D.W. "Community health aides in the ghetto: the Contra Costa project," *Med Care* 7 (1969): 332.

Morris, N., et al. "Alienation as a deterrent to well-child supervision," *Am J Public Health* 56 (1966a): 1874.

Morris, N., et al. "Deterrents to well-child supervision," *Am J Public Health* 56 (1966b): 1232.

Okada, L., et al. *Differential Patterns of Poverty and Health Care Utilization in Eight Urban Areas.* Paper presented at the meeting of the American Association for Public Opinion Research, Pasadena, Calif., 22 May 1971.

Olendzki, M., et al. "The impact of Medicaid on private care for the poor," *Med Care* 10 (1972): 201.

Richardson, W.C. "Poverty, illness and use of health services in the United States," *Hospitals* 43 (1969): 34.

Richardson, W.C. "Measuring the urban poor's use of physicians' services in response to illness episodes," *Med Care* 8 (1970): 132.

Roghmann, K.J. "The impact of Medicaid," chapter 7 in *Child Health and the Community.* Haggerty, R.J., et al. New York: John Wiley and Sons, 1975.

Taylor, D.G., et al. "A social indicator of access to medical care," *J Health Soc Behav* 16 (1975): 38.

U.S. Department of Health, Education and Welfare, National Center for Health Statistics. *Volume of Physician Visits by Place of Visit and Type of Service, United States—July 1963—June 1964.* Public Health Service Pub. No. 1000, Series 10, No. 18. Washington, D.C.: Government Printing Office, 1965.

U.S. Department of Health, Education and Welfare, National Center for Health Statistics. *Volume of Physician Visits, United States—July 1966—June 1967.* Public Health Service Pub. No. 1000, Series 10, No. 49. Washington, D.C.: Government Printing Office, 1968.

U.S. Department of Health, Education and Welfare, National Center for Health Statistics. *Physician Visits, Volume and Interval Since Last Visit, United States—1969.* DHEW Pub. No. (HSM) 72–1064, Vital and Health Statistics Series 10, No. 75. Washington, D.C.: Government Printing Office, 1972.

U.S. Department of Health, Education and Welfare. *EPSDT Summary of Second Progress Report for the Period Ending June 30, 1973.* Washington, D.C.: Social and Rehabilitation Service, Medical Services Administration, 1973.

Weiss, J.E., and Greenlick, M.R. "Determinants of medical care utilization: the effect of social class and distance on contacts with the medical care system," *Med Care* 8 (1970): 456.

Weiss, J.E., Greenlick, M.R., and Jones, J.F. "Determinants of medical care utilization: the impact of spatial factors," *Inquiry* 8 (1971): 50.

Zeckhauser, R.J., and Eliastam, M. "The productivity potential of the physician assistant," *J Human Res* 9 (1973): 95.

※ *Chapter 5*

Providing Primary Care
Practitioners for Children

Judy Baumann
David Calkins, M.D.

There are a number of approaches to solving the problem of unequal and insufficient access to primary health care services for children. Eliminating financial barriers to access is discussed elsewhere in this volume, as is improving the organization of health services. This chapter considers the personnel issue: Are there enough health care practitioners to deliver adequate primary care to children?[a] If not, what can be done to increase their supply?

The availability of a physician, of course, does not guarantee that medical problems will be recognized, diagnosed, or treated. The exact relationship between the number of health practitioners available to deliver care and the health status of the population is difficult to measure. Utilizing time-series data from a number of countries, for example, Stewart (1971) found no association between physician-population ratios (a common measure of the availability of health care services) and life expectancy. In examining mortality data across countries, Senior and Smith (1972) noted that of nine countries with a higher ratio of physicians to population than the United States in 1967, five had a higher general mortality and all nine had a higher infant mortality. The provision of adequate numbers of health care practitioners must be regarded, then, as only the first in a series of steps required to improve the health status of children.

[a] Primary care is first-contact, comprehensive, and continuing medical care. It is the point of entry into the health care system for the individual or family. It is generally ambulatory and includes such initial evaluation and treatment as can be carried out in an office or clinic setting. When more sophisticated services are required, the primary care provider will arrange for such services and participate in subsequent follow-up.

WHO DELIVERS CARE?

Physicians

Most primary care for children is provided by physicians. There were approximately 164 active physicians per 100,000 population in the United States in 1973, up from 128 per 100,000 in 1931.[b] Experts differ over whether there is currently an over-all "shortage" of physicians but increasingly they conclude there is not. The ratio of physicians to the population has gradually increased, although not at a steady rate. With the postwar increase in population there has been a leveling off of the curve upward. Since the 1960s, the declining population growth rate coupled with federal policies implemented to increase physician availability have caused the rate of increase to go up even more steeply than before.

Two actions of the federal government have had a substantial impact on the increase in numbers of physicians. The first was the change in immigration laws in 1965, which made it easier for foreign medical graduates to practice in the United States. Following changes in immigration policies the percentage of new physicians who are foreign medical graduates rose, from 18 percent in 1963 to 45 percent in 1973. At present nearly 25 percent of all active physicians serving patients directly and 40 percent of full-time hospital staffs are foreign medical graduates (Macy Commission, 1976). With the shift in emphasis away from the danger of a 'shortage,' the government has tightened up requirements for entry and practice in the United States by foreign medical graduates beginning in 1977. In the future, depending on how the new law is interpreted, there may be a decline in the numbers of physicians from this source. The government has also intervened to fund the training of physicians in the U.S.

Unfortunately, an increase in the over-all number of physicians does not necessarily guarantee an adequate supply of physicians providing primary care to children. While the supply has been increasing

[b] Estimates of the number of physicians per 100,000 population vary in the medical literature we reviewed. For the most part, these variations are due to differences in the definition of "physician" and "population." In some estimates, DOs and MDs are included in the physician totals; others include both active and inactive physicians. With regard to population, some estimates include U.S. citizens living outside the U.S. and its territories. Our figures are based on 1973 data for active MDs; our population estimates do not include U.S. citizens living outside the U.S. and its territories. Recently the surgeon general has been quoted as saying the figure for 1975 is 173 physicians per 100,000; it is unclear whether this more up-to-date figure includes inactive physicians or DOs or citizens residing outside the United States. For the sake of consistency, we have retained our 1973 estimates.

in recent decades, several other trends have affected the supply of primary care physicians for children.

First, there has been a trend toward specialization among physicians. For years medical school graduates have opted in increasing numbers for the surgical and other secondary or tertiary care specialties rather than primary care. This trend is best measured by the decline of the general practitioner. In 1931 general practitioners accounted for 72 percent of all physicians; in 1973 they represented only 14 percent of the physician pool. Where formerly the general practitioner provided the bulk of primary care for children, today it is provided to an increasing degree by specialists in pediatrics, family practice, and, to a limited extent, in internal medicine. These shifts in specialty choice by physicians are summarized in Figure 5-1.

To counter the shift away from primary care, the 'family practice' specialty was instituted in 1969, and more recently, residency programs in internal medicine and pediatrics have placed increased emphasis on primary care skills. The attention paid to the shortage of primary care physicians has had an effect. The number of filled first-year residencies in primary care has increased dramatically since 1968. The AMA estimates that 58 percent of medical school graduates entered primary care residency programs in 1974 (Nesbitt, 1975).[c] Less encouraging for children, however, is the fact that 31 percent of first-year residency positions are in internal medicine, a field with virtually no impact on the delivery of primary care to children because of the limited extent to which these doctors see children. Only 11 percent of graduates began residency programs in pediatrics; 10 percent began family practice training. The percentage of medical school graduates entering general practice residency programs, a nonspecialty, has declined to only 0.2 percent.

Second, there has been a shift away from traditional office-based practice by primary care practitioners. This shift is clearly seen among pediatricians. At present, only about 58 percent of pediatricians are in office-based practice. The pediatricians who are not in office-based care are not involved in delivering primary care to children. Ten percent are involved in administration and do not deliver services directly. Thirty-two percent are in hospital settings and rarely deliver primary care.

What effect do these trends have on the picture of availability of

---

[c]The AMA estimate is somewhat inflated, due to the inclusion of Canadian medical school graduates with U.S. graduates, and the inclusion of residents in obstetrics and gynecology as primary care physicians. (Our figures elsewhere in this chapter do not include this category). We estimate that the figure is closer to 50 percent, which is considerable improvement over the past.

Figure 5–1.   Active Physicians per 100,000 Population, 1931 and 1973, Primary and Nonprimary Care Providers

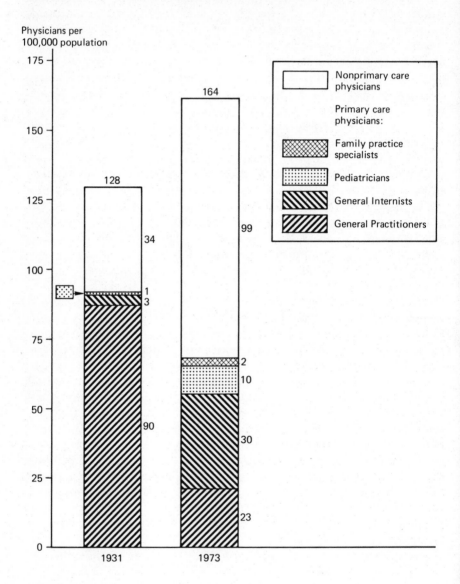

Source: Adapted from Macy Commission, 1976, and Roback, 1974.

children's primary care physicians? It is possible to calculate the number of full-time equivalent child health physicians by multiplying the number of general practitioners, pediatricians, internists, and family practice physicians by the fraction of time these physicians spend delivering primary care to children.[d] The results are shown in Table 5-1. Roughly 23,500 full-time equivalent child health physicians were delivering primary care in 1974.

Further, taking into account the 1974 level at which primary care physicians were being produced, we calculate that the equivalent of 1000 additional children's primary care physicians are trained per year; that is less than one child health physician for every ten medical school graduates (Table 5-2).

What has been the picture of availability of child health physicians over time? Rather than a gradual increase in the numbers of physicians delivering primary care to children, as is the case with physicians as a whole, the numbers have declined. In 1931 there were 18.6 full-time equivalent child health physicians per 100,000 population. By 1973 the number had fallen to 11.3 per 100,000. Thus, despite the increase in over-all numbers of physicians during this period, the number of child health physicians per 100,000 population had declined by a third.

While these numbers are useful in a certain sense because they enable us to determine whether there is currently a shortage of physicians and demonstrate the trends in supply over time, they do not show the full picture of availability of physicians. The fact is that nonprimary care physicians do deliver some primary care; further, geographic maldistribution has an effect on availability, as does the tendency of physicians to practice in urban rather than rural settings.

Large metropolitan areas have far more providers per population than rural areas, and the North and West have more than the South (Figure 5-2). In 1970, 132 rural communities reported the absence of any physician. Thus a large number of children as well as adults are without ready access to primary care services. The need to travel long distances to obtain care, much of which for children is preventive in nature, surely means that such services are used less often than would be desirable (Chapter 4).

As we've seen, the decline of the general practitioner and the in-

---

[d] One needed piece of research is another review of the time primary care practitioners spend on children. It may well be that with the increase in pediatricians and internists, and the continuing decline in general practitioners, there have been shifts in the mix of patients (adults and children) seen by each of these types of providers. The estimates in this chapter, from the National Ambulatory Medical Care Survey—1971, are valuable only insofar as they represent *trends* in the availability and current patterns of training of health practitioners.

Table 5-1.   Full Time Equivalent Child Health Physician Data, 1973

Type of Physician	Number[a]	Fraction of Time Spent Delivering Children's Primary Care	Number Full Time Equivalent Child Health Physicians
General Practitioner	48,192	$.19^b$	9,156
Pediatrician	20,849	$(.94)^b (.58)^c$	11,367
General Internist	61,735	$.03^b$	1,852
Family Practice	5,754	$.19^d$	1,093
		Total	23,468

Sources: [a]Roback, 1974; [b]National Center for Health Statistics, 1974 (percentage of time spent seeing children); [c]Parker, 1974 (percentage of pediatricians in office-based, i.e., primary care); [d]Estimated to be same as general practitioner, since family practice specialty not included in National Ambulatory Medical Care data.

Table 5-2.   Primary Care Residency Programs and the Number of Full Time Equivalent Child Health Physicians in Training, 1974

Type of Program	Number U.S. and Canadian Graduates of Medical Schools in First-Year Residency Programs[a]	Fraction of Time Spent Providing Primary Care to Children	Number Full Time Equivalent Child Health Physicians in Training
General Practice	23	$.19^b$	4
Pediatrics	1,252	$(.94)^b (.58)^c$	683
Internal Medicine	3,591	$.03^b$	108
Family Practice	1,124	$.19^d$	214
		Total	1,109

Sources: [a]Cooper, 1975; [b]National Center for Health Statistics, 1974; [c]Parker, 1974; [d]Estimated to be same as General Practitioner, since family practice specialty not included in National Ambulatory Medical Care Survey data.

Figure 5—2. Active Physicians *(MD and DO)* per 100,000 Population by Geographic Region: 1973

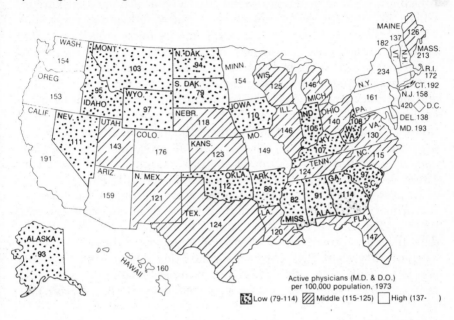

Active physicians (M.D. & D.O.)
per 100,000 population, 1973

Low (79-114) Middle (115-125) High (137-)

Source: Macy Commission, 1976, p. 69.

crease in primary care specialists has meant the decline of office-based physicians and their replacement by physicians who prefer group practice arrangements and hospitals. Since neither hospitals nor group practices are as prevalent in rural areas, the trend toward specialization has exacerbated the maldistribution of physicians. Further, even where the ratio of physicians to population may be high, as in urban centers, the number of office-based primary care physicians may be low. Office-based primary care physicians in Boston, for example, dropped from 194.3 per 100,000 in 1940 to 96.3 in 1961 (Parker, 1974). Thus even those children who live in cities may not necessarily have easy access to primary care services. The end result of these trends is that when poor urban children receive primary care, it is often provided by physicians or physicians-in-training outside of the traditional children's care settings. From 1962 to 1970 the number of outpatient visits doubled; from 1970 to 1974 use of emergency rooms increased 50 percent. The Macy Commission (1976) attributes this increase primarily to a lack of availability of private physicians.

Nonphysicians

Physicians, of course, are not the only providers of primary care for children. An expanding number of allied health personnel are involved in the delivery of primary care. These individuals carry such titles as physician's assistant, MEDEX, family nurse practitioner, and child health associate. The largest group involved in providing care to children are known as pediatric nurse practitioners (PNP). Pediatric nurse practitioners are usually registered nurses who have received additional academic and clinical training (a minimum of four months) enabling them to provide well-child care, diagnose and treat common illnesses, counsel parents, and handle problems generally presented to pediatricians over the telephone. Several programs exist to train personnel of this type (Silver et al., 1967; Connelly and Yankauer, 1969; Bergman, 1972; Bergeson et al., 1973; Kahn, 1973).

At present these physician-extenders represent only a small part of the primary care picture for children, but their numbers are growing rapidly. The first PNPs began training in 1967 in Colorado. Recent data from the American Academy of Pediatrics indicates a current level of fifty-eight PNP programs graduating nearly 1000 students per year, with total PNP graduates numbering about 3300 as of January 1977 (American Academy of Pediatrics, 1975a, 1975b, and 1977).

Compared with traditional office nurses, PNPs spend considerably more time in direct patient care. In one study, PNPs spent 47 percent of their time with patients as compared to 24 percent for other nurses in the same settings. This time tends to be spent largely in performing the sorts of patient care tasks usually handled by physicians. History-taking, physical examination, evaluation, and counseling occupied 60 percent of the patient contact time of PNPs, but only 11 percent of the patient contact time of other nurses (Silver and Duncan, 1971).

To the extent that they perform procedures usually done only by physicians, PNPs may be considered (in economic terms) a substitute for physicians. Ideally, they should be assigned those tasks in which they have the greatest relative efficiency, i.e., those tasks for which the ratio of cost when performed by extender to cost when performed by physician is least. Models applying this principle indicate that, when best employed, physician-extenders may increase the productivity of a practice in terms of patient visits 50 to 74 percent (Zeckhouser and Eliastam, 1973; Golladay et al., 1973). Gains should be greatest in group settings. In practices (mostly solo) where this has been studied empirically, the actual increase in productivity provided by a PNP is closer to 30 percent, although there is considerable variability among practices. Some pediatricians increase their practice load with the help of the PNP, while others devote more time to each patient or increase leisure activities (Yankauer et al., 1972a). As we will discuss, there are many factors, such as the availability of physicians to supervise PNPs, that will have an effect on whether PNPs can be employed to increase the productivity of a practice. Before looking at these prerequisites for employing PNPs, however, it is possible to estimate the numbers of full-time equivalent child health physicians available to deliver children's primary care from the pool of PNPs. Using the estimate that a PNP increases the productivity of a practice by 30 percent, it would take roughly three PNPs to perform the duties of one children's primary care physician. There are now 3300 PNPs, or the equivalent of 1000 full-time children's primary care physicians. An additional 1000 PNPs are trained each year; this is the equivalent of another 300 full-time equivalent children's primary care physicians. Combining the data on physicians and PNPs, there were 24,500 full-time equivalent child health physicians in 1974 and an additional 1300 being trained at current training levels.

Of course, PNPs, like physicians, are not uniformly available, and thus these figures do not show the whole picture of availability. Geographic maldistribution still appears a problem among the nonphysician group of primary health care providers, though precise data supporting this conclusion are lacking. It should not be surprising that such maldistribution might exist. Like physicians, physician-extenders are trained predominantly in urban settings and often elect to remain in such environments. In addition, large clinics and group practices (generally urban) have shown somewhat more interest than private physicians (more often rural) in hiring physician extenders. Since physician extenders must practice under physician supervision, they tend to be concentrated in urban areas where physicians are. However, there have been efforts by several programs (e.g., the University of Colorado Pediatric Nurse Practitioner Program) to place graduates in isolated rural settings, providing them physician support through telephone communication and periodic on-site visits. How widespread this approach will become is at present uncertain.

HOW MANY PHYSICIANS ARE ENOUGH?

How many child health physicians (or their equivalent) do we need? There is considerable argument on this point. Two standards might be offered as a basis for judgment. By specifying the types of primary care services that should be provided to children, the volume of such services, and then finally the number of physicians required to provide them, a group of physicians at Yale estimated the need for full-time child health physicians to be 37 per 100,000 population (Schoenfeld et al., 1972). Applying this "ideal world" standard to the expected growth in population suggests a need for 85,000 child health physicians by 1980.

A more empirical estimate of physician need may be obtained by examining staffing patterns of large prepaid group practices. The physician-population ratio of prepaid group practices should be regarded as a reasonable lower limit for a need estimate. Prepaid groups are able to achieve efficiencies of service delivery that cannot be attained in solo practice arrangements. Further, their patient populations are generally healthier than the population at large. Both of these factors should reduce their requirements for physician services. The child health physician-population ratio varies somewhat among prepaid groups, but is in the neighborhood of 20 per 100,000 population. Projected nationally, this would translate into a requirement of 46,000 child health physicians for an estimated population of 230 million in 1980.

If we define true need for child health physicians to be the number required to provide the level of services that would be demanded if such services were financially and geographically accessible, then that figure most likely lies somewhere between these two extremes (i.e., between 46,000 and 85,000). Since as of 1974 (as we have seen) there were only 24,500 full-time equivalent child health physicians available in the United States, this would suggest a need for 22,000 to 60,500 additional physicians (or their equivalent) by 1980. At 1974 training levels, less than 8000 additional full-time equivalent children's primary care physicians will be trained by 1980. We thus remain 14,000 to 52,500 shy of the number needed, geographic considerations aside.

WHAT ALTERNATIVES EXIST FOR INCREASING THE SUPPLY?

In general, three strategies have been suggested by policymakers for increasing the supply of primary care providers: train more physicians, increase the proportion of physicians who specialize in children's primary care, or expand the number of nonphysicians who provide children's primary care. Historically, federal policy has focused on the first of these alternatives. Beginning with the Health Professions Educational Assistance Act of 1963, which authorized direct aid (capitation) to medical schools, there have been a series of legislative acts providing scholarship and loan assistance as well as institutional and other kinds of help. These include the Health Manpower Act of 1968, the Comprehensive Health Manpower Training Act of 1971, and the Health Professions Educational Assistance Act of 1976.

The primary emphasis of these measures has been on the expansion of medical school enrollment. They have been successful in achieving this goal. Between 1965 and 1975 twenty-one new medical schools were established. Over the past decade the number of first-year medical school places increased from 8759 in 1965 to 14,937 in 1974 (Cooper, 1976). More recently, an effort has been made to influence the distribution of physicians among specialties and by geographic region. Current legislation ties federal medical school funding grants to requirements to increase residency positions in primary care, and creates loan programs to students tied to future practice in underserved areas. Relatively little attention has been given to the third alternative, expanding the role of nonphysicians in providing primary care.

Which of the above alternatives is most cost-effective? Training more physicians is clearly an expensive alternative. A study by the Institute of Medicine of the National Academy of Sciences (1974) put total education costs per medical students per year at $12,650. Since most medical schools still require four years for graduation, the total education cost per physician is $50,600. As mentioned previously, only 11 percent of medical school graduates entered pediatrics in 1974, 10 percent in family practice, and .2 percent in GP programs. If these "tastes" among medical school graduates remain constant, and adjusting for the amount of time these graduates spend on children and on primary care, it would be necessary to train at least ten medical students to achieve an increment of one in the number of child health primary care physicians. By favoring the admission of students with interests in children's primary care fields and developing a curriculum that reinforces these interests, however, it might be possible for medical schools to achieve the same result with a somewhat smaller expansion of enrollment.

Expanding residency training in family practice and primary care pediatrics is also an expensive proposition. Such programs require the development of suitable ambulatory care settings within existing hospital facilities or in remote sites. Faculty with experience in primary care delivery must be hired. Harvard Medical School recently estimated annual expenses at $30,000 for each trainee in primary care internal medicine or pediatrics. Robert Lawrence, director of the primary care residency program at Harvard, further estimates the value of the services provided by these trainees at $5000 per person per year (personal communication, 1975). This would result in a net cost to the institution of $25,000 per trainee per year, a full cost over three years of $75,000 per trainee. There are no published data regarding the cost of training residents in family medicine, but it is not unreasonable to assume that it would be similar.

The cost of training nurse practitioners is substantially smaller. Most PNP training programs require less than one full year of formal training. A 1972 survey of thirty-nine PNP training programs found that the mean cost per trainee was about $4000 (Dobmeyer et al., 1972).

Table 5−3 summarizes the above data. Cost is expressed in terms of the amount needed to train the equivalent of one full-time child health physician. Training additional pediatric nurse practitioners is the least expensive approach to take in increasing the supply of primary health care providers for children.

WHAT ARE THE EFFECTS OF PNP UTILIZATION?

It is reasonable at this point to ask what other effects would result from shifting a greater proportion of children's primary care to PNPs. Certainly, if the care provided by these individuals were infe-

Table 5−3. Comparison of Cost of Three Alternative Strategies to Increase Number of Full Time Equivalent Child Health Physicians

	Unit Cost	Adjustment Factor[a]	Cost of Training One Full Time Equivalent Child Health Physician
Expansion of medical school enrollment	$50,000	10	$500,000
Development of more primary care residency programs			
a. family practice	$75,000	5	$300,000
b. pediatrics	$75,000	1.4	$105,000
Training of more pediatric nurse practitioners	$ 4,000	3	$12,000

[a] number of 'units' which must be produced to obtain the equivalent of one full time child health physician.

rior to that provided by physicians, it would be unwise to suggest an increase in their utilization.

Quality assessment may take a variety of forms. It may focus on the basic qualifications of a physician-extender to provide a specific service through an examination of necessary knowledge and skills. A study of PNPs employing this methodology was in fact performed at St. Louis University. In a written examination concerning primary care pediatrics, a group of PNPs achieved scores comparable to those of pediatric residents and significantly better than those of senior medical students (DeCastro et al., 1974).

Quality assessment may also focus on job performance. Here judgments are made as to whether the processes followed by physician extenders adhere to accepted standards of medical practice. Such evaluation of PNPs has been performed in an informal sense in several practice settings, where physicians have been asked to give their opinion of the services provided by the PNPs with whom they were associated. In virtually every instance they have been "enthusiastic" in their assessment of the work of their new colleagues (Yankauer et al., 1970b). Evaluation of performance may, however, take a more formal nature. At the University of Colorado, children seen in a clinic setting were examined first by a PNP and then later (independently) by a pediatrician. Both made separate reports in the medical record regarding their findings. These records were then reviewed in order to identify any discrepancies in the two assessments. "Significant differences" were found in only 0.7 percent (two) of the cases. The PNP was correct in one case, the pediatrician in the other (Duncan et al., 1971).

Finally, quality assessment may focus on actual patient outcomes. Measures of the health status of children treated by physician-extenders is theoretically the best means of assessing their effectiveness. This technique has received limited use. A Pittsburgh study demonstrated that the health status of 110 infants in a low-income housing project who were cared for exclusively by a PNP was similar to the health status of infants in an upper-middle-class pediatric practice, when health status was determined on the basis of physical and laboratory parameters (Chappell et al., 1973).

Simply equating the quality of care provided by physician-extenders to that provided by physicians, however, tends to obscure an important point. There is some evidence to indicate that the nature of the product offered by PNPs may be an improvement over traditional physician services, since PNPs may add an element to primary care missing in the usual physician-patient relationship. Pediatricians and other physicians tend to be most attentive to patient's complaints that seem to have an organic basis. They may ignore those of an emotional or behavioral nature (Starfield and Borkowf, 1969). A PNP, perhaps because of his or her nursing training, may be more attuned to these areas of patient need (Bates, 1970). Compliance with medication has in some cases been shown to be higher in groups of patients followed by PNPs, perhaps in part because of their attention to the "whole patient" (Fink, 1969).

Furthermore, the involvement of a PNP in a pediatric practice may have a positive influence on the quality of care delivered by other professionals working in the same practice. The development of disease treatment protocols for PNPs may lead physicians to evaluate more carefully their own treatment practices. The presence of the nurse practitioner may serve as a subtle means of peer review. In addition, nursing personnel may be favorably influenced by their association with the PNP. One survey of nurses working in practices that employed PNPs indicated that 41 percent viewed the PNP as a stimulus for their own continuing education. Further, 52 percent thought the role encouraged other nurses to assert a greater degree of independence in their own practice, and almost two-thirds felt the PNP was a valuable resource to them (Turner et al., 1973).

A number of studies have been done to assess how patients feel about the services delivered by PNPs. A group from the University of Colorado carried out an opinion survey of sixty-eight families receiving care in a Denver pediatric practice that had added a graduate of the Colorado PNP program. Of the persons surveyed, 94 percent expressed satisfaction with the services provided them. In addition, 57 percent felt that the joint care provided by the pediatrician-PNP team was superior to the care provided by the pediatrician alone (Day et al., 1970). Studies of other pediatrician-PNP practices have shown similar degrees of patient satisfaction with the services of PNP (Karp et al., 1973).

Attention has also been given to the issue of provider acceptance of PNPs. One approach taken by researchers has been to survey physicians who have not worked with PNPs regarding the hypothetical addition of a PNP to their practice. Not surprisingly, these physicians show some hesitancy to delegate tasks. There is a particular reluctance to delegate well-baby care. Acceptance of the hypothetical PNP is greater among younger physicians and those practicing in groups (Schoen et al., 1973). On the other hand, survey of physicians who have actually utilized PNPs in their practices have shown almost uniform satisfaction with the relationship (Karp et al., 1973).

HOW CAN WE ENCOURAGE
UTILIZATION OF PNPs?

Several alternative strategies for increasing the supply of primary child health care providers have been considered. The training of physician-extenders (in particular, pediatric nurse practitioners) seems to be the best strategy to meet this need. We will now examine the factors likely to affect the training and employment of a larger number of PNPs, particularly in medically underserved areas, and the steps that must be taken to maximize their utilization.

Two elements are critical to increasing the supply of PNPs: nurses who will accept and prepare for an extended role, and training programs with sufficient positions to meet their needs. What is the state of the world today with regard to these two variables?

With regard to the first element, adequate nurses, the supply seems to be abundant. According to reports from directors of nurse practitioner training programs, the current ratio of applicants to enrollees is four to one (Dobmeyer, 1972). What is more, there would seem to be several sources of potential applicants in future years. According to the 1972 Inventory of Registered Nurses (reported by the Statistics Department of the American Nursing Association), only 778,470 out of 1,127,657 registered nurses were employed full or part time. Thus, nearly 350,000 registered nurses are currently inactive. Numerous factors explain this large pool of unemployed nurses, but of substantial importance are lack of perceived work opportunities in local settings, dissatisfaction with career limits, and unfavorable hours (Baker, 1970). It is likely that substantial numbers of these nurses could be attracted into careers as nurse practitioners, particularly if they were able to practice in their present communities. Anecdotal reports of such cases already exist (Oseasohn, 1971). Recent nursing school graduates are another potential source of nurse practitioners. There has been growing dissatisfaction in recent years with limitations and excessive routine of nursing in traditional settings, particularly among graduates of baccalaureate programs. The expanded role provided nurse practitioners might be appealing to this group.

The second element on the supply side of the question is the availability of training positions for nurse practitioners. The rapid growth of these programs during recent years has already been reviewed. A recent study indicated that enrollment in all nurse practitioner programs (the majority of which were PNP programs) was 1500 in 1973. This was expected to decrease somewhat, leveling off at about 1000 by 1976 (Dobmeyer et al., 1972). If these projections are accurate, a shortage of training positions may indeed exist, at least relative to the pool of interested applicants.

Such a shortage should be relatively easy to remedy, given the minimal financial and physical requirements of nurse practitioner training programs (in contrast to those of physician training). The likelihood of training too many nurse practitioners is small. In any case, programs could be reduced or eliminated fairly rapidly with minimal losses in terms of capital investment. Excess graduates would have difficulty finding jobs in which they could make full use of their skills, but given their training as registered nurses, they would certainly be able to find employment. The significance of training limitations will be considered further after we have examined the demand side of the equation.

At present, there seems ample demand for the services of nurse practitioners. In a recent survey, 75 percent of nurse practitioner program directors stated that there were too few graduates for the jobs available (Dobmeyer et al., 1972). Future needs, however, are less certain.

Several factors will affect physician demand for nurse practitioners. Three seem of particular significance: physician attitudes toward nurse practitioners, financial considerations in the employment of nurse practitioners, and legal provisions regarding the manner in which nurse practitioners may be utilized. We will consider the qualitative importance of each of these factors and, where possible, attempt to get some handle on their quantitative significance.

We have alluded briefly to physician attitudes toward PNPs earlier. Those physicians who have utilized PNPs have been uniformly enthusiastic in their assessment of the value of these new health practitioners. Future demand, however, will largely depend on the opinions of those who have not worked with PNPs. Here, as noted earlier, enthusiasm is somewhat less. In their 1967 survey of the Fellows of the American Academy of Pediatrics, however, Yankauer and his colleagues found that pediatricians were in general "prepared to move toward delegating patient care tasks to adequately prepared health workers" (Yankauer et al., 1970a, p. 539). Of those surveyed, 41 percent would hire a PNP full time, and 22 percent would hire one part time. The major obstacle to hiring was a shortage of capable personnel to whom tasks could be entrusted. If we extrapolate from this survey to the entire population of some 16,000 pediatricians expected to be available in 1980, there seems to be a theoretical demand for about 10,000 pediatric nurse practitioners on a full-time or part-time basis. It is reasonable to assume, however, that the continued expansion in the use of personnel will increase the number of pediatricians who desire to employ PNPs. If we further assume that some pediatricians may wish to hire more than a single PNP (e.g., to staff multiple outreach clinics) and that a few may be hired by family physicians, the demand for PNPs by 1980 may reach 12,000 to 16,000.

Financial considerations, particularly could reduce actual demand below this theoretical level. An important aspect of the financial feasibility of PNPs in actual practice is the policy of third-party payers (government and private) with regard to the reimbursement of physicians for services provided by these individuals. At present a physician may usually be reimbursed for these services provided he is physically present in the same building where the care is provided. Reimbursement has, however, been denied in instances where the supervising physician is in a location separate from that of the assistant. It has been argued that specific legislation authorizing the PNP or other assistant to provide care in a defined manner in a remote setting should constitute sufficient assurance to third parties that these services have professional approval and should, therefore, be covered (Ott, 1973).

Concern among physicians regarding the financial soundness of physician-extender utilization seems to be real. In a survey of physicians in the state of Washington, economic concerns were cited by forty-one of those responding as the major obstacle to the hiring of a physician-extender (Appel and Lewin, 1975).

Another factor that will influence the extent to which PNPs are utilized is the legal framework within which they practice. This is largely determined by state law. Three approaches have been taken by states in regulating the activity of PNPs and other physician-extenders. General delegatory statutes simply amend the state medical practice act to allow for the delegation of routine patient care functions to qualified personnel who are not physicians. Regulatory authority statutes authorize specific organizations (e.g., the state board of medical examiners) to establish rules and regulations with respect to the education and employment of physician-extenders. As of 1973, seven states had laws allowing delegation and seventeen states had laws conferring regulatory authority statutes. A third approach is the actual licensure of physician-extenders (i.e., the establishment of education and practice standards through legislation). Only one state has taken this approach, and then with reference to only one category of physician-extender (the Colorado Child Health Associate Law) (Dean, 1973).

Debate rages in the literature over which of these various approaches is optimal. At one extreme are those who argue for "benign neglect" of the physician-extender. One medical-legal scholar has written: "It is best in the evolution of professional groups to start with registration and move to licensure only after the professional group is fully matured, clearly defined in its responsibilities and capable within its own educational and training programs of meeting the reasonable manpower needs in its field of practice" (Curran, 1970, p. 1085). At the other extreme are those who argue that licensure is essential for these new health practitioners to achieve their full potential. Silver points to the Colorado Child Health Associate Law, claiming that it has actually broadened the role of these practitioners by allowing them to prescribe certain medication independently (Silver, 1971).

It is apparent that excessive regulation in any form may limit the use of physician-extenders. California is a case in point. Under the California Physician Assistant Law (a regulatory authority statute) the state board of medical examiners established restrictive policies regarding the practice of these professionals. This law has served to discourage the further development of physician-extender training programs in that state (Ott, 1973).

One final factor that may limit the utilization of PNPs is the threat of malpractice suits against physicians as a result of PNP activities. While it is clear that physicians are responsible for the clinical actions of their assistants (Curran, 1972), there has been no rash of malpractice claims stemming from the increased use of physician-extenders. In fact, as of 1973, there had been no suits against the graduates of university-affiliated physician-extender programs or against their employers. Nurse practitioners and other physician-extenders, by promoting better relations between provider and consumer, may even make malpractice claims less likely. Therefore, some have argued that not only will there be few claims against physician-extenders, but also the over-all incidence of malpractice litigation will be reduced (Ott, 1973).

Let us now return briefly to the question of supply and demand for PNPs. As of January 1977, a total of 3300 individuals had been graduated from pediatric nurse practitioner training programs. Annual PNP output seems to be stabilizing at about 1000. By 1980, we could therefore expect about 6300 pediatric nurse practitioners to be available for practice, perhaps somewhat fewer depending on the degree of attrition due to career dissatisfaction, family responsibilities, and other factors. This is well short of what is needed, suggesting that a case might be made for intervention in order to increase the supply of PNPs.

SUMMARY

Little attention has been paid to the effects of recent physician training trends on children. The increases in the training of primary care physicians have not improved the availability of children's health services.

While the total numbers of physicians in the U.S. increased to 164 per 100,000 in 1973, the number of full-time equivalent child health physicians actually declined from 18.6 per 100,000 in 1931 to 11.3 per 100,000 in 1977. Currently, 50 percent of medical graduates are going into residency programs in primary care. This represents a significant shift over the past ten years. However, much of the increase is due to the increase in the number of general internists, who rarely see children; in 1974, 30 percent of medical graduates entered training programs in this primary care specialty.

Children's primary care is delivered by general practitioners, pediatricians, and family practice specialists. The number of GPs is declining rapidly; in 1974, only 0.2 percent of U.S. graduates went into GP training programs. Pediatricians are increasing, but 32 percent of pediatricians have opted for service in hospitals, where they deliver almost no primary care. The family practice specialty is increasing, but these specialists divide their time between children and adults.

Of course, not all primary care is, or will be, delivered by physicians. Allied health professionals play an important role. The most significant nonphysician health provider for children is the pediatric nurse practitioner (PNP). There are currently 3300 PNPs in the U.S. and 1000 more are trained annually.

A variety of techniques may be used to estimate shortages in health care personnel. Using the most conservative of these techniques, we find that there will be a shortage of at least 14,000 full time equivalent child health physicians by 1980. Three approaches have been suggested to meet the need for additional providers of health care: an increase in the over-all number of medical school graduates; an expansion of residency programs in primary care; and an increase in the training of allied health professionals. The third strategy is clearly the most effective from the standpoint of cost; further, evidence now available suggests that the quality and acceptability of the care provided by pediatric nurse practitioners is good.

The expansion of PNP utilization deserves more attention than it has received. Particularly, legal and financial barriers to the full utilization of pediatric nurse practitioners should be eliminated. The development of programs to encourage nonphysician health practitioners to practice in underserved areas and to encourage physicians to hire and use effectively these assistants should be initiated and funded.

REFERENCES

American Academy of Pediatrics. *Lengthening Shadows*. Evanston, Ill.: author, 1971.

American Academy of Pediatrics. *An Accumulative Listing of Programs for the Pediatric Nurse Associate, Medical Assistant in Pediatrics, and Pediatric Aide.* Evanston, Ill.: Office of Allied Health Manpower of the American Academy of Pediatrics, 1975a.

American Academy of Pediatrics. *Summary Report of Pediatric Nurse Practitioner Graduates and Training Programs.* Evanston, Ill.: Office of Allied Health Manpower of the American Academy of Pediatrics, 1975b.

American Academy of Pediatrics. Unpublished data on Pediatric Nurse Practitioners compiled by the Office of Health Manpower. Evanston, Ill., 1977.

American Nurses Association. "Guidelines on short-term continuing education programs for pediatric nurse associates" (joint statement with the American Academy of Pediatrics), *Am J Nurs* 71 (1971): 509.

Appel, G.L., and Lowin, A. *Physician Extenders: An Evaluation of Policy-Related Research.* Minneapolis: Interstudy, 1975.

Baker, A.S. "Editorial: Primary care by the nurse," *N Engl J Med* 290 (1970): 282.

Bates, B. "Doctor and nurse: changing roles and relations," *N Engl J Med* 283 (1970): 129.

Bergen, S.S., Jr. "Primary health care: suggested organization structure," in *Primary Care: Where Medicine Fails*, edited by S. Andreopolos. New York: John Wiley and Sons, 1974.

Bergeson, P.S., et al. "A pediatric nurse associate program for Arizona," *Ariz Med* 30 (1973): 333.

Bergman, A.B., et al. "Time-motion study of practicing pediatricians," *Pediatrics* 38 (1966): 254.

Bergman, A.B., et al. "Pediatric manpower problems are solvable," *Pediatr Clin North Am* 19 (1972): 281.

Burnett, R.D. "Pediatric manpower needs: can they be met?" *Pediatr Clin North Am* 16 (1969): 254.

Chappell, J.A., et al. "Evaluation of infant health care by a nurse practitioner," *Pediatrics* 49 (1972): 871.

Comptroller General of the United States. *Report to the Congress: Progress and Problems in Training and Use of Assistants to Primary Care Physicians.* Washington, D.C.: Government Printing Office, 1975.

Connelly, J.P. and Yankauer, A. "Allied health personnel in child health care," *Pediatr Clin North Am* 16 (1969): 921.

Cooper, T. Statement of the Assistant Secretary for Health, Department of Health Education and Welfare, before the Subcommittee on Health of the Committee on Labor and Public Welfare, U.S. Senate, September 16, 1975. Washington, D.C.: Government Printing Office, 1976.

Curran, W.J. "New paramedical personnel—to license or not to license?" *N Engl J Med* 282 (1970): 1085.

Curran, W.J. "Legal responsibility for actions of physicians' assistants," *N Engl J Med* 286 (1972): 254.

Day, L.R., et al. "Acceptance of pediatric nurse practitioners," *Am J Dis Child* 119 (1970): 204.

Dean, W.J. "State legislation for physicians' assistants: a review and analysis," *Health Serv Rep* 88 (1973): 3.

DeCastro, F.J., et al. "An evaluation of new primary pediatric paraprofessionals," *J Med Educ* 49 (1974): 192.

Dobmeyer, T.W., et al. *A Report of a 1972 Survey of Nurse Associate Training Programs.* Minneapolis: Interstudy, 1972.

Duncan, B., et al. "Comparison of the physical assessment of children by pediatric nurse practitioners and pediatricians," *Am J Public Health* 61 (1971): 1170.

Fein, R. *The Doctor Shortage: An Economic Diagnosis.* Washington, D.C.: The Brookings Institution, 1967.

Fine, L.L., and Silver, H.K. "Comparative diagnostic abilities of child health associate interns and practicing pediatricians," *J Pediatr* 83 (1973): 332.

Fink, D., et al. "The management specialist in effective pediatric care," *Am J Public Health* 59 (1969): 527.

Golladay, F.L., et al. "Allied health manpower strategies: estimates of the potential gains from efficient task delegation," *Med Care* 11 (1973): 457.

Haggerty, R.J., et al. *Child Health and the Community.* New York: John Wiley and Sons, 1975.

Kahn, L. "Washington University pediatric nurse practitioner training program, development and experience," *Mo Med* 70 (1973): 658.

Karp, S.S., et al. "The pediatric nurse practitioner in the private office," *J Med Soc N J* 70 (1973): 773.

Machotka, P., et al. "Competence of child health associates. I. Comparison of their basic science knowledge with that of medical students and pediatric residents," *Am J Dis Child* 125 (1973): 199.

Macy Commission. *Physicians for the Future.* New York: Josiah Macy, Jr., Foundation, 1976.

Mason, H.R. "Effectiveness of student aid programs tied to a service commitment," *J Med Educ* 44 (1971): 575.

National Academy of Sciences. *The Physician's Assistant.* Washington, D.C.: author, 1970.

National Academy of Sciences. *Cost of Education in the Health Professions.* Washington, D.C.: Institute of Medicine of the National Academy of Sciences, 1974.

National Center for Health Statistics. *National Ambulatory Medical Care Survey: Background and Methodology.* Series 2, No. 61. Washington, D.C.: Government Printing Office, 1974.

Nesbitt, T.E. Statistics of the American Medical Association presented as a supplement to the testimony of T.E. Nesbitt, M.D., before the Subcommittee on Health of the Committee on Labor and Public Welfare, U.S. Senate, November 18, 1975. Washington, D.C.: Government Printing Office, 1976.

Oseasohn, R., et al. "Rural medical care: Physician's assistant linked to an urban medical center," *JAMA* 218 (1971): 1417.

Ott, J.E. "New health professionals in pediatrics," *Adv Pediatr* 20 (1973): 39.

Parker, A.W. "The dimensions of primary care: blueprints for change," in *Primary Care: Where Medicine Fails*, edited by S. Andreopoulos. New York: John Wiley and Sons, 1974.

Patterson, P.K., and Bergman, A.B. "Time-motion study of six pediatric office assistants," *N Engl J Med* 281 (1969): 771.

Roback, G.A. *Distribution of Physicians in the United States, 1973*. Chicago: American Medical Association, Center for Health Services Research and Development, 1974.

Schoen, E.J., et al. "The health care team: the role of nurse practitioners as viewed by California pediatricians," *Calif Med* 118 (1973): 62.

Schonfeld, H.K., et al. "Numbers of physicians required for primary medical care," *N Engl J Med* 286 (1972): 571.

Senior, B., and Smith, B.A. "The number of physicians as a constraint on the delivery of health care: how many physicians are enough?" *JAMA* 222 (1972): 178.

Silver, H.K. "Use of new types of allied health professionals in providing care for children," *Am J Dis Child* 116 (1968): 486.

Silver, H.K. "New allied health professionals: implications of the Colorado Child Health Associate Law," *N Engl J Med* 284 (1971): 304.

Silver, H.K., and Duncan, B. "Time motion study of pediatric nurse practitioners: comparison with regular office nurses and pediatricians," *J Pediatr* 79 (1971): 331.

Silver, H.K., and Hecker, J.E. "The pediatric nurse practitioner and child health associate: new types of health professionals," *J Med Educ* 45 (1970): 171.

Silver, H.K., et al. "A program to increase health care for children: the pediatric nurse practitioner program," *Pediatrics* 39 (1967): 756.

Starfield, B., and Borkowf, S. "Physicians' recognition of complaints made by parents about their children's health," *Pediatrics* 43 (1969): 168.

Stewart, C.T. "Allocation of resources to health," *J Hum Res* 6 (1971): 103.

Turner, I., et al. "Evaluation of the nurse associate in a variety of health care settings," unpublished, 1973.

Yankauer, A., et al. "Pediatric practice in the United States," *Pediatrics* (Suppl) 45 (1970a): 521.

Yankauer, A., et al. "The practice of nursing in pediatric offices—challenge and opportunity," *N Engl J Med* 282 (1970b): 843.

Yankauer, A., et al. "The outcomes and service impact of a pediatric nurse practitioner training program—nurse practitioner training outcomes," *Am J Public Health* 62 (1972): 347.

Yankauer, A., et al. "The costs of training and the income generation potential of pediatric nurse practitioners," *Pediatrics* 49 (1972b): 878.

Zeckhauser, R., and Eliastam, M. "The productivity potential of the physician assistant," *J Hum Res* 9 (1973): 75.

Chapter 6

Financing Children's
Health Care

John A. Butler

How do we as a nation pay for the health care of our children and what have we learned about the public financing of children's care? This chapter gives a brief overview of the private and public components of expenditure, reviews the Medicaid experience in its implications for increasing medical care access among low-income children, and explores the evidence regarding prepayment and capitation as favored financing mechanisms. The discussion provides background information at a time when policymakers are considering major revisions in the nation's system of health care financing. In this dialogue it may be useful to introduce data specifically oriented to the needs of children.

PRIVATE AND PUBLIC CHILD
HEALTH EXPENDITURES

The Social Security Administration reports that in 1975 about 15.4 billion dollars were spent on the health care of children and youth under nineteen years of age. This represents approximately 15 percent of the total 103.2 billion dollars spent for all age groups. Of the amount spent on children, 76 percent is from private sources, 9 percent is from state and local funds, and 15 percent from the federal government (Mueller and Gibson, June 1976). Approximately half of the expenditures that can be traced to private sources are in the form of out-of-pocket payments, usually in fee-for-service arrangements.

Private health insurance among children is much more likely to cover hospital costs than primary care costs. Almost three-quarters of American children are covered by some form of private insurance for hospitalization, but less than 30 percent for doctor visits. Income-related differences in private health insurance coverage remain pronounced (National Center for Health Statistics, 1975).

Out-of-pocket health care expenditures for children and youth are not uniformly distributed. Instead, the data suggest a very skewed distribution of private expenditures (Table 6–1). In 1969, 18 percent of children and youth showed no health-related expenditures at all; two-thirds had expenses not exceeding $100; and only 8.7 percent had expenses in excess of $250. Hence the $105 average per child masks an important reality: most children have little or no out-of-pocket health care expenditure, and only a few children have high expenditures.

There are also major differences in personal expenditure per child by income group and residential area, as seen in data from the 1970 Survey of Health Care Utilization and Expenditures (Table 6–2). Total expenditure estimates from these data are lower than the ones reported by the Social Security Administration, both because they are from an earlier year and because estimation techniques were somewhat different in the two surveys.[a] But we may assume that proportions from free and nonfree sources are essentially the same in both surveys.[b] The table suggests many possible bases for equity comparisons; among children and adults, or various subgroups of

[a]The Social Security Administration and the University of Chicago's Center for Health Administration Studies are widely recognized sources of information on personal health care expenditures. The research efforts of these two groups yield estimates based on different samples and differing data collection techniques. The SSA data are for the entire population of the United States and estimates of expenditures per patient are taken from providers, physicians and hospitals. The CHAS/NORC data are for the noninstitutionalized population, and estimates are based on consumer interviews. SSA estimates are consistently higher than those from the CHAS/NORC survey, even adjusting for inflation, and it is difficult to know how much of the difference should be attributed to differing research strategies and how much to possible generalized under-reporting of expenditures in the CHAS/NORC survey. For a further discussion, see Appendix D of Andersen, R., et al. *Expenditures for Personal Health Services: National Trends and Variations: 1953–1970.* DHEW Pub. No. (HRA) 75–3105. Washington, D.C.: Government Printing Office, October 1973.

[b]The CHAS/NORC analysis makes an important distinction between free and nonfree services. Free services include Medicaid, tax-supported hospital services and clinics where there is no third-party payment and where services are free, and certain other small sources, such as vocational rehabilitation, care for members of the armed forces, and OEO health center care or other care in categorical programs. Thus, free care is "medical goods and services provided to the family at no direct cost or at substantially reduced rates and without benefits being provided by any type of [private] health insurance plan" (Andersen et al., 1973, p. 54). Nonfree care is every other type of care. The separation of free and nonfree is essentially a public/private split in the original source of funds.

Table 6–1. Percent Distribution of Persons Under Seventeen Years of Age by Intervals of Total Annual Out-of-Pocket Health Expense (Including Insurance Premiums), Average Expense for Persons with Expense, and per Capita Expense by Family Income: United States, 1970

Family Income	Total Population in Thousands	No Expense	Health Expense						Average Expense for Persons with Expense	Per Capita Expense
			Less than $50	$50–$99	$100–$249	$250–$499	$500–$999	$1000 or more		
			Percent Distribution							
All incomes[a]	66,716	18.0	25.9	23.3	24.2	6.2	1.7	0.8	$128	$105
Less than $3000	5,387	47.4	28.7	11.9	8.1	b	b	b	$ 86	$ 45
$3000–$4999	6,677	34.4	30.2	16.2	15.1	3.5	b	b	$ 89	$ 58
$5000–$6999	10,501	27.2	29.6	18.7	14.7	6.1	2.3	b	$153	$111
$7000–$9999	15,104	14.7	26.9	27.7	24.3	4.9	b	b	$109	$ 93
$10,000–$14,999	18,497	6.8	25.7	26.4	31.4	6.8	1.8	b	$134	$125
$15,000 or more	8,572	4.5	14.9	27.1	37.8	11.6	3.3	b	$161	$154

[a]Includes persons with unknown incomes.   [b]Figure does not meet standards of reliability or precision.

Source: Monthly Vital Statistics Report, Volume 22, No. 1, Supplement, April 2, 1973
Health Interview Survey—Provisional Data from the National Center for Health Statistics.

Table 6—2. Mean Expenditure for All Personal Health Services per Person by Source of Payment, by Age, by Family Income, by Residence: 1970

	Free			Nonfree			All		
	Central City	Other Urban	Rural	Central City	Other Urban	Rural	Central City	Other Urban	Rural
Birth to 17									
Income									
0–5999	76	58	5	25	66	41	101	124	46
6–10,999	23	5	8	65	103	90	89	107	97
11 plus	2	2	8	107	175	163	110	177	172
All Ages and Incomes	44	43	13	195	248	187	239	291	200

Source: Anderson et al., 1973.

children, or according to various components of expenditure. Of course, expenditures may not be strictly comparable in what they produce. Price per unit service may differ, illness and other needs may differ, consumer preference may differ. Bearing this in mind, it is still obvious that low-income children in rural areas and near-poor children in central cities have very low average health care expenditures. Andersen et al. (1973) point out that nonwhite children wherever they reside must also be added to this list.

Despite the relatively low cost of children's care, per child expenditures continue to rise. Table 6—3 shows percentage increases in out-of-pocket expenditures from 1953 to 1963 and then from 1963 to 1970. Categories of expenditure most relevant to primary care are for physician and dentist services; hospital estimates in this table include inpatient as well as outpatient services.

From the table, two facts are clear. First, for children and adults increases in expenditures were steeper from 1963 to 1970 than from 1953 to 1963, and these increases were largest for hospital care. From the most recent Social Security Administration data, we know the rate of increase in hospital costs for children continues, from a 10 percent increase in 1974 to 15 percent in 1975 (Mueller and Gibson, June 1976). Second, private expenditures on physician's services for children from birth to age five have gone up disproportionately. This, too, is a reflection of medical care inflation, although it is also perhaps a reflection of improved standards of care for this age group, with resultant increase in the demand for services. Total private expenditure for children from birth to five has been rising faster than the population average, while total expenditure for those six to seventeen has been rising somewhat more slowly.[c]

Low-income families are less apt to have out-of-pocket expenditures, and when they do they tend to pay less, although they still pay

---

[c]Although there has been an average annual increase of approximately 11 percent in the personal health expenditures of children and youth, the rate of increase has diminished gradually from 1968 to 1973, somewhat more rapidly than the rate for adults:

	Percent Increase in Aggregate Expenditures	
Fiscal	*All Ages*	*Under 19*
1968	12.1	9.8
1969	12.4	9.6
1970	13.6	14.9
1971	11.1	10.7
1972	10.8	7.7
1973	10.0	7.6
		(Wilson, 1974)

Table 6-3.   **Percentage Increases in Nonfree Expenditures for Selected Age Groups: 1953 to 1963 and 1963 to 1970, Adjusted for Inflation**

	Birth to Five		Six to Seventeen		All Ages	
	1953-63	1963-70	1953-63	1963-70	1953-63	1963-70
hospital	6%	28%	3%	20%	8%	16%
physician	3	14	2	6	3	7
drugs	8	1	8	0	6	4
dentist	0	22	4	7	4	8
other	7	20	4	4	2	9
all services	5	16	4	8	5	10

Source: Adapted from Andersen, et al., 1973.

a higher proportion of family income for the care received. From 1954 to 1970, not only has there been a larger proportion of family income paid by the poor than by the rich, but this proportion rose, both absolutely and relative to the rise experienced among affluent families. As Andersen et al. (1973) point out: "In 1970 families below the near poverty line were spending about twice as high a percentage of their income for medical care as those above the near poverty level" (p. 12). Interestingly, this inequity has not been diminished by the advent of Medicare and Medicaid: "Results show that in 1970 as in the earlier studies the poor continued to spend much more of their income on medical care than the rest of the population" (p. 12).

THE MEDICAID EXPERIENCE

Public sources contributed 3.7 billion on health care for children in 1975. Fifty-six percent of these public funds came from public assistance under the Medicaid program. Half of the federal funds were Medicaid matching grants, and almost three-fourths of state funds were for Medicaid (Table 6-4).

Although Medicaid expenditures for eligible children are proportionately less than for adults, children represent a large percentage of those on the Medicaid rolls. In 1969 in Rochester, for instance, even though poor children accounted for only about 10 percent of total costs, they comprised about 50 percent of all persons on Medicaid (Haggerty et al., 1975). Moreover, a high percentage of states offer at least some Medicaid benefits for children. Wallace, Goldstein and Oglesby (1975) report that almost all states reimburse individual

Table 6–4. Estimated Personal Health Care Expenditures Under Public Programs, by Program and Source of Funds, for Children Under Nineteen and All Ages; 1975

Program	All Ages			Under Nineteen		
	Total	*Federal*	*State and Local*	*Total*	*Federal*	*State and Local*
Total	$40,924	$28,578	$12,346	$ 3,749	$ 2,391	$ 1,358
Health insurance for the aged and disabled	14,121	$14,121	—	3	3	—
Temporary disability insurance	73	—	73	—	—	—
Workmen's compensation (medical benefits)	1,830	51	1,779	—	—	—
Public assistance (vendor medical payments)	12,487	6,692	5,795	2,098	1,125	974
General hospital and medical care	5,492	1,090	4,492	518	320	198
Defense department hospital and medical care (including military dependents)	2,989	2,989	—	726	726	—
Maternal and child health services	535	272	263	365	186	179
School health[a]	—	—	—	—	—	—
Veteran's hospital and medical care	3,206	3,206	—	—	—	—
Medical vocational rehabilitation	190	157	33	38	31	7

[a]School health costs cannot be distinguished from education costs and hence are not represented in this chart.

Source: Mueller and Gibson, June 1976, p. 23.

physicians and hospitals for selected services, and over half offer some benefits via clinics, NHCs, and group practice settings.

Let us review the evidence on how this system of public third-party reimbursement has affected the utilization of services among children and ameliorated the inequities of access to the medical care system.

Access to free care has been extended to many AFDC families, but eligibility criteria, scope of benefits, and level of payment vary widely from state to state. States vary greatly in their standards for Medicaid eligibility and in specifying the scope of benefits. Wilson (1974) points out that state variations in the ratio of Medicaid child recipients to children in low-income families are great, with states like California and New York far more generous in the numbers of children actually receiving benefits than states in the southern and northern mountain regions.

Wilson has devised a "risk" index for states according to three indicators of medical care need and inability to pay:

1. The rate of families classed as "low income" (according to the Office of Management and Budget definition) exceeds the national rate by 25 percent or more.
2. The proportion of women twenty-five years of age or older who completed eight years or less of school is above the national proportion.
3. The infant mortality rate, averaged for the years 1964—68, places the county among the top 40 percent of counties in this respect.

Table 6—5 indicates the level of variability among states in 1972 according to risk level and Medicaid eligibility and payment. There is a clear correlation between higher need, lower recipient ratios, and lower levels of payment. Those states with highest risk also tend to be those with lowest ratios of Medicaid recipients to low-income children; the same states also show lower average per child payments.

The data presented in Table 6—5 refer to Medicaid reimbursement for all types of care, primary, secondary, and tertiary. What more can be said about primary care alone? Data from a subsample of states in each risk category were analyzed by Wilson to compare physician visits alone. High-risk states reported almost the same number of visits per Medicaid recipient as other states (approximately three), with low-risk states showing marginally fewer visits (2.72). This result is interpreted by Wilson as an indication of the greater restrictiveness of the program in high-risk areas and the tendency among recipients in high-risk states to be sicker when they go to the physician. The data are consistent with the interpretation that overutilization will not necessarily result from generous eligibility and benefit criteria.

At present, Davis (1975) estimates that about one-third of the poor are not receiving Medicaid benefits—"mostly two-parent families of childless individuals with low incomes who are ineligible for AFDC assistance, and hence for Medicaid coverage" (p. 7). The program has tended to concentrate on the elderly and disabled, and on hospital benefits. Adults and children on AFDC receive only about one-fourth of the total Medicaid benefits although they constitute over half the total beneficiaries of the program. "Average Medicaid expenditures for medical services of AFDC children on public assistance are about 20 percent below medical expenditures for all children in the United States" (p. 7).

More detailed data on public expenditures for those under fifteen years of age show that inequities continue among subgroups of children: rich and poor, white and nonwhite, urban and rural, and according to other background variables. Notably, racial differences in use exist at all age levels (Table 6-6). Among child recipients, racial inequities are found mostly outside large SMSAs, with rural areas and the South again showing highest disparities. These same areas tended to show fewest poor children receiving any Medicaid benefits at all: only one-tenth of the Mississippi children who are poor receive Medicaid benefits, while almost all of the poor and even some near-poor families in New York do.

The problem of imbalances between large SMSAs and rural areas is reinforced by CHAS/NORC data on the percentage of personal health expenditures paid by Medicaid and other free care in different residential areas (Table 6-7). Among central city children, about three-quarters of health care expenditures are now paid by Medicaid, while in rural areas the percentage paid by Medicaid is only about 11 percent. Inequity in percent of expenditure paid by Medicaid is far more pronounced for children outside metropolitan areas and greater than for adults.

In spite of gains in access among poor children, serious inequities of utilization persist. Ample data exist to demonstrate that gains have been made by poor children in rates of utilization, but unequal utilization persists both within the Medicaid-eligible population and between that group and more affluent Americans (Chapter 4). Those whose families were below the federal poverty line averaged 2.7 visits per year. By 1971, visits for the same group had risen to 4.0 (National Center for Health Statistics, 1965, 1968, and 1972). In contrast, during the same interim physician visits for children from families of

Table 6–5.   Medicaid Rates for 'High-Risk,' 'Medium-Risk,' and 'Low-Risk' States

	Average	High Risk	Medium Risk	Low Risk
Dependent children receiving Medicaid services in fiscal year 1972:				
Per 1,000 children under twenty-one on 7/1/72	97	56	66	114
Per 100 children under eighteen in low-income families, 1970	76	24	39	118
AFDC child recipients who received Medicaid services in fiscal year 1972:				
As percent of Medicaid recipient children	88.1	97.3	87.5	87.4
Per 100 AFDC recipient children (monthly average)	91.2	57.4	74.5	101.1
Medicaid payments for dependent children in fiscal year 1972:				
Average per child receiving Medicaid services	$150.14	$87.30	$112.46	$162.41
Average per child under eighteen in low-income families in 1970	$113.89	$21.02	$ 44.07	$191.59

Table 6–5. continued (Notes)

Data are missing for Alaska and Arizona (no Medicaid programs in 1972) and for Alabama and Massachusetts (reports not submitted).

Sources:

1. U.S. Bureau of the Census, *Current Population Reports: Population Estimates and Projections.* Series P–25, No. 500, May 1973. U.S. Government Printing Office, Washington, D.C. Table 1.

2. U.S. Bureau of the Census, Census of Population: 1970. *General Social and Economic Characteristics.* Final Report PC(1)–C1 United States Summary. U.S. Government Printing Office, Washington, D.C. 1972. Table 182.

3. Average for the twelve-month period of figures published in the monthly *Public Assistance Statistics,* NCSS Report A–2. National Center for Social Statistics, Social and Rehabilitation Service, U.S. Department of Health, Education and Welfare, Washington, D.C.

4. *Number of Recipients and Amounts of Payments Under Medicaid, 1972.* NCSS Report B–4 (CY72). National Center for Social Statistics, Social and Rehabilitation Service, U.S. Department of Health, Education and Welfare, Washington, D.C., May 23, 1974. Tables 6, 13 and 24.

5. Data for Virginia obtained from the National Center for Social Statistics.

Table 6–6. Medicaid Payments for All Medical Services per Recipient, by Race, Age, Region, and Residence, 1969[a]

	All Ages		Under Twenty-One		Twenty-One to Sixty-Four		Sixty-Five and Over	
	White	Nonwhite	White	Nonwhite	White	Nonwhite	White	Nonwhite
All Areas	$375	$213	$130	$117	$447	$341	$697	$328
	ratio: 1.76		ratio: 1.11		ratio: 1.31		ratio: 2.12	
Residence								
City, 400,000 or more	333	221	122	126	381	355	763	400
Other SMSA	426	228	141	114	532	376	679	351
Non-SMSA	406	179	136	86	525	275	660	233
Region								
Northeast	362	205	132	120	421	303	982	401
North Central	449	249	135	122	576	442	731	453
South	322	180	117	102	387	289	413	209
Mountain	303	213	1000	117	383	362	587	417

[a]Based on data from twenty-four states with Medicaid programs in 1969 and reporting data by race.

Source: Calculated from unpublished State Medicaid reports by K. Davis.

Table 6–7. Percent of Expenditures for All Personal Health Services Paid by Medicaid or Free Care among Low-Income Families, by Age Group: 1970[a]

Age	SMSA, Central City	Other Urban	Rural
Birth to seventeen	75.2%	46.8%	10.9%
Eighteen to sixty-four	43.9%	23.6%	32.9%
Sixty-five and over	12.1%	11.6%	6.6%

[a]low-income = family income below $6000.
Source: R. Anderson et al., 1973.

above median income increased only marginally, from 4.5 to 4.8. Medicaid reimbursement explains most of the increased utilization among the poor. This increase was for the most part among central city residents.

The fact that children consistently show lowest absolute rates of utilization for any age group should not in itself be taken as an indication of inequitable treatment for this age group as compared to others. Appropriate utilization must be adjusted according to estimates of medical need. It is worth noting, however, that in one estimation of utilization adjusted to health status, poor children continued to show lowest levels of utilization (Davis, 1975). Use data also suggest that there are greater and more persistent inequities between poor and affluent children than between poor and affluent individuals in other age groups. Following federal subsidies for the medical care of the poor, low-income adults and the aged have moved from the lowest to the highest utilizing group. The effect for children has been less pronounced. Although the gap in utilization has been closed noticeably, poor children still remain lower in utilization than affluent children; the average difference between use of rich and poor still remains larger than for other age groups.

Differences arise partly from differing state eligibility criteria and reimbursement formulae, as we have seen, and partly because of the many familiar nonmonetary barriers to access. Under a federalized Medicaid or some other new national financing scheme it is likely that state plans for eligibility and reimbursement would be more homogeneous, reducing these disparities, but we must assume that differences attributable to nonmonetary barriers to access would tend to persist.

There has been no serious overutilization as a result of Medicaid, but also no significant shift among children in appropriateness of use. Because it is known that use of health services by the poor is particularly sensitive to the out-of-pocket component of expenditure (Bice et al., 1972), it was hypothesized by many prior to the passage of Medicaid that public third-party reimbursement would result in serious overutilization. This was likely to be especially true, it was reasoned, for those groups needing a high degree of previously un-subsidized acute care, among them children. As it has turned out, however, overutilization for minor acute care has not been a serious problem for any age group, and has probably been less of a problem for children than for others.

Rabin and Schach (1975) report data from a Baltimore area health interview survey of use of health services among Medicaid eligibles and persons from two other income groups, lower and middle-to-upper. When all age groups were pooled, Medicaid recipients were sickest and had higher physician use, in part because they were more apt to have visits suggested by a physician, in part because they were more often asked to return, and in part because they were given more injections. The evidence for adult Medicaid eligibles who were mildly ill points toward some overutilization, but for children in-creased use could be largely attributed to justifiable preventive care such as immunization visits.

It is true that at the initiation of the Medicaid program in many cities, utilization rates jumped most for children and others who en-joyed fewest previous sources of public financial support. Olendzki (1974) summarizes a ten-year study of a cohort of welfare cases in New York City which explored the impact of Medicaid on health care utilization more among the younger and less sick members of the study group. The author suggests, however, that this indicates a ceiling effect on utilization among the older and more sick which had been approached prior to the passage of Medicaid. By now, average rates of use have tended to stabilize for all age groups at levels that do not appear excessive.

But data on appropriate use of preventive care services among Medicaid-eligible children are not particularly encouraging. The Roch-ester health studies data (Haggerty et al., 1975) permit us to ask not only about number of physician visits for Medicaid children but also what type of visits these were and how the distribution of types of visits differs among Medicaid recipients and more affluent children in the same area. In 1969, Medicaid children averaged 3.7 visits and non-Medicaid children, 5.4. The difference between the groups was made up for the most part by higher numbers of preventive care visits by non-Medicaid children, with only a small component of the differ-ence being additional acute care visits. It is ominous that the princi-pal differences occurred in the realm of preventive care, which as the authors point out is apt to be more important for children than for other age groups. Fewer than three-quarters of the Medicaid-eligible children in the Rochester area were immunized against smallpox as compared to over 90 percent of the non-Medicaid group. Medicaid children, the authors report, had about 40 percent fewer preventive visits per year and 20 percent fewer illness-related visits, and for dental care this difference was even greater, with Medicaid children showing only about one-third the number of visits of children covered by Blue Cross-Blue Shield. The differences in part reflect patterns of parent initiative, but more significantly they reflect the very substantial barriers to availability and access which remain for the poor in this country even after financial barriers have been lowered. It is not known whether this pattern of preventive care use has been significantly altered by better implementation of the Medicaid program of Early and Periodic Screening, Diagnosis and Treatment (EPSDT).

Medicaid eligibility has not significantly increased the access of poor children to private care and has exerted minimal impact on patterns of use of various provider arrangements. The Medicaid program has not resulted in a massive reallocation of children's visits back to private provider arrangements. There have been modest increases in the use of private physicians, but the general trend has been for aid recipients to seek care in hospital-based service outlets unless a comprehensive care center is accessible. Discouraging the return to private practitioners are the shifting aid eligibility requirements, the likelihood that some out-of-pocket expenditures may still be necessary for GP visits or other private practice visits, and the simple absence of private practitioners in central city residential areas.

National data from 1969 leave no doubt that income-related disparities persist in level of private care use among the rich and poor (Table 6−8). Only 68 percent of physician visits among poor children under seventeen were to private physicians as compared to almost 90 percent of those children from families above the median income. Aid status exerted minimal impact on the likelihood that a visit would be to a private practitioner or that a poor child would see a pediatrician.

In the Rochester studies, the authors discovered that in 1966 half as many Medicaid children as children above the median income reported a private practitioner as usual source of care. By 1971, numbers of Medicaid children with a private practitioner had diminished to about 30 percent. This trend reflected in part the tendency of private practitioners to leave the central city, and in part suggested that those in private practice did not seek out or encourage a Medicaid clientele. Some evidence also exists for the active exclusion of

Table 6—8.   Percent Physician Visits to Selected Kinds of Physicians, by Income: 1969

	General Practitioner (All ages)	Pediatrician (Under Seventeen)	Obstetrician/ Gynecologist (Women Seventeen to Forty-Four)
All persons	59%	32%	21%
Under $5000	70	18	13
Aid	73	21	6
No aid	70	17	14
$5000–9999	61	30	23
$10,000–14,999	51	40	24
$15,000 and over	41	39	23

Source: K. Davis, 1975. Calculated from the 1969 Health Interview Survey, National Center for Health Statistics.

poor children from private practice settings. On a more positive note, the percentage of Medicaid children with a regular source of care increased in the same interval, reflecting in part the initiation of the neighborhood health centers and in part increased use of hospital outpatient facilities.

In another study, welfare families in New York City were examined longitudinally to ascertain the impact of Medicaid in opening up private care for the poor (Olendzki et al., 1972). Families reporting a private doctor increased slightly over the interval of the study (from 1 percent before to 10 percent after), but for the most part families continued to use hospital clinics and other public sources of care. Many respondents said that they would feel uncomfortable or out of place in a private physician arrangement because they perceived such an arrangement as unfamiliar, unwelcoming, inappropriate, undeserved, or even illegal.

Roghmann (1967) showed that among those Medicaid enrollees using the emergency room inappropriately, few had made any attempt to find a private doctor or had changed their regular source of care after the initiation of the program. The conclusion of this earlier study was borne out in the experience of the next five years: "enrolling the poor and paying for their care is one thing; improving either the quality or the availability and accessibility of care is another" (Haggerty, et al., 1975, p. 202). Without understanding precisely the dynamics of consumer choice, we may conclude that although use-rate differentials have been altered by Medicaid, differentials in site of care generally have not. Instead there has been a solidification of the present system in which sites of care for the poor remain substantially separate from sites for other income groups.

The EPSDT program has not succeeded in providing preventive care and screening to a large proportion of Medicaid eligibles. Moreover, it has recreated the danger of separating preventive and screening efforts from sources of comprehensive care. In 1969, Medicaid benefits for children were supplemented by EPSDT. Under the program, providers are reimbursed for offering screening and diagnosis of health care needs as well as treatment. All Medicaid-eligible children are entitled to EPSDT benefits.

Although the impetus behind passage of the EPSDT legislation was admirable—to shift the balance of care under Medicaid toward early case finding and preventive care rather than acute care—the results have been disappointing. Major problems with the program first were encountered in its implementation. States did not wish to incur additional Medicaid cost-sharing responsibilities, physicians did not wish to participate in the program because of low reimbursement schedules, and the Department of Health, Education and Welfare under a cost-conscious administration acted to some extent as an ally in slowing the implementation process (Foltz, 1975; Steiner, 1976). Law suits were filed in several states demanding reasonable compliance, and finally the matter of inadequate implementation was brought to the attention of Congress. Although implementation in the 1970s has been better, the program still has reached less than half of the Medicaid-eligible child population, which in turn represents only a portion of the total poverty population.

Particularly frustrating in some states have been the difficulties of gaining reimbursement for traditional screening programs in health departments and schools. There have been demonstration projects reimbursing school health programs, but three bureaucratic obstacles make school reimbursement complex: (1) the guideline that services under EPSDT can only be reimbursed if they do not substitute for already existing screening and preventive care efforts, meaning that traditional school health programs often do not qualify for funding; (2) the difficulty of determining reimbursement formulae for school populations with some children AFDC-eligible and others not (this is a problem analogous to setting school eligibility standards under Title 1 of ESEA); and (3) the rule in many states that only a physician may be reimbursed for services, ruling out a system of service provision or independent billing by nurses and nurse practitioners. With few exceptions, the schools have not been able to qualify as suitable provider arrangements.

If traditional sources of preventive care are not allowed to benefit, forced implementation can create incentives to minimal legal compliance. In many states the response of state officials to EPSDT has been predictably bureaucratic: they have been motivated mainly to comply with federal regulations and have tended to set up a substantially separate delivery apparatus for the program, creating another fragment in an already fragmented system, or duplicating services already provided, or both. Separate screening programs and a separate agency structure for screening efforts assures that whatever the effectiveness of the screening, it runs the risk of failure at the stage of referral, subsequent diagnosis, and treatment because it is not clearly integrated with any ongoing, regular care source for the child. This problem is the same one mass screening efforts have faced in the past.

EPSDT is significant in a period preceding national health insurance. It clearly highlights some of the problems inherent in trying to employ a financing mechanism to provide an appropriate mix of services for children. For preventive care and early detection, two activities that should dominate much of children's care, we may learn that minimal improvement can come from legislative initiatives that alter only our methods of medical care financing without simultaneously considering mechanisms for appropriate service delivery.

Some Implications of the Medicaid Data

Reviewing the full implications of Medicaid, it would be wrong to conclude that disparities among children in levels of use and access would not be helped under national health insurance. Any scheme that generalized to all states the benefit structure of the most generous states, whether by reform of Medicaid or by formation of a new national program, would immediately extend eligibility to a large number of poor children and offer an improved benefit structure for many already on the Medicaid rolls. But Medicaid data cast doubt on the notion that any financing scheme, however homogeneous, can eradicate differences in levels of use and public reimbursement resulting from differences in provider availability and nonmonetary access factors as they vary by residential areas and regions. It appears that the enhancement of appropriate utilization is not merely a matter of reducing financial barriers but rather is multifactorial, requiring that we consider various aspects of access simultaneously. That is not to say, of course, that reducing financial barriers to care is not a good place to start, or that of the many determinants of correct utilization behavior, financial considerations are not among the most important.

PREPAYMENT AND CHILDREN'S CARE: RESEARCH FINDINGS

Weber (1975) has argued that under a national public financing scheme prepaid practice is the provider mode most likely to assure rational use of services by children and families, and capitation reimbursement—a form of provider prepayment—is the reimbursement mode most likely to control costs and problems of federal administration while simultaneously tending to unify the delivery of preventive and acute care. It is valuable to explore the pros and cons of this argument, to better understand the extent to which a financing scheme can be engineered to bring about more equity of child access and better reasoned public expenditure on children's primary care.

Advocates of prepaid practice have argued that it is in the public interest to promote health maintenance organizations (HMOs). By pitting two sets of incentives against each other—one to enlist new subscribers and the other to control cost—the HMO holds forth the promise of maintaining appropriate benefit packages at competitive prices while still maintaining a ceiling on aggregate medical care costs. The same incentives should work, it is reasoned, to make HMO plans a good buy for the federal government under National Health Insurance or other forms of national medical care financing. Cost control and service maximization are also anticipated from rural medical care foundations, although the logistical and administrative advantages of a large multispecialty practice in a single location can not be achieved and hospital costs not so easily controlled.

It is also reasoned that the HMO is ideally suited to the medical needs of children. To the extent preventive and ambulatory acute care can avoid more costly secondary and tertiary care, it is in the HMO's self-interest to be oriented to the simpler types of care, which are precisely the types most often required by children. Children's care is largely predictable, ambulatory, and low cost. About half of the five or so visits to the physician a child averages each year are for health supervision. Likewise, parents who are HMO subscribers should be more motivated to use preventive care services for their children. Having paid for these benefits they are more likely to take advantage of them, a fact that could have major consequences for children's medical care equity. Preventive care is the component of services most often neglected by parents and also, as we have seen, the component explaining most of the utilization gap between rich and poor children.

Does the medical care research literature support these arguments, casting a favorable light on prepayment and the HMO as a provider arrangement for children? By and large the answer is yes, although it is important to understand that this answer is contingent on the realities of the medical care market as it currently operates. First let us review some conclusions from the research literature and then speculate about whether these conclusions would be likely to remain valid under new assumptions introduced by an enlarged system of public financing.

There is ample evidence in the research literature that families benefit from participation in HMOs. Roemer and Shonick (1973) point out that HMOs have proven especially attractive to young families. The benefits of comprehensive care are greatest for families requiring prenatal and postnatal care and those with children under six (Moustafa et al., 1971). In the Kaiser plan, rates for child dependents are slightly more than half the rate for the subscriber, without regard to numbers of children in the family.

Evidence on quality of care for the HMO remains sketchy and indirect, but various indicators suggest that in most prepaid practice arrangements care for children is excellent. Criteria for physician hiring in the large HMOs are very exacting, requiring for instance that GPs be qualified under the new specialty board in group practice. The only reported problems with level of physician competency have been in a few highly commercial HMOs organized to provide services to Medicaid beneficiaries in California (Nelson, 1973). These cases were minor exceptions to a general pattern of high standards.

It can also be argued that physician stability is an indicator of quality and here HMOs compare favorably with other practice arrangements. Prybil (1971) found in a national survey of private multispecialty practice arrangements that yearly turnover among HMO physicians was less than 5 percent. Mechanic (1972) found prepaid physicians most satisfied of all subgroups of physicians, although survey results showed just as high a rate of solos very satisfied with their jobs. Cook (1971) reported less than a 10 percent turnover among Kaiser Permanente physicians in Northern California from 1966 to 1970. Roemer and Shonick (1973) conclude that "with the steady growth of open-market private group practice (now up to about 20 percent of clinical physicians, according to the AMA Survey reported in 1972) and the general national promotion of the HMO idea, participation in PPGP will become regarded as less and less 'deviant,' will attract more doctors, and will become associated with greater stability" (p. 280).

Higher quality of care for children is also presumably a function of incentives to provide complete preventive care services. It remains unclear whether it is actually in the long-term financial interest of HMOs to promote the use of preventive care and early detection on the theory that this will lower the probability of severe and costly health problems among subscribers later in life or later in the cycle of disease or disability. This cost-benefit calculation depends on complex factors ranging from the amount of cohort attrition among subscribers as they grow older, to the number of problems treated in later life for which preventive care early in childhood actually would reduce HMO costs; here we have a difficult question of medical care discounting. But from a purely empirical standpoint it seems clear that prepaid practice plans are the form of family health insurance most apt to lead to proper utilization of preventive care services by children. Roemer et al. (1973) suggest that according to a "preventive service index," computed by factor scores of various preventive care services for all age groups, the HMO is more oriented to prevention than other insurance coverage plans. Donabedian (1973) states that there is evidence from the HIP plan suggesting that HIP subscribers are more likely to use general checkups and prenatal and postnatal care than are persons in a general New York population. In addition, Cauffman and Roemer (1967) report that among a sample of Los Angeles children with minor disabilities detected in school-based multiphasic screening, children of families in prepaid group practice plans were more likely than others to have had a checkup recently.

Parent attitudes toward the quality of care are very positive. In general, those parents who sign up tend to be willing to trade some increase in impersonality for the comprehensive benefit package. Certain administrative and managerial problems are perceived as irksome, but these irritations do not alter the view of most parent subscribers that care is excellent.

Cost Control and Appropriate Use. One critical question is whether HMOs serve children as well as they do adults in controlling cost while at the same time increasing appropriate utilization. Because most care for children is ambulatory and outpatient-oriented, the most important aspect of this question is whether the HMO has encouraged appropriate use of preventive and acute care services for children, discouraging both overutilization and underutilization, while at the same time containing net costs. It is also important to estimate likely effects of HMO membership among rich and poor clients on the present income-related gap in appropriate use of preventive care.

Assuming once again the conditions of the present medical care market, the evidence suggests that the HMO yields lower hospital use, relatively more use of ambulatory and preventive services, and lower over-all cost than normal fee for service arrangements. There is also some evidence of economies of scale in HMO arrangements, although this hypothesis still has not been conclusively demonstrated, in large part because of lack of consensus about a cost-effectiveness paradigm that would enable such comparisons.

For children, whose use of secondary and tertiary care is slight, prepayment and the HMO offer the promise of a net increase in ambulatory care with little loss of desired hospital services. The evidence suggests that excess hospitalization under fee-for-service arrangements as compared to prepaid group practice often can be traced to the same surgical procedures and types of acute care where children are apt to experience overreferral.

Although the final verdict is far from being rendered, the prevailing pattern in the various studies of admission rates for the Health Insurance Plan of New York (HIP), as compared with other types of practice organization in New York City, was substantially lower in precisely those diagnostic categories most often suspected to comprise unnecessary admissions— tonsillectomies and upper respiratory infections (Roemer and Shonick, 1973, p. 281).

Simply by providing fewer hospital beds for children and no financial incentives to hospital use, children's care perhaps may be enhanced.

The evidence on appropriate use of ambulatory care services is also positive, although findings are more diverse and open to interpretation. In general, rates of ambulatory care utilization are higher among prepaid practice subscribers than others, especially if the subscribers are highly educated and well-informed about the scope of PPGP benefits. Estimates of increase in utilization of various forms of ambulatory care among children under a prepaid group practice arrangement at a university medical center suggest that hospitalization may indeed be controlled but that ambulatory care visits, in this situation without any constraint on physician use, will be higher than for a nonprepaid group (Perkoff, Kahn and Mackie, 1974). In this study, the significant difference between experimental and control children under fourteen was for all components of ambulatory care except ambulatory surgery. Kahn and Perkoff (1974) report the same pattern among children in a university-based pediatric prepaid group practice. Fee-for-service and prepaid client groups were assigned randomly when the Medical Care group of the Washington University School of Medicine in St. Louis was begun. The two groups were then compared on various aspects of utilization. It was discovered that the prepayment group made almost twice as many ambulatory care visits as the other group, but that they used more than 50 percent fewer hospital days. Again, in a university setting, with a more informed client group and fewer initial cost control incentives or for-profit care incentives operating in the prepayment group, ambulatory care was allowed to reach a high rate.

The cost of general increases in ambulatory care are not limited to costs of physician services in handling acute care. For all age and income groups among Kaiser-Portland subscribers, for instance, patterns of lab service use by physicians showed that in 1970, 58 percent of lab tests were for routine health supervision. General medicine, pediatrics, and OB/GYN, the three categories of lab testing most likely to reflect use by mothers and children, represented over 90 percent of all lab tests ordered. In spite of increased use of laboratory services by PPGP clients, there is no evidence of inappropriate utilization of these services.

Equity of Use Among Income Groups. If the use of ambulatory care for children generally increases somewhat but remains appropriate, what can be said about the utilization gap between rich and poor children? On the one hand, in a prepaid practice arrangement where both groups have access to essentially the same services, there is in principle a higher likelihood of equity and equality of services used. On the other hand, one of the principal dangers of the HMO is the potential for underserving a client group, and it would be reasonable to expect that in the present semipublic market for services, children of highly educated parents of middle income or above are apt to seek care more frequently and perhaps more appropriately than children of poor parents, who have no personal insurance investment and are not as likely to be in the habit of fulfilling all of their children's medical care needs. As Roemer points out, the use of outpatient services is more sensitive than other services to parental education and socioeconomic status: "It would appear that better educated and probably more sophisticated persons are able to make greater use of ambulatory care in the relatively complex framework of the large prepaid group practice plans found in California; this is less true under conventional conditions of private medical practice" (in Roemer and Shonick, 1973, p. 291).

Sparer and Anderson (1973) summarize the findings of the OEO experiment with prepayment in four community based prepaid practice plans: Kaiser-Fontana, Kaiser-Portland, Group Health of Puget Sound, and HIP. Kaiser-Portland enrolled 1500 families, the others about 500 families apiece. After a six-month period of stabilization, the low-income group members reached a pattern of utilization much like that of regular plan members. Cost savings were reported for the prepayment groups because of reduced length of stay in the hospital and reduced laboratory and X-ray procedures, which also were lower than averages for regular members, perhaps as a result of larger numbers of children in the low-income families.

These results are generally taken as a positive comment on cost control and appropriate use among income groups. From another standpoint, however, they could be interpreted as suggesting underutilization of ambulatory care by the poor. In an analysis adjusting the utilization rates to simulate results if enrollees were representative of the national poor population in terms of age and sex, it was discovered that in every case except Puget Sound, utilization rates were lower than national averages. In addition, physician utilization rates for the HIP plan, the largest plan to enroll Medicaid clients and arguably the least prone to Hawthorne effects in the experiment, show sizable differences in physician access between regular plan members and low-income subscribers (Table 6—9). For the poor, the use of nonphysician personnel made up the difference in total utilization. This is not necessarily evidence of a two-track system, but it does suggest caution in predicting long-term equalities in income-related patterns of ambulatory care use.

The area where prepayment schemes seem most able to regulate cost is in the inpatient hospitalization sector, but "fine tuning" of the system may occur in the ambulatory care sector, with fewer visits promoted if cost-cutting is important. It is in this sector that under-doctoring of the poor and especially of children may need to be guarded against in the future. Hester and Sussman (1974) suggest that much of the research reported so far with positive results is based on small-scale programs, and conclusions of these studies have limited generalizability to large-scale programs:

> The special concessions made in setting up the demonstrations, e.g., guaranteed eligibility of all enrolled for the duration of the project, and the problems which only appear when the problem reaches a certain scale, make these demonstrations of very limited use in anticipating the implementation problems in statewide or citywide operations (p. 418).

Despite this concern, the equity benefits of HMOs in the cities are almost certain to be better than among fee-for-services private practice arrangements. Differential treatment of rich and poor will be much more difficult to monitor and regulate in smaller office-based practice arrangements. In rural areas, the medical care foundation concept shows the greatest promise among payment arrangements of net redistributional benefits for the poor. In at least one study, Gartside and Proctor (1970) found that a higher percentage of all physicians from the foundation area, especially pediatricians and other specialists, were serving Medicaid children than was the case in a matched control area. The authors interpret the evidence as indicating that equity may be well served by foundations:

> These findings would suggest that, in the nonmetropolitan type of county where medical foundations have tended to develop, they exert a positive influence on the qualifications of doctors serving the poor; similar disciplinary influence might possibly apply to the care of all patients in foundation-type HMOs (in Roemer and Shonick, 1973, p. 280).

In summary, research conclusions on prepaid practice and the HMO concept are sometimes tentative but generally positive. They suggest that prepayment ought to be preferred as a health care financing mode by a large proportion of young parents, families and children. They also suggest that such arrangements are in the public

Table 6–9.   Annual Utilization Rates per Member for the Four Plans[a]   (Low-Income and Regular Members)

Services	HIP, NY		Group Health of Puget Sound		Kaiser Fontana		Kaiser Portland	
	Low Income	Plan Members	Low Income	Plan Members	Low Income	Plan Members	Low Income	Plan Members
Medical-physician	2.88	4.20	4.00	3.91	4.12	3.72	3.29	3.14
Nonphysician	1.74	NA	0.66	1.00	1.20	NA	0.70	NA
Totals	4.62	4.20	4.66	4.91	5.32	3.72	3.99	3.14
Laboratory	1.77	4.01	2.24	4.33	NA	NA	3.49	4.08
X-ray	0.27	NA	0.50	0.66	NA	NA	0.97	0.97
Prescriptions	NA	NA	NA	0.33	3.78	3.21	NA	4.14
Home health	1.70	—	2.30	—	3.37	—	1.34	—

[a]Plan-members data relate to 1971. Low-income utilization relates to 12 months ending March 1972, except for Puget Sound (12 months ending July 1972). NA indicates data not available and not applicable.
Source: From Sparer and Andersen, 1973. Reprinted with permission of *N Engl J Med.*

interest to promote. Does this suggest that strong incentives to prepayment should be built into any national public financing scheme? Let us consider the prospects for this payment mode under an enlarged system of publicly financed care for children.

Prepayment and Public Assistance— Some Problems

As a financing paradigm, prepayment is usually considered a contract between consumer and provider. A set of incentives exists by which both are likely to benefit. The problems of prepayment under a system of publicly financed care all relate to the fact that this paradigm now becomes more complex: the government pays some or all of the prepayment on the consumer's behalf. This means that third-party reimbursement of the HMO or other prepaid practice arrangement requires full cooperation of four actors: the consumer, the provider, the health plan, and the local agency. The difficulties of such cooperation may have the effect of creating among an enlarged group of eligibles certain problems currently experienced in Medicaid prepayment plans.

Hester and Sussman (1974) summarize certain inauspicious shortcomings of three efforts to enroll Medicaid patients into prepaid group practice arrangements: the Kaiser and HIP experiments and the conversion of Martin Luther King Health Center in New York City into a prepayment program for its Medicaid client population. Problems included limited enrollment growth and high rate of client turnover, underutilization of services, use of out-of-plan services, absence of adequate regulations surrounding the quality of care, and failure of the prepayment mechanism as a means of cost control. The authors conclude that it is dangerous to assume that Medicaid prepayment will operate the same as privately financed prepayment. It can be further argued that this may be especially true among children.

It can be predicted that the three kinds of abuse most likely to be found among Medicaid providers may continue to be difficult to regulate or control adequately under any public system of provider reimbursement. These are fraud (claims for services not performed), unsatisfactory quality, and overutilization (especially when superfluous services potentially involve formal or informal "kickback" networks). As Hester and Sussman (1974) point out: "None of the agencies responsible for Medicaid are capable today of monitoring to an adequate degree the quality of care delivered by a large-scale, multi-group, and geographically dispersed pre-payment program" (p. 417). It is also true that none is able to monitor adequately the appropriateness of care or to regulate referral networks.

Bellin and Kanoler (1971), in a report on Medicaid practitioner abuses in New York City, cite an example of overreferral within a fee-for-service group practice. Every Medicaid child presenting symptoms of uncomplicated acute otitis media was referred to the group otolaryngologist, adding twenty dollars to the total Medicaid bill. Other instances of "ping-ponging" under Medicaid are numerous, with laboratory costs an especially likely area for abuses in children's care. Large prepaid practices, which negotiate levels of capitation reimbursement from the government at frequent intervals, may prove only slightly more likely than private fee-for-service providers to discourage this type of abuse.

Client turnover in most HMOs is so great that the assumption of a stable client group, especially among families with young children, cannot be sustained (Roemer and Shonick, 1973). Moreover, it is increasingly acknowledged that many families will remain as HMO subscribers while their children are young and then move to a less comprehensive scheme when the children reach school age and become somewhat lower utilizers (Moustafa et al., 1971). Client turnover under Medicaid has also been related to changes in eligibility.

There are also persisting problems of out-of-plan use, with many HMO clients seeking supplementary care in other settings. Various studies (Greenlick, et al., 1972; Roemer et al., 1973) tend to indicate somewhere between 10 and 15 percent of subscribers have some out-of-plan use, more for ambulatory care. Among Medicaid clients, this percentage can be significantly higher. The data in Table 6–10 sug-

Table 6–10.   Annual Out-of-Plan Utilization by HIP Medicaid Enrollees at Fee-for-Service Providers: 1973

	Per Capita Visits	Cost Per Visit	Total Cost
Out of HIP			
1. Voluntary hospital clinics[a]	1.3	$29.40	$2,200,000
2. Municipal hospital clinics[b]	.7	$28.40	$1,000,000
3. Private physicians[b]	1.8	N/A	N/A
Total	3.8		$3,200,000
In HIP	2.0	$34.50	$3,900,000
Total Utilization	5.8		$7,100,000 ($127/enrollee)

[a] Estimate based on one-month sample of bills.
[b] Estimate based on five-month sample of bills.
Source: Hester and Sussman, 1974. Reprinted with permission of *Milbank Mem. Fund Q.*

gest that HIP provides only about one-third of the medical care visits of its enrollees:

If it had paid the claims, the city would have paid other providers for claims a sum greater than the HIP capitation payments. Some of these services and claims are valid because the benefit package covered by the capitation contract does include some services, but this can only account for a small fraction of out-of-plan use shown in [the] table (Hester and Sussman, 1974, p. 428).

Thus, under any enlarged system of provider reimbursement, the poor would lack a strong incentive to enroll in a prepayment plan committing them to a single source of care, and those who did make this commitment would be likely to some extent to seek care from other sources. To police multiple use would require administrative mechanisms sophisticated enough to audit multiple use and prevent the reimbursement of several different providers for identical services to a single child.

The history of HMO legislation to the present does not suggest that we yet know how to regulate PPGPs without seriously threatening their attractiveness as a mode of practice. At present the growth of HMOs is seriously challenged by 1973 legislation requiring that HMOs qualifying for government support at start-up provide not only physicians' services, hospitalization, emergency care, and diagnostic and laboratory services, but also home health services, family planning, and preventive dental care for children. This is so large a package of services that it is difficult to offer in the early years of a plan, and assures that premiums must be high enough to cut a significant portion of the competitive edge the HMO might have against various private insurance alternatives. Under an enlarged public system of health care financing, of course, the situation could not get better and might well get worse if relatively low deductibles or comprehensive coverage removed altogether the incentive for consumers to prefer such arrangements.

Capitation Reimbursement

Along with comprehensive coverage and prepayment, capitation reimbursement has been mentioned as a desirable mode of national health care financing and one likely to benefit children. Capitation payment as a federal reimbursement option is usually contrasted with the "usual and customary fee" criterion used in many cases for Medicaid reimbursement.

Under capitation, each child has an assigned comprehensive care reimbursement rate, and providers would be entitled to collect this capitation fee for every child enrolled. Every provider contracts to become an HMO of sorts. The administrative mechanisms of reimbursement could vary, with providers first being given vouchers by parents or otherwise being required to present proof that a child was enrolled. The amount of the capitation fee for various groups of children also could vary, with risk factors justifying higher capitation for certain children or capitation add-ons being offered as an incentive for primary care providers in underserved areas.

The attractions of capitation are four. First, it is administratively simpler in some regards than other modes of reimbursement. Direct formula reimbursement to providers via local national health insurance agencies would be relatively straightforward; indeed, to the extent service is not based on capitation, paperwork and budgeting problems may be staggering. It is also clear that if the legislative intent of national health insurance is to circumvent the private insurance companies, capitation minimizes their potential role as intermediaries. If it is concluded that the government rather than the private sector should reimburse providers, it also of course falls to the government in the first instance to monitor quality. Differences of opinion persist about the relative effectiveness of the public and private sectors to carry out this charge.

Second, capitation holds forth the promise of an easier mechanism for controlling costs. Rational planning may be allowed if an over-all budget constraint first can be established; capitation reimbursement rates can be set without having to predict piecemeal the incremental cost of services or having to combat an inflation of "reasonable rates." Providers in turn have some incentive to reduce their own costs. As one example, capitation payment has been shown to be the most efficient for four methods of payment for Head Start dental services (Ross, 1971). Contrast was between "usual and customary" fee arrangements typical of agency contracts and capitation methods contracted with a local dentist group, which used significantly more auxiliary personnel. The capitation method resulted in the same services being provided at major reductions in cost.

Estimates of potential capitation costs for children under national health insurance enable a politically persuasive case that with this financing mode all of the country's children could be offered full financial access to comprehensive medical services at a total government expense not exceeding the total currently spent on various categorical programs plus the children's component of Medicaid. Weber (1975) estimates that $225 per child per year would be sufficient for complete comprehensive coverage, which would total 7 billion dollars for all children from birth to nine. Total outlays are already higher than this nationally if we consider all private and public health expenditures.

Third, capitation provides incentives both to provider and consumer to establish a regular source of comprehensive care for each child. To the extent out-of-plan use is discouraged, families and children will be limited to a single regular source of care or agent of care, and the recipients of capitation fees will be unable to collect without some demonstration that comprehensive services have been rendered. Thus, it can be argued that capitation is the best means of fostering continuity of care. Assuming a comprehensive care package for children under NHI, it may even be possible to specify a provider agency responsible for overseeing the care of every American child.

Finally, capitation reimbursement is the strongest financing option available to combat provider maldistribution and problems of access in areas of provider scarcity. In principle it is possible to arrange capitation incentives so that "bounties" on children in underserviced areas and populations are higher than for other children, offering an economic incentive for those who would provide them with care.

These potential advantages are not inconsiderable. Up against them, however, there remain an imposing set of problems. The most immediate and serious is the problem of supplementation. Unless a ceiling is placed on all per child health expenditures, affluent families will be inclined to add to capitation quotas, seeking private care outside the NHI system. This could rapidly lead to an even more clearcut dual system of care than at present, further engraining patterns by which the poor receive care which is largely public, and the rich, care which is largely private (Mechanic, 1972).

Another serious problem is in the likely advantage that capitation gives to larger practice arrangements, able to offer a full range of services. Small providers would be forced to reinsure and in general assume higher risk. The solo practitioner or other small practice physician will have to insure against the costs of additional care for clients with an independent insurance source, while in larger arrangements the variability in actual costs as they fluctuate around the mean of predicted costs will be accommodated internally. This trend could lead rapidly to control of children's medical care by organizational arrangements which many consider to be the wrong ones: financial partnerships and shared professional facilities.

Finally, capitation may not be as successful as has been assumed in controlling costs. From the federal standpoint, it is important not to put a plan unduly at risk at the time of start-up. Only after a year or two of operation will it be possible to set capitation rates with reasonable exactness. Until such a rate can be calculated, there is no source of leverage to keep costs at a minimum. Even after reasonable capitation levels have been established, variable reimbursement rates may have to be instituted if there is any attempt to foster a pluralism of provider arrangements, and annual or semiannual renegotiation of capitation levels may be required to avoid chasing physician groups out of the NHI medical care market into private care based on supplementation. Continual reequilibration of such a system suggests a spiral of ambulatory care costs.

In the meantime, profit maximization may cause practitioners to seek enrollees who are minimally at risk. The poor child and the child with probable need for special medical care is not likely to be pursued by providers without strong incentive reimbursement, with the result that these children may once again find themselves at the end of the queue. Migration rates are also higher for poor children than others, presenting additional problems of continuity of care.

None of these problems is sufficient in itself to enable a simple rejection of the capitation proposal. All, however, should cause policymakers to think carefully before adopting such a scheme too readily.

In sum, while evidence supports the notion that prepayment and capitation indeed are preferable modes of payment for children's care, more attention must be given to realistic means by which these modes of payment may be implemented in publicly financed health care for children.

THE "CHILDREN'S HMO"

In principle a prepaid practice arrangement for children need not possess any of the attributes of the HMO or Medical Care Foundation except that it receives a capitation fee for each child and serves as a point of coordination, case advocacy, and provider reimbursement. The children's HMO demonstration project proposal of Mount Sinai Hospital in New York is a case in point (Daniels et al., 1976). A separate agency would be established to enroll children and provide capitation reimbursement to providers.

The demonstration project is not intended as a provider of services but as a coordinating mechanism. Approximately 2000 Medicaid eligible persons of elementary and high school age at four local schools have been identified as the target group, along with other dependent children in their families. These young people would be invited to participate in a program that offers comprehensive health care benefits at optional combinations of provider facilities. Primary care providers include a local medical group, a neighborhood health center, and the Mount Sinai Hospital. The HMO will provide up to $2500 worth of free care per child, financed by the state Medicaid system. Providers are reimbursed by capitation fees from the central agency. The coordinating agency itself is to be provided by a foundation grant.

There are several advantages to this model. First, there is no need to introduce additional sites of care in an already dizzying array of service outlets; second, emphasis is placed on individual responsibility for targeted children with all the same incentives to cost control which currently exist in the HMO; third, the cost savings of combining school-based screening with clinic and hospital-based backup are preserved; fourth, such a system may be better equipped than the large HMO to build upon a network of neighborhood-based primary care units, public and private, rather than becoming centralized in a large hospital complex. Such a plan is one reasonable solution to the problem of reorganizing services. It offers incentives to those who would assist children in threading their way effectively through the present system of care. There is no reason why such a system could not be oriented to families instead of children alone.

Such a scheme is not a panacea. It does not avoid altogether the problem of out-of-plan use and introduces serious administrative complexities. But the children's HMO concept is deserving of attention because it is a serious attempt to maximize the potential advantages of prepayment and capitation without a major redesign of the primary care delivery system. Under a capitation system, the possibility of a consumer rather than provider-organized prepayment system also is attractive—a health care cooperative. Under this system, which would be substantially similar to the prepayment network just described, consumer groups would negotiate capitation contracts with providers and offer subscribers alternative mixes of services according to family needs.

REFERENCES

Andersen, R., et al. *Expenditures for Personal Health Services: National Trends and Variations, 1953–1970.* DHEW Pub. No. (HRA) 74–3105. Washington, D.C.: Government Printing Office, 1973.

Bellin, L., and Kanoler, F. "Medicaid practitioner abuses and excuses vs. counterstrategy of the New York City health department," *Am J Public Health* 61 (1971): 2201.

Bice, T., et al. "Socioeconomic status and use of physician services: a reconsideration," Med Care 10 (1972): 261.

Cauffman, J., and Roemer, M. "The impact of health insurance coverage on health care of school children," Public Health Rep 82 (1967): 323–28.

Cook, W. "Profile of the Permanente physician," in The Kaiser-Permanente Medical Care Program, edited by A. Somers. New York: Commonwealth Fund, 1971.

Daniels, M.S., et al. A New Model for School Health. Paper presented at 104th annual meeting of the APHA, Miami, Fla., 21 October, 1976.

Davis, K. "A decade of policy developments in providing health care for low income families," (draft for A Decade of Federal Anti-poverty Policy: Achievements, Failures and Lessons, edited by R. Haveman. Madison: University of Wisconsin Institute for Research on Poverty, 1977), xerox, 1975.

Donabedian, A. "An evaluation of prepaid group practice," Inquiry 6 (1969): 3.

Donabedian, A. "An examination of some directions in health care policy," Am J Public Health 63 (1973): 243.

Foltz, A.M. "The development of ambiguous federal policy: early screening, diagnosis and treatment (EPSDT)," Milbank Mem Fund Q 53 (1975): 35–39.

Gartside, F., and Procter, D. Medicaid Services in California Under Different Organizational Modes: Physician Participation in the San Joachim Prepayment Project. Los Angeles: University of California School of Public Health, (xerox), January 1970, cited in Roemer and Shonick, 1973.

Gaus, C.R., et al. "Contrasts in HMO and fee-for-service performance," Social Security Bulletin (May 1976): 3.

Greenlick, M., et al. "Comparing the use of medical care services by a medically indigent and a general membership population in a comprehensive prepaid group practice program," Med Care 10 (1972): 187.

Haggerty, R.J., et al. Child Health and the Community, New York: John Wiley and Sons, 1975.

Hester, J., and Sussman, E. "Medicaid prepayment: copayment and implementation," Milbank Mem Fund Q 52 (1974): 415.

Holahan, J. Financing Health Care for the Poor: The Medicaid Experience. Lexington, Mass.: Lexington Books, 1975.

Hurtado, A., et al. "Unscheduled use of ambulatory care services," Med Care 12 (1974): 498.

Kahn, L., and Perkoff, G. "The pediatric experience of an experimental prepaid practice in a medical school setting," Pediatrics 53 (1974): 319.

Mechanic, D. Physician Satisfaction in Varying Settings. Madison: University of Wisconsin, undated c. 1972.

Moustafa, A., et al. "Determinants of choice and change of health insurance plan," Med Care 9 (1971): 32.

Mueller, M.S., and Gibson, R.M. "National health expenditures, fiscal year 1975," Social Security Bulletin (February 1976): 3.

Mueller, M.S., and Gibson, R.M. "Age differences in health care spending, fiscal year 1975," Social Security Bulletin (June 1976): 18.

National Center for Health Statistics. *Volume of Physician Visits by Place of Visit and Type of Service, United States: July 1963–June 1964.* Public Health Service Pub. No. 1000, Series 10, No. 18. Washington, D.C.: Government Printing Office, 1965.

National Center for Health Statistics. *Volume of Physician Visits, United States: July 1966–June 1967.* Public Health Service Pub. No. 1000, Series 10, No. 49. Washington, D.C.: Government Printing Office, 1968.

National Center for Health Statistics. *Volume of Physician Visits, United States—1969.* DHEW Pub. No. (HSM) 72–1064, Vital and Health Statistics Series 19, No. 75. Washington, D.C.: Government Printing Office, 1972.

National Center for Health Statistics. *Current Estimates from the Health Interview Survey: United States 1974.* DHEW Pub. No. (HRA) 76–1527. Washington, D.C.: Government Printing Office, 1975.

Nelson, H. "Investigation of prepaid health programs asked: possible fraud in some cases hinted by L.A. county unit," *Los Angeles Times*, February 1973.

Olendzki, M. "Medicaid benefits mainly the younger and less sick," *Med Care* 10 (1974): 163.

Olendzki, M., et al. "The impact of medicaid on private care for the urban poor," *Med Care* 10 (1972): 201.

Perkoff, G., et al. "Medical care utilization in an experimental prepaid group practice model in a university medical center," *Med Care* 12 (1974): 471.

Prybil, L. "Physician terminations in large multispecialty groups," *Med Group Management* 18 (September 1971).

Rabin, D., and Schach, F. "Medicaid, morbidity, and physician use," *Med Care* 13 (1975): 68.

Roemer, M., et al. *Health Insurance Effects: Services, Expenditures, and Attitudes Under These Types of Plan.* Ann Arbor, Mich.: University of Michigan School of Public Health, 1973, cited in Roemer and Shonick, 1973.

Roemer, M., and Shonick, W. "HMO performance: the recent evidence," *Millbank Mem Fund Q* 51 (1973): 271.

Roghman, K. *Emergency Room Survey.* Rochester, N.Y.: University of Rochester, Rochester Child Health Studies, xerox, 1967.

Ross, B. "A comparative study of four dental payment mechanisms in a Headstart program," *Am J Public Health* 61 (1971): 2176.

Shinefield, H., and Smillie, J. "Prepaid group practice and the delivery of health care," *Adv Pediatr* 20 (1973): 205.

Social Security Administration. *Chartbook on Medical Care: expenditures, prices and costs.* Washington, D.C.: Department of Health, Education and Welfare, 1975.

Sparer, G., and Anderson, A. "Utilization and cost experience of low income families in four prepaid group-practice settings," *N Engl J Med* 289 (1973): 67–72.

Steiner, G. *The Children's Cause.* Washington, D.C.: The Brookings Institution, 1976.

Wallace, H., Goldstein, H., and Oglesby, A. "Child health care in the United States: expenditures and extent of coverage with selected comprehensive services," *Pediatrics* 55 (1975): 176–81.

Weber, J. *An Evaluation of an Expanded Public Role in the Financing of Health Care Services for Children.* Paper presented at the Sun Valley Health Forum, Sun Valley, Idaho, August 1975.

Wetherville, R.I., and Nordly, J.M. *A Census of HMO's.* Minneapolis: Interstudy, 1975.

Wilson, R. *Statistical Data Prepared for the Child Health Task Force.* Washington, D.C.: Division of Analysis, National Center for Health Statistics, mimeo, 1974.

Chapter 7

Children and National Health Insurance

Theodore R. Marmor[a]

To understand how the leading national health insurance proposals will affect children, concerns about children's health must be set in the broader political context in which national health insurance is being discussed. Has the concern about the health circumstances of children—their health status and their care—significantly contributed to the growth in the 1970s of demands for national health insurance? The short answer is that it has not.

If children's health problems have had little to do with the origins of national health insurance as an issue in American politics, what has? Second, what is the relationship between the problems of American medicine and the health insurance proposals that are taken seriously by contemporary political elites? The leading proposals are the Kennedy-Corman, CHIP, and the Long-Ribicoff. What problems do they address and how? Third, what likely effects will these plans have on the costs of medical care, its quality, organization, and distribution?

NATIONAL HEALTH INSURANCE
AND AMERICAN POLITICS

The conflict over national health insurance is best understood as an example of "redistributive" American politics. The disputes over

[a] A number of people generously contributed to the drafting and revision of this chapter. At Chicago, Lynn Carter and Jenny Brorsen were particularly capable research assistants and editors. Within the Harvard Child Health Project, Rich Thompkins and John Butler made extraordinarily extensive comments for

Social Security, the long battle over federal aid to education, the fight over Medicare, and now the conflict about NHI exemplify this type of political issue. The question of the scope of government involvement in organizing, financing, and redistributing services is the fundamental theme in all of these seemingly disparate issues.

Sixty-Five Years of Debate

NHI was first a campaign issue for Theodore Roosevelt on the Bull Moose ticket. In 1977, sixty-five years later, it remains a controversial legislative issue. Conflict between national interest groups has been both intense and emotional. The redistribution of income, influence and status, and the legitimacy of highly valued political beliefs and symbols have been at stake in NHI debates. On one side there are those whose basic objective has been to shift medical care financing from privately controlled institutions to the federal government. A central theme in their argument has been that private financing of medical care has produced intolerable inequities. From their perspective, universal government-financed health insurance is the most important missing element in the set of social welfare schemes initiated with the Social Security Act's social insurance and public assistance programs ("The social security revolution," 1965). They argue that medical services should be prepaid through a national tax system assuring everyone, regardless of socioeconomic circumstances, both equal access to needed care and freedom from fearfully expensive medical bills.

Historically, large industrial labor unions, the CIO and later the United Auto Workers (UAW) have spearheaded the recurrent demands for NHI. More recently, their special aim has been to eliminate health insurance costs, generally the most expensive fringe benefits, from contract negotiations with management. They are convinced that a compulsory, tax-financed health program would provide their membership with comprehensive coverage at lower cost to union families.

A number of prominent individuals have linked national health insurance to the predevelopment of a mature Social Security system.[b] They were involved in the development of the Social Security

---

which I am very grateful. In many respects John Butler is a co-author of this chapter, deserving much of the credit for its merits, and a bit of the blame for its remaining problems.

[b]This group includes Wilbur Cohen (Secretary of Health, Education and Welfare, 1968–69), I.S. Falk (Social Security Administration, 1936–54), Robert Ball (Commissioner of the Social Security Administration, 1962–73), and Nelson Cruikshank (Advisory Council Social Security Financing, 1957–58; Health Insurance Benefits Advisory Council, 1965–72).

Act of 1935 and almost every other social welfare program since then, including Medicare and Medicaid in 1965. For forty years they have been advising presidents and members of Congress on social welfare matters and advocating government-financed health insurance. The industrial unions and social insurance reform leaders have been regularly bolstered by a loose coalition of "liberal" church, professional, service, and "consumer" organizations.

Organizations representing physicians, hospitals, insurance companies, and other segments of the health industry have historically opposed comprehensive government health insurance. They have regarded government-financed health insurance as a dire threat to their professional status and to the discretion they have traditionally had in providing and regulating medical services. Anti-NHI groups have persistently argued that the market structure of American medicine is responsible for the high quality of care enjoyed by most Americans. They allege that government-financed health insurance means lower quality, more depersonalized medical service, and their major objective has been to prevent such financing. In that effort, the health industry pressure groups have had allies from other "conservative" and business-oriented national organizations, ranging from the Chamber of Commerce and the National Association of Manufacturers to the Young Americans for Freedom.

The historical NHI debate is extraordinary in its stability of interest group alignment and argument. But although debated in political, academic, and public arenas, it has rarely proceeded beyond the predecisional stage in the federal policy process. The intensity of the struggle has been evident whenever legislative action seemed even remotely feasible. For two decades after World War II government health insurance proposals were salient, whether for all, the elderly, or the poor. The enactment of Medicare in 1965 brought a temporary halt to the long-standing cleavage between the coalitions, and for nearly five years the public discussion of medicine centered on the problems of implementing Medicare and Medicaid and dealing with the unprecedented level of inflation that followed their enactment.

National Health Insurance in the 1970s
Opinion surveys in the early 1970s suggested that a large majority of Americans agreed there was a health crisis but did not regard it as their own (Nixon, 1969; Meany, 1971; Andersen et al., 1971). They have worries: access to a physician, waiting time, cost, and impersonality. Other polls indicate concern, particularly among physicians, about catastrophic financial consequences of serious or lingering ill-

ness, understandable since a large proportion of the population have work-related or Medicare insurance, which do not offer adequate major medical protection (Strickland, 1972).

But it is not patient concerns about access or catastrophe that dominate the crisis conception of American medicine before congressional committees. The problem highlighted here is one of over-all cost, expressed in the testimony of government program managers, insurance company executives, and union leaders. Hospitals and physicians are increasingly under attack as the alarm over rising medical care costs leads to the question of how efficiently and effectively the health industry delivers its services.[c]

Medical Care Problems

This assertion of crisis and the listing of problems have become the standard prologue for national health insurance advocates. National health insurance is required, they argue, because the costs, quality, distribution, and organization of American medicine are so critically flawed.

But the citation of these problems as if they were signals for a particular national health insurance plan is misleading. The plans address different aspects of America's health concerns. They do not agree on crisis, problem, or solution.

Cost.   Consider, for example, the most frequently cited problem: rising medical care costs. That total expenditures for medical care have increased explosively in the past two decades is undeniable. Americans spent more than $118 billion on medical care in fiscal year 1975 (Council on Wage and Price Stability, 1976). That means average expenses per person of $558 in 1975, compared with $485 in 1974. The proportion of the gross national product (GNP) devoted to medical care increased by more than 80 percent in the past twenty years, from 4.6 percent to 8.3 percent in 1975.

But costs understood as total national expenditures is the language of statisticians, not citizens. What Americans worry most about are the prices of their own office visits, appendectomies, insurance premiums, or the costs of a severe illness (cancer, a broken hip, cerebral

[c]The intensity of the health care issue is increasing. Between 1972 and 1975 the proportion of those who regarded health care as a critical problem increased from 42 to 55 percent. Fifty-five percent of the respondents ranked health care as a "very very important issue" (5 on a 5-point scale) compared to 42 percent three years ago. See remarks by Dorothy Lynch in National Health Council, A Declaration of Interdependence: Developing America's Health Policy, Proceedings of the Twenty-Fourth Annual National Health Forum, March 16–17, 1976, Philadelphia, Pennsylvania, p. 36.

palsy). They fear the consequences of medical inflation in these personal terms, linking rising prices with out-of-pocket costs to their own family. And they worry about an insurance plan expiring just when it is essential, in the rare financially catastrophic case. (Fewer than 1 percent spend more than $5000 a year on medical care. See Meyer, 1974.)

Governments likewise are more concerned about the cost to them than about total health expenditures. As Table 7–1 illustrates, the public sector has become the largest source of payment for health care. Governments at all levels now account for 40 percent and the federal government alone is approaching 30 percent of total health expenditures. The dramatic growth is particularly evident at the federal level. Eleven years ago, Medicare and Medicaid represented federal budget outlays of $5.9 billion; in 1975, approximately $25 billion. While the state and local share of personal health expenditures stabilized around 12 percent between 1966 and 1975, the federal share tripled (United States, Executive Office of the President, 1975).

Cost control preoccupies Medicare and Medicaid administrators. Although government expenditures have increased, so have the needs of their poorer clientele. In fact, the real value of Medicaid benefits per capita, taking inflation into account, has slightly declined between 1968 and 1974 despite the annual dollar increases in program expenditures (Table 7–2). The major focus on costs has meant that primary care, issues of humane treatment, and the special problems of poor children have not had priority in the debate. Yet these are precisely the aspects that preoccupy child health advocates.

Maldistribution and Fragmentation. For both children and adults there is worry about maldistribution of medical services, both by geography and by specialty. There are serious shortages of physicians in rural areas and the inner cities, and the traditional family doctor appears to be declining. Only 70,000 of the 295,000 MDs practicing in the U.S. are pediatricians or general practitioners (AMA, 1974). The complaint about the under-supply of primary care physicians is common in both the pediatric and adult medicine literature. Though cost problems have not been central for children, the fastest growing portion of children's health expenditures at present is for secondary and tertiary services.[d]

Changes in medical school training programs and the interests of

---

[d]Secondary care is referral care, whether as an inpatient or an outpatient. Tertiary care is care at a still higher level of skill—intensive care, or care in specialized hospitals. All inpatient hospital care is secondary or tertiary.

Table 7–1. The Growth of Personal Health Care Expenditures by Source of Payment[a] (Dollar sums in millions)

Fiscal Year	Total	Private Sector						Public Sector			
		Out of Pocket		Insurance Benefits		Industry and Philanthropy		State and Local		Federal	
		Amount	Percent of Total	Amount	Percent of Total	Amount	Percent of Total	Amount	Percent of Total	Amount	Percent of Total
1950	10,400	7,107	68.3	879	8.5	312	3.0	1,124	10.8	979	9.4
1955	15,231	8,992	59.0	2,358	15.5	412	2.7	1,886	12.4	1,583	10.4
1960	22,729	12,576	55.3	4,698	20.7	525	2.3	2,828	12.4	2,102	9.2
1965	33,498	17,577	52.5	8,280	24.7	683	2.0	4,118	12.3	2,840	8.5
1966	36,216	18,668	51.5	8,936	24.7	720	2.0	4,542	12.5	3,349	9.2
1967	41,343	18,786	45.4	9,344	22.6	753	1.8	4,991	12.1	7,471	18.1
1968	46,521	19,098	41.1	10,444	22.5	780	1.7	5,797	12.5	10,401	22.4
1969	52,690	20,957	39.8	12,206	23.2	824	1.6	6,421	12.2	12,283	23.3
1970	60,113	24,272	40.4	14,406	24.0	890	1.5	7,142	11.9	13,403	22.3
1971	67,228	26,307	39.1	16,728	24.9	964	1.4	7,827	11.6	15,401	22.9
1972	74,828	28,141	37.6	18,620	24.9	1,035	1.4	8,906	11.9	18,126	24.2
1973	82,490	30,348	36.8	20,955	25.4	1,125	1.4	9,884	12.0	20,178	24.5
1974	90,088	31,310	34.8	24,100	26.8	1,220	1.4	10,499	11.6	22,959	25.5
1975	103,200	33,599	32.6	27,340	26.5	1,337	1.3	12,345	12.0	28,578	27.7

[a] Amounts shown are smaller than total health care expenditures due to exclusion of prepayment and administrative expenses and government public health activities which were approximately 15 percent of personal expenditures in 1975.

Source: Mueller and Gibson, February 1976.

Table 7–2. Federal Outlays per Medicaid Recipient in Constant Dollars, Fiscal Years 1968–1974
(Total outlays and recipients in thousands)

	1968	1969	1970	1971	1972	1973	1974
Medicaid: Total outlays in constant dollars	$1,922,642	$2,284,713	$2,539,438	$2,929,961	$3,650,583	$3,648,704	$4,404,845
Number of recipients of services	11,500	12,060	14,507	18,223	20,632	23,537	27,187
Outlay per recipient	167	189	175	161	177	155	162

Source: L.B. Russell et al., 1974, p. 64.

medical school students have encouraged those who advocate greater emphasis on primary care. For example, between 1968 and 1974, the number of first-year positions filled by primary care training programs nearly doubled, from 4600 to 8800. In 1975, 56 percent of the 12,700 graduating medical students entered programs in primary care fields (*Medical World News*, 23 February 1976). These developments may, however, be less profound changes than they appear.[e]

Quality of Care. The quality of treatment usually comes to public attention through suits for malpractice and accounts of the high cost of malpractice insurance. But errors of medical competence may be rarer and cause less social harm than questionable and inefficient medical services. Drugs are not always prescribed wisely or in moderation; surgery is not always necessary.

However, despite the crisis language, there is no agreed spectre in health except high and rising costs. The various other "problems" are just that, defects that any sensible analyst would recognize, but not uniformly worsening so as to justify a fear of disaster. This is particularly true about access, where the gap between rich and poor adults has been substantially reduced in the past decade (Chapter 4).

Competing NHI Remedies

The most straightforward way to describe national health insurance proposals is to compare their benefits, beneficiaries, financing, and administrative arrangements along simple grids. The Department of Health, Education and Welfare regularly publishes such digests of congressional proposals, and public finance experts attach cost estimates and impact projections.

Three basic types of bills now dominate the public debate over national health insurance. They can be usefully distinguished by the degree of centralization of governmental authority they propose.

Minimum Public Control. The first group of proposals reflects the shared assumption among national health insurance contestants that government should redistribute the current costs of illness. The American Medical Association has prominently advocated plans of this sort. Its Medicredit proposal, first presented in the early 1970s

---

[e]The strong, long-term trend toward specialization has reappeared within the so-called primary care fields, illustrated by the tendency of young internists to bypass general internal medicine in favor of subspecialties like hematology, oncology, and endocrinology. This trend is demonstrated by the sharp increase in the number of physicians taking subspecialty examinations by the American Board of Internal Medicine: 200 in 1970 to 2000 in 1974.

(Table 7−3), was designed as a federal tax subsidy of health insurance premiums in hopes of stimulating the purchase of more comprehensive plans. It would have replaced the present tax deduction for medical care expenses with a tax credit to offset in whole or in part the premiums of qualified health insurance plans. The amount of the credit was graduated in reverse: the higher the income tax bracket, the lower the tax credit.

According to the Medicredit scheme, the American medical care system would respond to a more broadly distributed capacity to buy

Table 7−3. AMA "Medicredit" Plan (Fulton-Broyhill-Hartke Bill)

Program would provide credits against personal income taxes to offset the premium cost of a qualified private health insurance policy providing specified benefits. Employers would be required to provide qualified policies to retain favorable tax treatment.

BENEFITS	Tax credits of 10 to 100 percent of the cost of qualified health insurance policy; amount of credit depends on annual tax payments with higher benefits given to those with lower taxable income. Voucher certificates for purchase of insurance issued to those with little or no tax liability. Policies to provide sixty days hospitalization or (substituted on a two-for-one basis) skilled nursing facility; physician care; dental care for children; home health services; laboratory and X-ray; ambulance service. Catastrophic coverage of unlimited hospital days and an additional thirty days in a skilled nursing facility.
POPULATION COVERED	All U.S. residents, on a voluntary basis.
FINANCING	Tax credits from federal general revenues. Employers must provide qualified policies to take full premium cost as a normal business deduction.
COST SHARING	$50 deductible for hospital or skilled nursing facility stay. 20 percent coinsurance for physician care, home health services, laboratory and X-ray, ambulance, dental care. For catastrophic coverage, a deductible which varies by income. Total coinsurance limited to $100 per family for combined physician/lab/X-ray services; $100 per family for hospital outpatient, home health and ambulance; and $100 per family for dental care. Medicaid to pay all cost-sharing for cash assistance recipients.
ADMINISTRATION	Private carriers issue policies. State insurance departments certify carriers and qualified policies. DHEW issues voucher certificates. New federal board establishes standards.

Source: Waldman, 1975.

its services. By increasing consumer purchasing power, particularly among lower-income groups, the problem of inaccessibility to care would be overcome. A decade ago the plan would have generated criticism within the medical profession for its encouragement of more third-party medical financing.

Also within the minimum public control class are proposals to protect against financially catastrophic expenses. Other governmental programs and private health insurance would cope with the rest of the medical care industry's problems (Meyer, 1976). The catastrophic portion of the Long-Ribicoff bill covers hospitalization stays beyond sixty days and annual medical expenditures of more than $2000 (Table 7—4). The major risk insurance proposal (MRI) by Martin Feldstein would protect against disaster while requiring direct patient payment for most medical expenses, thereby, it is hoped, reducing the rate of medical inflation. Feldstein's MRI is a comprehensive universal health insurance policy with a very high deductible; it would pay all medical bills that exceed 10 percent of annual income (Feldstein, 1971; Marmor and Kudrle, 1975). Quite similar, though administered by the IRS as a tax credit scheme for large medical expenses, is the bill sponsored by Senator William Brock of Tennessee (Waldman, 1975).

Catastrophic insurance is effective and relatively inexpensive but only because its benefits are limited. Most versions are predicted to be less than $5 billion in federal cost. The catastrophes it covers are financial rather than medical. The Long-Ribicoff proposal, for example, leaves almost intact the present subcatastrophic system, with all its problems. Feldstein's MRI plan appears to do the same, but with a major qualification: in suggesting the removal of current tax incentives for insurance, Feldstein attempts to shift the burden of medical-financial decisions from physician to more cost-conscious patients. By using a deductible that is high in relation to average yearly medical expenditures (expenditures that are short of catastrophic), it also seeks to combat medical inflation with consumer restraint. If these policies were to be fully implemented, they would reintroduce the financial barriers to care which many national health insurance advocates see as the access problem in the first place.

Major Government Intervention. In contrast to this first group of proposals are those which call for major intervention on the part of the federal government. The most ambitious is the Kennedy-Corman bill (Table 7—5) which proposes a government monopoly of the health insurance business. To insure that "money would no longer

Table 7–4. Long-Ribicoff-Wagonner, Catastrophic Protection

	Catastrophic Insurance Plan	*Medical Assistance Plan*
BENEFITS	Hospital in-patient *after* first sixty days. One hundred days of skilled nursing facility care for persons who received catastrophic hospital benefits. Physician services, lab and X-ray, home health services. Medical supplies and ambulance services except Medicare limit of $250/year for outpatient psychiatric services in one year retained.	Hospital inpatient care (sixty days). Skilled nursing facility care, intermediate care facility, physician's services, lab and X-ray, home health services. Full cost of benefits under catastrophic plan for recipients not covered by catastrophic insurance, and cost sharing for recipients who do have catastrophic insurance.
POPULATION COVERED	Persons insured or receiving benefits under Social Security.	Low-income individuals and families regardless of age or employment status, with aid to families who have incurred heavy medical expenses relative to income.
FINANCING	Special tax on wages and self-employment income subject to Social Security tax. Rate initially 0.3 percent, to rise to 0.4 percent.	State and federal general revenues.
COST-SHARING	Coverage begins only when expenses reach specified catastrophic proportions (after first sixty days of hospitalization with unlimited further days covered and $21 per day copayment; skilled nursing facility benefits for those who have received catastrophic hospital benefits, with $10.50 per day copayment). Total coinsurance limited to $1000 annually per person; $2000 medical deductible.	$3 copayment for first ten visits to a physician per family.
ADMINISTRATION	Through the Medicare program with private carriers handling claims.	

Source: Adapted from Waldman, 1975; Holahan, 1975.

Table 7–5.   Kennedy-Corman Bill

A universal health insurance program administered by DHEW, financed by federal general revenues and payroll taxes. Broad benefits with no cost-sharing and few limitations. Would establish a national health budget under which funds would be allocated to regions and localities.

POPULATION COVERED	All U.S. residents, without regard to whether they have contributed to the program through taxes.
BENEFITS	Hospital care (limited for psychiatric inpatient care to forty-five consecutive days per spell of illness), and 120 days of care in a skilled nursing facility. Physicians (comprehensive, including checkups, immunization, well-baby and family planning services; psychiatric is limited to twenty visits per spell of illness but unlimited if furnished by HMO hospital, OPD, or mental health clinic). Dentists for children under fifteen and eventually for entire population. Home health services. Other health professionals. Laboratory and X-ray. Medical supplies and ambulance services. Optometrists and eyeglasses. Prescription drugs for chronic and other specified illness.
FINANCING	Tax on payroll (1.0 percent), unearned income (1.0 percent), self-employed (2.5 percent), with employers paying 3.5 percent tax. Income subject to tax is the first $15,000 per year for individuals, and the total payroll for employers (state and local governments do not pay employer tax). Federal revenues equal to the total receipts from taxes.
COST-SHARING	No deductibles or coinsurance.
ADMINISTRATION	Federal government, by a special board in DHEW with regional and local offices to operate program.

Source: Adapted from Waldman, 1975; Holahan, 1975.

be a consideration for a patient seeking any health service," the Kennedy-Corman plan would establish a national health insurance program with universal eligibility and unusually broad coverage of service, financed jointly by payroll taxes and general revenues. There would be no cost-sharing by patients so that care under the plan would be "free" at the point of service, with the federal government paying providers directly. Further provisions of the bill address problems of cost escalation (by limiting the total budget for medical care), distribution (by creating incentives for comprehensive health service organizations and for health personnel in underserved areas), and quality (by policing the standard of care) (S.3; H.R.23, 1975).

Hybrid Proposals. The third and final group of proposals includes a mixture of strategies that call for increased government regulation and partial federal subsidy of the present medical care system. The leading hybrid proposal to date is the Ford administration's Comprehensive Health Insurance Plan (CHIP) (Table 7−6). It calls for employer contributions, larger financial contributions from patients as the incomes of welfare families rise, and controls costs by state regulation and the encouragement of prepaid group practice.

The mandated employer plans are a way of insuring vast numbers of families for health expenses with a minimum impact on the federal budget. For example, employers under CHIP would be required to offer policies with broad benefits and pay three-quarters of the premium. The employee would pay one-quarter of the premium and would be responsible for substantial cost-sharing at the time of use. More modest payment scales would obtain for families in lower-income categories. Whatever the specific features, such plans share the current health expenditures among patients, employers, and the government. They do not lower health costs but they appear to do so because the federal price tag is so much lower than under Kennedy-Corman, for example.

Saying that CHIP costs $45 billion and Kennedy-Corman $100 billion is misleading. It would be accurate only if unions dropped their present benefits and accepted the cost-sharing of CHIP. It is more likely that under CHIP employers would supplement the federally mandated plan. In this case total health expenditures would be nearly the same under both CHIP and Kennedy-Corman, and neither would radically inflate our present $118 billion health expenditures.

Very similar to the Ford CHIP bill is the 1974 proposal of Senator Kennedy and Representative Wilbur Mills (Table 7−7), a more politically acceptable version of the Kennedy-Corman bill. The Kennedy-Mills proposal is similar to CHIP in the structure of benefits and out-of-pocket payments but differs in the financing. The estimated federal cost of Kennedy-Mills at $77 billion vastly exceeds that of the CHIP plan at $43 billion, though both are lower than the estimated $103 billion federal cost of Kennedy-Corman (1974 estimates by the secretary of DHEW).

National health insurance cannot solve all the shortcomings of the health industry. The AMA has recognized that improving "any system of medical care depends basically on balancing three strong and competing dynamics: the desire to make medical care available to all, the desire to control cost, and the desire for high quality care" (AMA, 1971). The competition among these goals is such that serving any two of them works against the third:

Table 7–6.   Comprehensive Health Insurance Plan (CHIP): Ford Administration Proposal

A three-part voluntary program which would include: (1) a plan requiring employers to provide private insurance for employees, (2) an assisted plan for low-income and high-medical-risk families and individuals, and (3) an improved federal Medicare program for the aged.

	Employee Plan	*Assisted Plan*	*Plan for Aged*
BENEFITS	Hospitalization Physician services (excluding physical exams for adults) Laboratory X-ray Prescription drugs and medical supplies Home health visits (100/year) Post-hospital extended care (100 days/year) Well-child care to age six; eye, ear and dental care to age thirteen Family planning Prenatal and maternity care Hospitalization (inpatient mental health, thirty full or sixty partial) Physician services (outpatient mental health: thirty visits to community center; fifteen to private practitioner) Vision, hearing, and dental exams (to age thirteen)		
POPULATION COVERED	Full-time employees	Low-income families, employed or unemployed; Families and employment groups who are high medical risks; All others who wish to enroll on payment of premiums	Aged persons insured under Social Security
FINANCING	Employer-employee premium (employer paying 75 percent)	Federal and state revenues, and premiums from enrollees according to family income groups	Payroll tax and premium payments by the aged (with federal and state financing of premiums for low-income aged)

COST-SHARING	Deductible of $150 per person coinsurance; 25 percent total cost-sharing limited to $1500 per year per family	Maximum provisions as in employee plan but reduced according to individual or family income	Deductible $100 per person coinsurance. 20 percent total cost-sharing limited to $750 per person per year. Reduced cost-sharing for lower-income aged
ADMINISTRATION	Insurance through private carriers supervised by states under federal regulations	Administered by states using private intermediaries, under federal regulations	Administered by federal government

Sources: Adapted from Marmor, 1974; Waldman, 1975; Holahan, 1975.

Table 7–7.   Kennedy-Mills Bill

A two-part program consisting of (1) a national health insurance plan for the general population and (2) a revised Medicare plan for aged and disabled including a long-term care benefit.

	NHI	Medicare, regular	Medicare, long-term
BENEFITS[a]	Comprehensive, as in CHIP		Extensive provisions for home and institutional care services
POPULATION COVERED	Persons insured or eligible for Social Security, working full-time or on AFDC or SSI	Aged and disabled, as under present Medicare program	
FINANCING	Payroll tax (3 percent for employers, 1 percent for employees), self-employment and unearned income (2.5 percent), and AFDC and SSI payments. Income taxable up to $20,000.	Continuation of same financing provisions	Enrolled pay $6 monthly premium. Balance from federal and state revenues (90 percent and 10 percent respectively)
COST SHARING	Deductible $150 per person Coinsurance $25 Total cost-sharing limited to $1000 per family but eliminated for low-income families. No cost-sharing for preventive care	Same as present Medicare program but eliminated or reduced for low-income families	No cost-sharing, except Social Security or SSI benefits reduced for persons receiving institutional services
ADMINISTRATION	Administered by an independent SSA with insurance carriers processing claims		New community centers provide or arrange for services under state and SSA supervision

[a]Excluding physical exams for adults.
Sources: Adapted from Waldman, 1975; Holahan, 1975.

When you link the quest for easy and universal access with a desire to maintain quality of care. . . . that combination of factors works against cost controls. . . . If you link quality with vigorous efforts to control cost, then there has to be pressure on access . . . (AMA, 1971, p. 1951).

Proposals and Problems: Likely Effects

What would be the effect of the various plans on the cost, quality, organization, and distribution of medical care? Would any of these plans reduce the more than $10 billion annual increase in the national health care bill? The answer is not optimistic. In Canada and Sweden, government financing on a large scale has not reversed the upward spiral in prices and expenditures, especially since financing is dispersed among different units of government (Marmor, Heagy and Hoffman, 1975; Marmor, Wittman and Heagy, 1976). There is evidence that where financing is concentrated at one governmental level and service providers are directly budgeted (rather than reimbursed by insurance), expenditures and the rate of medical inflation are lower. With its National Health Service, England in the last fifteen years has spent a third less of its resources on medical care and experiences roughly a third the rate of inflation of Canada, Sweden, or the United States (Table 7—8) (Zubkoff, 1976). To the 16 percent of Americans who favor putting doctors in an English-style system, this will be a welcome argument (Lynch, 1976). But even to others, the experience of Great Britain suggests a financing concentration desirable in a future national health insurance program. Thus, the "conservative" emphasis on controlling inflation may best be accomplished by a greater degree of governmental centralization than even many "liberals" favor.

Of the leading U.S. plans the Kennedy-Corman bill, with its federal financing concentrated in a single governmental agency, affords the best theoretical prospects for curbing inflation. But to be effective it must be fully implemented, which is at present unlikely. The Feldstein plan aims at containing costs by placing financial responsibility on patients in order to restrain inflation. But to work, such a plan must bar supplementary insurance, and this is not an acceptable measure politically.[f] Hence, the promising anti-inflation proposals are politically the least likely to emerge in the United States.

National health insurance is likely to be more successful in improv-

[f]Interviews with HEW officials suggest that any efforts to change the current tax advantages of health insurance meet with fierce resistance. This resistance has led Stuart Altman, deputy assistant secretary for Health, Office of Planning and Evaluation, HEW, to conclude that more drastic constraints on insurance would have a near-zero probability of enactment.

Table 7-8.   Total Expenditures for Health Services as a Percentage of the Gross National Product, Seven Countries, Selected Periods, 1961-69

Country	WHO Estimates[a]		SSA Estimates[b]		McKinsey Estimates[c]	
	Year	Percentage of GNP	Year	Percentage of GNP	Year	Percentage of GNP
Canada	1961	6.0	1969	7.3	1973	7.8
United States	1961-62	5.8	1969	6.8	1973	7.7
Sweden	1962	5.4	1969	6.7	1971	7.0
The Netherlands	1963	4.8	1969	5.9	1972	7.3
Federal Republic of Germany	1961	4.5	1969	5.7	1968	6.1
France	1963	4.4	1969	5.7	1973	5.8
United Kingdom	1961-62	4.2	1969	4.8	1973	5.3

Source: [a] Abel-Smith, 1967; [b] Simanis, 1973; [c] Maxwell, 1975.

ing access than in containing costs. But financial barriers are only part of the problem. Equally serious is the poor distribution of medical personnel (National Health Council, 1976). No proposed remedy has worked well. Educational loan forgiveness for service in underdoctored areas has been tried, also the substitution of rural or ghetto medical service for physicians' military obligations and subsidies for medical centers in underserved locales. Poor distribution remains even after the medical purchasing power of poor city neighborhoods and remote rural areas is improved (U.S. Congress, 1975b). Young doctors have good professional and social reasons for continuing to prefer specialty practices in affluent suburban neighborhoods.

In sum, the quality of medical care depends much more on professional self-regulation and consumer awareness than on the regulations of any conceivable health insurance plan. Adequate financing cannot insure that the care received is good.

But skepticism need not justify inaction. The major aim of insurance is to calm fears of financial disaster. Some have argued that national health insurance without incentives for prevention and for improvement of health is not worth having. But would anyone argue that automobile insurance, for example, is not worth having if it does not prevent accidents and improve the quality of our automobiles?

WHAT WOULD NATIONAL INSURANCE MEAN FOR CHILDREN?

Children's concerns have been at the periphery of the preoccupation with medical care costs this past decade. Those interested in children have worried that typical NHI plans would not simply ignore but would negatively affect children's health care. This worry should be noted before we turn to what in fact the leading NHI proposals might mean for children's health concerns: access, distribution of providers, and quality of care. Finally, one should point out that medical care for children differs from that of adults in stressing preventive care and monitoring services. Programs designed for children cannot easily deal with the consequences of the increasingly expensive, sophisticated, hospital-based services that most Americans identify with modern health care.

What are the likely effects on children of the three types of plans that have just been reviewed? Presently under congressional scrutiny are catastrophic schemes (Long-Ribicoff), universal first-dollar comprehensive plans (Kennedy-Corman), and national comprehensive schemes with significant patient cost-sharing (CHIP and Kennedy-Mills). These represent respectively the minimum public controls, the major government intervention, and the mixed breeds.

Children's Health Status

Children now use medical services which comprise a relatively small share of the nation's health expenditure budget (U.S. DHEW, 1975). Children get sick more frequently than adults, and younger children more than older children. When acute illness is defined as any illness limiting activity, children are almost twice as likely as other age groups to get sick (Figure 7–1).

Figure 7–1.   Decline in Acute Illness with Advancing Age *(Data from the National Health Surveys)*

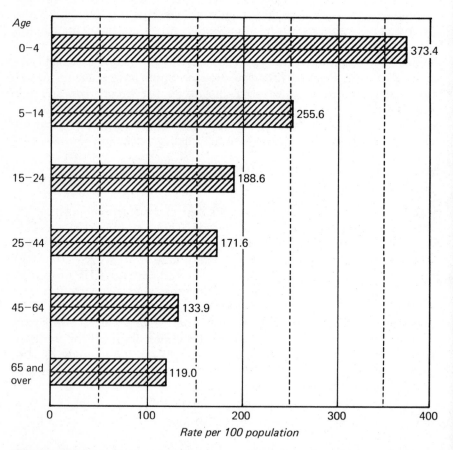

Note: In this survey, illness is defined as some symptom that takes a person to the physician or limits activity for one or more days.

Source: Green and Haggerty, 1968.

Yet the vast majority of children's illnesses, perhaps as much as 80 percent of presenting problems, are easy to diagnose, tend to be self-limiting, and cause little disability. Common respiratory illness is about three times as frequent as any other problem (Green and Haggerty, 1968). For the most part, children's acute care is for a distribution of illnesses weighted heavily to routine problems. This means that the acute care needs of children are more predictable than those of adults. It is somewhat surprising to discover that the list of pediatric deficiencies in ordinary care is long.

In 1973, about one out of every three U.S. children was not fully immunized against polio, measles, rubella, diphtheria, whooping cough, and tetanus. Levels of immunization against polio have dropped alarmingly since the middle 1960s. Between 10 and 20 percent of U.S. children have some form of chronic handicapping condition; it is estimated that at least a third of these problems could be corrected by appropriate intervention in the preschool years, and another third by appropriate continuous care until age eighteen. In one group of children selected from a central city Washington, D.C. population, it was discovered that 18 percent suffered from conductive hearing loss, which except in rare cases derives from untreated middle ear infections. Levels of rheumatic fever among U.S. children are expected to reach over one million cases by 1980 according to one estimate of the American Academy of Pediatrics; all of these cases should be avoidable.

Beyond these problems is what Haggerty et al. (1975) refer to as "the new morbidity," those conditions that are occurring more frequently or are more evident with the control of more serious diseases. Among these are learning disorders, behavior problems, vision and hearing problems, management of chronic disease or handicap, social adjustments in adolescence, and battered children. Moreover, it is now estimated that two-thirds of all childhood fatalities result from accidents, homicides, and suicides. These changing problems are of central importance in appraising the effect of NHI on children.

Utilization of Children's Health Services

Physician services and hospitalization comprise roughly a third each of total medical expenditures for children. The proportions highlight the relatively more important role physicians play in the medical care for children and youth. While physician services accounted for some 23 percent of the medical care expenses of all age groups, and hospital services 45 percent, the ratio of physician to hospital expenses for children is 32 percent to 31 percent (Weber, 1975).

The character of children's health services can be quickly grasped from national surveys. In 1972 children (infants to age seventeen) used approximately four physician visits per person, an estimated 265 million visits as compared to the 136 million visits for those in the survey aged twenty-five to sixty-four (Weber, 1975).

Most of these visits, for those seventeen and under, were to general practitioners and about one-third to pediatricians. This pattern differs, however, by income class. Children and families with less than $5000 annual income saw a general practitioner 65 percent of the time and a pediatrician 19 percent of the time. These figures contrast with 37 percent for general practitioners and 41 percent for pediatricians among the children from families of income over $15,000. A National Opinion Research Center (NORC) survey showed that only 60 percent of low-income children aged one to five saw a physician during the survey year, while 83 percent of high-income children did so. It should be noted that this direct relation between income and physician visits no longer holds for the under-sixty-five adult population.

This portrait of income inequalities in relation to utilization of physicians is important background to the assessment of NHI plans for children. The extent of physician consultations, a quarter of which are by telephone, means there may be opportunities to substitute nurse practitioners and physician-extenders for doctors' services. The application of upper-income models of child health care may mean an extraordinary expansion in the volume of medical care services delivered to children, a fact that itself may prompt more efficient use of physician manpower. But use of these medical personnel may not have a significant impact on the number of providers because of stringent supervision requirements and concerns about malpractice liability (Chapter 5).

The relatively infrequent hospitalization of children means that only very sick children would be markedly affected by hospitalization insurance, whether catastrophic or first-dollar (Table 7—9). For children under eighteen, the use of hospitals varied substantially with income, the poorer using hospitals twice as much. Those interested in primary care for children should ask first: What impact would the competing plans have on the access to preventive, well-baby, and routine acute care by children? Tables 7—10 through 7—12 detail the benefit provisions in each of the major NHI proposals under consideration.

Table 7—9. U.S. Hospital Discharges by Age Group, 1972

Age Group	Short-Term Hospital Discharges Per 100 Persons
0—17	7.0
17—24	14.7
25—34	16.6
35—44	15.2
45—64	16.0
65 and over	26.2

Source: United States Department of Health, Education, and Welfare, 1973.

Access to Care

The impact of NHI on access to care depends substantially on the degree of patient cost-sharing and on the supplementary insurance that would be bought concurrently.

The Comprehensive Health Insurance Plan (CHIP) would diminish financial access of children currently covered under Medicaid, because families would have to spend as much as 9 percent of income on medical care before they would be eligible for the plan's benefits (Davis, 1975b) (Table 7—10).

Kennedy-Mills is somewhat more advantageous than CHIP in its cost-sharing provisions for the near poor (Table 7—11). The plan as it would affect children is much like CHIP. No payments would be required for a family of four with income below $4800. For those above this amount a deductible of $150 per person and a 25 percent coinsurance rate would go into effect (no more than two $150 deductibles allowed per family). The generosity of the plan comes principally in the ceiling it imposes on costs, which would never exceed 25 percent of the difference between family income and $4800 and is limited to $1000 per family. For most families with children this would be a major source of financial security in the face of high medical costs for their children, but would matter little if, as in most cases, children's care did not cost more than $100 or so per year. In addition, the plan offers no incentive to increased earnings. This is as much a problem here as with the CHIP proposal, since both gear family cost-sharing to earnings.

The Kennedy-Corman plan (Table 7—12) would, in theory, most dramatically improve the financial access for children to medical care services. It would in fact provide all children the wide range of benefits and the removal of financial barriers that Medicaid currently

Table 7–10. CHIP Bill: Selected Benefit Provisions

Service	For General Population		Limited to Children	
	Provisions	Cost-Sharing	Provisions	Cost-Sharing
Basic services:				
Hospital inpatient	No limitations	Common $150 deductible per person for all benefits of proposal and 25 percent coinsurance		
Skilled nursing facility	100 days			
Physicians' services	No limitations			
Laboratory and X-ray	No limitations			
Prescription drugs	No limitations			
Specialized services:				
Maternity care	No limitations			
Physical exams			Under age six	
Dental services			Under age thirteen	Common $150 deductible per person for all benefits of proposal and 25 percent coinsurance
Vision services			Under age thirteen, exams and eyeglasses	
Hearing services			Under age thirteen, exams and hearing aids	

Source: Waldman, 1974.

Table 7–11. Kennedy-Mills Bill: Selected Benefit Provisions

Service	For General Population		Limited to Children	
	Provisions	*Cost-Sharing*	*Provisions*	*Cost-Sharing*
Basic services:				
Hospital inpatient	No limitations	Common $150 deductible for all benefits of proposal, and 25 percent coinsurance. No more than two deductibles per family per year.		
Skilled nursing facility	100 days			
Physicians' services	No limitations			
Laboratory and X-ray	No limitations			
Prescription drugs	For treatment of chronic illnesses			
Specialized services:				
Maternity care	No limitations			
Physical exams			Under age six	25 percent coinsurance
Dental services			Under age thirteen	
Vision services			Under age thirteen, exams and eyeglasses	
Hearing services			Under age thirteen, exams and hearing aids	

Source: Waldman, 1974.

Table 7–12.   Kennedy-Corman Bill: Selected Benefit Provisions

Service	For General Population		Limited to Children	
	Provisions	Cost-Sharing	Provisions	Cost-Sharing
Basic services:				
Hospital in-patient	No limitations			
Skilled nursing facility	120 days			
Physicians' services	No limitations	None		
Laboratory and X-ray	No limitations			
Prescription drugs	For treatment of chronic illness[a]			
Specialized services:				
Maternity care	No limitations	None		
Physical exams	No limitations			
Dental services			Under age twenty-six[b]	None
Vision services	Includes exams and eyeglasses	None		
Hearing services	Includes exams and hearing aids			

[a]Full range of drugs covered if provided by an HMO or professional foundation.
[b]Coverage initially limited to children under age fifteen. Phased in, over a five-year period, to persons under age twenty-six. Within seven years of enactment of bill, a timetable for phasing in the entire population must be established.
Source: Waldman, 1974.

brings many poor children. But while Kennedy-Corman would represent an improvement for low-income children whose family insurance is currently limited, its universal coverage means that these
children would have to compete with other citizens whose effective
demands for health care would also have been increased.

Canadian experience with Kennedy-Corman type programs has not
shown the poor results of that competition feared by some child
advocates. Two developments are likely in children's access to care
under the Kennedy-Corman type of program. One is that poor children may somewhat improve their access relative to other children
(Table 7—13). The other is that, compared to the elderly, children
may use a slightly smaller proportion of resources under conditions
of universal financial accessibility to health care. Table 7—14 shows
that in Quebec child health expenditures relative to those of the
elderly have fallen somewhat between 1971 and 1973.

The over-all result in Quebec province suggests that children at
risk are responded to. Of particular significance, according to Enterline, is the "increased frequency with which patients were seen for
. . . common and important medical symptoms. This suggests that
the removal of economic worries may actually improve the general
health level of the population" (Enterline et al., 1973). But, since
most children do not use the most expensive medical care facilities
regularly, it should be expected that equal financial access might
slightly disadvantage children as a class. In Saskatchewan, the evidence corroborates the conclusions drawn from Quebec. Beck (1973)
has shown that the degree of nonuse has equalized during the first

Table 7—13. Redistributive Effects of Medicare Measured by Average Annual
Visits to a Physician by Income Group Before and After Medicare, 1969—72
*(in Montreal metropolitan area, province of Quebec. Percentage change as
increase or decrease over approximately a two-year period)*

Income in Dollars	Average Number of Visits	Percent Change in Visits	
$0—3000	7.8	18	gain
$3000—5000	6.0	9	gain
$5000—9000	4.7	No change	
$9000—15,000	4.9	4	loss
$15,000 and over	4.8	9	loss
All income groups	5.0	No change	

Source: Modified from Castonguay, table 4, p. 117, in Andreopoulos, 1975.

Table 7−14. Allocation of Costs by Age Group, Province of Quebec, 1971−73

		Physician Services	Dentist Services	Optometrist Services
1971	0−14	17.0%	29.3%	17.8%
	65−over	12.7%	2.2%	7.4%
	Total	$269,987,793	$2,307,690	$7,792,437
1972	0−14	15.7%	26.2%	16.6%
	65−over	12.8%	2.0%	7.5%
	Total	$297,043,726	$2,822,327	$8,930,316
1973	0−14	15.6%	24.2%	16.3%
	65−over	12.7%	2.1%	7.6%
	Total	$334,798,961	$2,869,870	$10,414,372

Source: Regie de l'Assurance Maladie du Quebec, 1974.

five years of universal health insurance, though he also mentions that poor children did less well in improving their immunizations levels.

The Long-Ribicoff plan (Table 7−15) is generally regarded as the most conservative in extent of coverage and as having the least effect on financial accessibility. While this is true, the plan still has implications for children's care not substantially different from those of the CHIP and Kennedy-Mills plans. There would be no premiums for families with incomes less than $4800, and the benefit package for children would contain much the same services as in the other plans, but the copayment for the first ten outpatient visits for a poor family would be $3 for each visit. This figure is so low that it probably would not deter a family from seeking acute care, but it might well affect utilization of preventive care services.

The Long-Ribicoff catastrophic plan (Table 7−16) does, however, relate payment directly to the difference between family income and the baseline for poverty status. If medical expenditures exceed the difference between these two, additional expenses will be covered. This system, as experienced under Medicaid, amounts to a step-sliding scale of income-related deductibles (Holahan, 1975). Protection is quite.generous for the poor, but there are steeply reduced benefits for the near-poor.

The pattern of care for most children, in short, would be unaffected by the enactment of a catastrophic plan. But the much more crucial access issue here is the impact of catastrophic coverage on new medical technology and the treatment of severe illnesses that affect a small number of children. The case of hemophilia comes to

Table 7–15. Long-Ribicoff Bill, Medical Assistance Plan: Selected Benefit Provisions

Service	For General Population		Limited to Children	
	Provisions	*Cost-Sharing*	*Provisions*	*Cost-Sharing*
Basic services:				
Hospital inpatient	Sixty days	None		
Skilled nursing facility	No limitations	None		
Physicians' services	No limitations	$3 per visit for first ten visits		
Laboratory and X-ray	No limitations	None		
Prescription drugs				
Specialized services:				
Maternity care	No limitations	None		
Physical exams			Under age eighteen	None
Dental services				
Vision services			Under age eighteen, exams and eyeglasses	None
Hearing services			Under age eighteen, exams and hearing aids	None

Table 7–16.   Long-Ribicoff Bill, Catastrophic Plan: Selected Benefit Provisions

Service	For General Population		Limited to Children	
	Provisions	Cost-Sharing	Provisions	Cost-Sharing
Basic services:				
Hospital inpatient	No limitations	First sixty days of hospital care		
Skilled nursing facility	One hundred days			
Physicians' services	No limitations	First $2000 in medical expenses		
Laboratory and X-ray	No limitations			
Prescription drugs	—	—		
Specialized services:				
Maternity care	No special limits	No special cost-sharing		
Physical exams				
Dental services				
Vision services				
Hearing services				

mind. Bone marrow transplants are another illustration of a relevant, highly specialized, and expensive procedure. In fact, schemes like Long-Ribicoff provide an alternative source of funds beyond the current categorical and research support for tertiary care affecting small numbers of children.

The special case of children's access to care for kidney failure brings out the impact of catastrophic health insurance plans. Children affected incur tremendous financial costs (approximately $215 per session two or three times per week). Estimates for outpatient treatments in 1972 vary from $10,000 to $40,000 per year. Estimates for home care, after an initial expensive year, drop to approximately $5000 a year.

The technique of dialysis is still new enough that no "usual fees" are reliable. Since outpatient treatment instead of home care can triple the cost, there are substantial incentives to reduce outpatient modes of care. But there are no incentives for the patient or physician to use home care. Some have suggested that reimbursement under the current Medicare kidney program be limited in amount to what would only cover home care. This, however, could evict from 20 percent to 60 percent of the patients from their current sites of care. Moreover, 10 percent to 15 percent of the patients suitable for home care must return at times to outpatient departments because of complications (Friedman and Kountz, 1973).

All of these issues are relevant to government financing programs for conditions like renal failure, and for other diseases like hemophilia, bone marrow transplants, long-term cancer treatment, various chronic crippling conditions, mental retardation, and chronic psychotic disorders. Most children receiving dialysis, for example, would meet the hospital service deductible under the Long-Ribicoff bill, but only if their outpatient dialysis were regarded as hospitalization.

To the extent insurance schemes cover hospitalization preferentially, hospitalization will be encouraged. To the extent large (though income-related) deductibles are employed (as in the Feldstein Major Risk Insurance scheme), children suffering from chronic conditions will remain a substantial, continuing financial burden on their families. Both catastrophic plans most seriously mentioned—Long-Ribicoff and Feldstein's MRI—have made very poor provision for lingering chronic disease. The expression of benefits in annual terms virtually ignores the cumulative problems which a very small proportion of families face.

Data from a national health survey conducted in 1970 by the Center for Health Administration Studies and the National Opinion Research Center (Table 7-17) show the small incidence of cata-

Table 7–17. 1970 Family Expenditures for Medical Care by Family Income

Family Income	Gross Expenditure[a] Greater Than $5000	Outlay[b] is $1000 or More	Outlay is 15.0 Percent or More of Family Income	Income Distribution of All Families
Under $2000	5%	1%	38%	10%
$2000–$3499	8	4	25	11
$3500–$4999	3	6	13	9
$5000–$7499	20	13	14	16
$7500–$999	8	12	4	15
$10,000–$14,999	18	28	3	22
$15,000 and over	38	37	4	17
Total	100%	100%	100%	100%
N	(47)	(209)	(451)	(3765)

[a] Charges for care, including what a third party may have paid.

[b] The actual out-of-pocket amount spent by a family in 1970 for hospital care, physician services, prescribed and nonprescribed drugs, dental care and other medical goods and services. Outlay also includes what the family paid for health insurance premiums.

Source: Kasper, Andersen and Brown, 1975 (unpublished).

strophic medical expenditures, defined as amounts in excess of $5000 per family during a one-year period. Data from that same survey indicate that only 1 percent of all children (infants to age seventeen) have total medical expenditures exceeding $1000 for a one-year period. Curiously enough, it is the Kennedy-Corman bill which most generously treats the catastrophic financial consequences of chronic illness (although it does not focus on that set of problems) because of its universal coverage for a broad range of benefits. There are limits, however, to the psychiatric benefits.

Preventive Care

How will the various NHI proposals affect preventive care services for children? The tables below summarize the preventive care provisions in the major proposals under consideration.[g]

[g] There is little evidence to support the enthusiasm for preventive care. Primary prevention—for example, prenatal care—effectively prevents some maternal, infant, and child problems. But there is evidence that mass screening programs and even the annual physical checkups are economically wasteful and only occasionally detect conditions that are aided by early treatment. Economists Ralph Andreano and Burton Weisbrod (1974) conclude that preventive care can increase costs without significantly raising the level of health.

If administered the way it is proposed, the Kennedy-Corman plan is neutral on the patient's choice of preventive versus acute care (Table 7—18). But its reward of HMOs and belief that HMOs provide preventive care for children makes Kennedy-Corman appealing to those advocating a shift of emphasis toward simple, important preventive services. The Medi-Cal (California's Medicaid program) fiascos with some prepaid plans have raised doubts about the capacity of the HMO industry to grow properly in response to significant financial incentives (Goldberg, 1975). On the other hand, if an implemented Kennedy-Corman program were to pay fee-for-service providers more generously, the HMO incentives would be relatively weaker and the encouragement of preventive services through HMOs less evident. Since poor children use less preventive care than experts approve, these developments are particularly crucial to watch in the enactment and implementation of plans like Kennedy-Corman.

The Long-Ribicoff bill (Table 7—19) does not encourage preventive care but responds instead to disastrous illness. Indeed, it can be said to discourage the expansion of preventive care for children. In this case it resembles CHIP and the Kennedy-Mills schemes which, while not excluding preventive services, will, because of substantial deductibles, discourage their relative growth.

Table 7—18. Kennedy-Corman Bill: Coverage of Preventive Services

	Benefit		
Service	*Coverage Status*	*Other Information*	*Cost-Sharing*
Physical exams (adults)	Covered	No limitations	\
Well child care	Covered	No limitations	
Prenatal and maternity care	Covered	No limitations	
Family planning	Covered	Excludes drugs,[a] may include devices[b]	None
Vision exams	Covered	No limitations	
Hearing exams	Covered	No limitations	
Dental exams	Covered	Under age sixteen[c]	/

[a] Drugs covered only if provided by an HMO or professional foundation.
[b] Under the bill, coverage of medical devices will be determined by regulation.
[c] Coverage extended to persons under age twenty-six over a five-year period. Once eligible, coverage continues throughout lifetime. Within seven years after enactment of bill, a timetable for phasing-in the entire population must be established.

Table 7–19. Long-Ribicoff Bill: Coverage of Preventive Services

| | Catastrophic Plan | | | Medical Assistance Plan | | |
| | Benefit | | | Benefit | | |
Service	Coverage Status	Other Information	Cost-Sharing	Coverage Status	Other Information	Cost-Sharing
Physical exams (adults)	Not covered			Not covered		
Well-child care	Not covered			Covered	Under age eighteen	
Prenatal and maternity care	Not covered			Covered	No limits	None
Family planning	Not covered			Covered	Includes drugs and devices	
Vision exams	Not covered			Covered	Under age eighteen	
Hearing exams	Not covered			Covered	Under age eighteen	
Dental exams	Not covered			Not covered		

Public Health Departments. The effects of NHI will also be conditioned by what happens to the largest single deliverer of well-child medical services: public health departments. Children come into contact with local public health agencies through a variety of special programs: school health examinations, vision and hearing tests, and immunization drives. These programs are extensive, accounting for as much as 18 percent of the contacts children have with primary care (Chapter 3). Yet despite the large number of children affected, public health programs are typically quite limited in the scope of services they provide. By contrast, there are intensive programs that are publicly funded (maternal and infant care projects, crippled children's programs) but are very limited in the number of children served (Davis and Carney, 1974). Will any of these programs be able to adjust from local tax-based or federal categorical funding to take advantage of universal third-party payment? The probable answer is no.

No insurance scheme is well suited to support present child-oriented medical care arrangements in the public sector. Preventive care providers in schools and health departments will not be able to benefit from NHI except by receiving contracted services from other sectors. Neighborhood health centers, C and Y projects, and other comprehensive care sources will probably find third-party reimbursement difficult, although it promises to be much easier under any plan that is fully federal. If NHI involves matching state monies then it is likely that all the frustrations of Medicaid reimbursement will be reinvented. Less than 15 percent of current expenditures for children in NHCs and C and Y projects are reimbursed by Medicaid.

If we assume that a large proportion of poor and near-poor children at present receive preventive care services in a local school, health department clinic, or federally initiated program, but that NHI would provide for reimbursement of a single primary care provider for all medical care services, then the choice is stark. Either NHI funds are not allowed to go directly to local programs and agencies providing less than complete services, or someone must supervise the allocation of per child funds to avert massive duplication of effort and cost across provider arrangements. Imagine, for instance, the child whose GP collects the capitation grant for his comprehensive care, but who also attends a Follow Through program in the school which performs routine vision and hearing screening and requires reimbursement. Or the preschool child whose mother is a member of an HMO but also takes him to the well-child clinic of the local health department.

Under any but a comprehensive coverage plan, the net effect

would be to strongly reinforce the current fragmentation between preventive and acute care providers. All three cost-sharing plans would preclude the automatic free provision of preventive care to any but poor children, making reimbursement of school and health department programs complicated and requiring that local tax-based preventive care remain an independent effort.

Under a comprehensive coverage plan, NHI may have the net effect of putting out of business those state and local agency programs that provide preventive care, or else it will have to find ways to subsidize them to perform services that would otherwise be provided by the child's regular source of care. The only alternative, it would seem, is to offer incentives to regular providers to pool their preventive care budgets and subcontract certain services to the school or health departments. Such a solution might enable economies of scale, but would present a logistical nightmare, especially for smaller providers.

Effect of National Health Insurance on Distribution of Providers and Services

Two cautionary comments should be made before discussing the distributive consequences for children of the three types of NHI plans under discussion. The first is that, while the "maldistribution" of providers both topographically and organizationally is widely cited, it is unlikely that NHI will dramatically affect those conditions.

Financing mechanisms are at best a weak indirect means of reallocating physicians by region and residential area. On the basis of Medicaid data, Davis has concluded:

> Rural residents and minorities facing nonfinancial barriers to access to medical care have been least assisted by financing approaches and most assisted by health services delivery programs which have established health centers in their neightborhoods (1975a, p. 85).

It may also be predicted as a result of the present distribution of service arrangements that benefits will be higher for urban residents than rural residents and, similarly, greater for whites than nonwhites. Davis notes that only among those poor and rural families living in the catchment areas of neighborhood health centers or other federally sponsored projects do utilization patterns correspond to those of more advantaged parents and children.

The implication is clear: equal financial access would not guarantee equal utilization, or equally appropriate utilization. It certainly would not assure compensatory access or utilization for the poor. Medical resources would continue to be much more plentiful in the areas where high-income persons lived and worked, and indirect costs of obtaining care would continue to be higher for the poor, minorities, and those in rural areas. There is also some evidence to support the notion that physicians prefer to treat patients from the same socioeconomic class and will, on average, provide less service for the same price to the poor (Davis, 1974).

The second point is that policies concerning the distribution of medical providers generally can be discussed with or separate from NHI proposals; distributive schemes can be added as components to different plans. The picture is somewhat more complex with respect to child health concerns. The more the benefits are targeted on primary care, the more financial inducement there is for physicians to enter pediatrics and general practice. The more the benefit package focuses on tertiary care services, the more the reverse incentives apply. Children also raise special issues in that many of their providers are fungible; that is, general practitioners and internists already supply a very large proportion of children's services and can supply more or less depending on the other claims on their time.

Presumably, whatever small differences can be brought about in the distribution of children's providers would be greatest under those plans with broad eligibility requirements and a minimum of patient cost-sharing. It is clear that the Kennedy-Corman plan, with its extensive preventive package and costlessness to patients, would in theory reallocate providers more than any of the other proposals. It may also redirect patient demand to preventive services. The evidence that bears most directly on the likely result of these policies is Canada's medical insurance experience since the late 1960s. LeClair (1975) acknowledges that universal medical insurance's "greatest benefit has been the provision of financial accessibility to health care . . .: no longer do people wait to seek care because they cannot afford it and a sudden illness or accident is not a financial catastrophe for an individual or a family." But he also shows that with government health insurance the public has come to expect better distribution of physician services, especially in rural areas. The general dissatisfaction with the high specialist distribution has put pressure on medical schools to emphasize family practice. This plus the students' hope of building up a remunerative family practice in a relatively short time has stopped the decline in the ratio of general practitioners to specialists, which to date remains virtually unchanged.

The large deductible plans, CHIP and Long-Ribicoff, virtually ignore the direct redistribution of manpower. However, under both

Kennedy-Mills and Kennedy-Corman a health resources development board would be established to help increase health resources and improve service delivery. The board would receive a percentage of the total national health insurance program funds (1 percent under Kennedy-Mills, 5 percent under Kennedy-Corman) to finance its operations. Their responsibilities would include making grants and loans for the development and construction of health maintenance organizations, and conducting special manpower training programs. It is unclear what the impact of these modest provisions will be on the distribution of providers.

ORGANIZATIONAL ISSUES

How do the competing NHI plans and their financing schemes deal with different modes of care, particularly HMOs (Health Maintenance Organizations) and fee-for-service practices? What services will the plans pay for, and for whom? How will quality of care be affected?

Modes of Care

It seems unlikely that national health insurance will head off the major professional trends of the last thirty years: the decline of solo practice and the expansion of large financial partnerships in medicine with or without multispecialty and prepaid features. There has also been great enthusiasm for the development of multispecialty HMOs. These organizations make a prepaid contract with clients to provide comprehensive health services for some defined period, do so for an enrolled population, and have a clearly stated benefit package.

The Kennedy-Corman plan specifically rewards health maintenance organizations in its provision for provider reimbursement. The reimbursement proposal is for capitation pools in every part of the country, which local health districts spend first by reimbursing prepaid group practices on a per capita basis. This arrangement means that the fee-for-service providers would have to share the amounts that remain and incur pro rata reductions where their total fees exceeded those amounts. This reward of prepaid practices is obviously associated in Kennedy-Corman with an anti-inflationary policy of a limited total budget for health, a "cap" on governmental expenditures.

Yet while the Kennedy-Corman plan would reward prepaid group practices if enacted and implemented along these lines, the general impact of free comprehensive national health insurance programs on prepaid group practice is stultifying. First-dollar coverage alone, as the Canadian experience over the last decade has amply shown, retards the rapid development of HMOs unless they are given special privileges (Andreopoulos, 1975).

The attractions of the HMO for parents in urban areas are the same as those in any large multispecialty practice or hospital-based clinic: the assurance of a single source of care for comprehensive services (perhaps at a single location), twenty-four-hour availability, and a wide range of clinical and specialty services.

The principal attraction of prepayment prior to NHI was to minimize parents' uncertainty about medical care expenses in a world where their children's care by and large is *not* insured. Prepayment is insurance against any out-of-pocket expenditure. After passage of an NHI plan, prepayment should in principle remain a good buy for parents to the extent cost-sharing persists and children's care still involves out-of-pocket expenditure. One would consequently expect the expansion of HMOs. But this has not been the case for Canada's community health centers, which parallel our HMOs.

The Comprehensive Care Paradox. The documentation of this nonexpansion is quite extensive in the Canadian literature and highlights what might be called the comprehensive care paradox. Under a comprehensive care plan that assured free care for children at any preferred source of care, prepaid practice arrangements would no longer enjoy a competitive edge, unless convenience or perceived quality of services entered in. Parents may prefer some other care source or multiple sources of care. Thus, NHI plans that pay for practically all care reduce the financial incentives to join HMOs.

CHIP and Kennedy-Mills, with their high deductibles, have in contrast some built-in competitive advantages for the development of HMOs. NHI cost-sharing rewards HMOs that save on lower hospitalization costs and pass these savings to subscribers in the form of more generous benefit packages.

This advantage would arise for all HMO users, regardless of age. The higher the deductible, the more advantageous to the efficient HMO. This generalization should be qualified only to the extent that high deductibles are likely to mean supplementary insurance and low out-of-pocket expenses. But generally the comparative advantage of the HMO is less in the first-dollar coverage plans and greater in ones with significant patient cost-sharing.

HMOs and the Feldstein Major Risk. The remarks that apply to CHIP and Kennedy-Mills hold even more strongly for Feldstein's Major Risk Insurance scheme, which is, after all, nothing but universal health insurance with a large cumulative deductible. HMOs can benefit from such a scheme only if the actuarial value of Feldstein's plan were transferable to HMOs willing to take on the risk of catastrophic financial cost. The details of such actuarial equivalents have never been widely or usefully presented and constitute an implementation issue of considerable significance. This is particularly the case where the expected costs vary substantially by age and income class, a point of obvious relevance to our discussion of children.

Long-Ribicoff and Medicare. The Long-Ribicoff plan presents the same problem of actuarial equivalence. Under Medicare there has been a reluctance to provide HMOs with substantial financial incentives. The appeal of capitation is counterbalanced by a fear of unseemly "profits" from excessive rates for the elderly. Hence the hesitancy of parts of the Congress, particularly the Senate Finance Committee, to accept capitation payments 95 percent of the average annual Medicare expenditure per capita.[h] The Long-Ribicoff Bill is conceptually linked to the current Medicare benefit package, starting where Medicare leaves off. Unless the problems just discussed are more ably handled, we should expect little encouragement of HMO growth in schemes of the Long-Ribicoff sort. It would be a mistake to assume that because the government pays for medical care it can shape at will the arrangements in which nongovernmental professionals provide care.

Quality of Care
Financing medical care, whether privately or publicly, cannot assure that the services one receives are good. Assessing the impact of alternative national health insurance plans on the quality of care for children raises this same problem in a particular demographic context. Since it is very hard to define quality of care without a specific case in mind, it may help to say what good care is not.

There are three conceptions of poor quality care: patient abuse, questionably efficacious patterns of service, and inefficient medical practices. Abuse refers to the gross deprivation of needed care or inappropriately performed clinical actions. Malpractice considerations are relevant here. Between abuse and inefficiency is what may be called questionable care, care that is risky in relation to its medical benefits. Two classic examples are overprescribing pharmaceuticals, especially antibiotics, and inappropriately high rates of surgery, as with tonsillectomies. By inefficient use of resources is meant medi-

[h] Interview with Walter McClure, 1975.

cal care practices which could be done more cheaply or the cost of which could finance more effective health-enhancing interventions. Renal dialysis or cardiac by-pass surgery are good examples of the latter; hospitalization for X-ray therapy is an illustration of the former. National health insurance, according to expert Canadian opinion, will not have much effect on the incidence of abusive care. By making care more accessible, it will have some positive effect on deprivation of care.

Inefficient use of medical care resources does not entail direct detrimental consequences for individual patients. Rather, it means that opportunities for more effective health-enhancing activities are foregone through expenditures for less effective or more expensive modes of care. The Canadian experience suggests this issue is posed by contrasting the effects on children's health status of, for example, lead paint control programs with frequent checkups for well children by expensive physicians. Whereas one might reasonably say that the factors that determine the quality of care provided should be separated from those that determine the health status of the child population, efficiency issues are increasingly at the center of discussions of "quality." Our own discussions of excessive hospital expenditures and the demand for more primary care for children exemplify this concern in the current American discussion.

The relationship between quality and the organization of care is particularly complicated for children in one respect. The most important care given to children will show up in their health status later on; well-baby care and good preventive treatment have what I call "longitudinal benefits." The organizational mode most favored for its health-enhancing (as opposed to curative) perspective is prepaid group practice. Prepayment encourages full consumer use of services, including preventive care services for children. But in principle, incentives still exist for providers to offer as little care as possible. This could lead to skimping on the less visible and more routine aspects of children's care, especially if high patient turnover means that long-term benefits of preventive care are not captured by the child's current HMO. Professional norms and protocols will militate against the incentive to deprive consumers of care, but the implications of this issue for children deserve further consideration.

The quality of care and its impact on children's health depends on factors beyond financial accessibility. Some problems arise from the inappropriate response of patients to medical care providers, apparently a serious matter in the Medicaid program. Housing, nutrition, and psychosocial factors have health impacts too.

This returns us to the lessons of sobriety raised earlier. The dream of national health insurance enthusiasts is to use national financing to prod American medical care into new delivery modes. The most reasonable prediction is that national health insurance will finance in most areas what is already available. Only with special zeal will it prod the system into new shapes. Indeed, if Karen Davis's favorable report on Title V Child Health Programs is to be taken seriously (Davis and Carney, 1974), it may be more important to figure out how to use NHI funding to continue good locally based child care than to direct one's attention to using NHI to finance innovations in the organization of care. Likewise, if dramatic cost increases have been the main source of the demand for national health insurance, advocates of child health concerns ought to address themselves explicitly to how programs for children would affect the medical inflation problem.

PROGRAMS FOR CHILDREN
THROUGH NHI

There are four hybrid national health insurance proposals that focus on improved health care services for children. None of these are embodied in the plans discussed so far. The first involves comprehensive health insurance for preschoolers and pregnant women, and catastrophic coverage for all others. The second calls for the federalization of Medicaid. The third is an extension of current federal categorical programs for children. The fourth combines federalization of Medicaid and comprehensive primary care coverage for children.

The issue is not simply whether child insurance plans have merit, but whether programs for them can meet the fiscal, administrative, and political constraints that have stalemated the enactment of national health insurance. On that count, it is crucial to emphasize that the care children most need is readily producible, relatively cheap, and reasonably likely to have an improving effect on the current and future health status of preschoolers.

Each of the proposals under review remains embryonic, but if formally developed might be a politically viable version of NHI beneficial to children. Each deserves careful analysis prior to selection of a new national financing scheme.

Comprehensive Coverage for Children
and Catastrophic Insurance for All Others

The most fully developed of these plans, suggested by Marmor,[i] would involve comprehensive coverage for children and a catastrophic

[i]For a detailed explication of the Marmor proposal, see Theodore Marmor, "Children and national health insurance: the case for beginning with youngsters,"

insurance for all others.[j] Under the first part of the plan, children aged zero to six would receive all medical services free regardless of family income. The plan for adults would be a true insurance, a hedge against high and unanticipated medical care costs. The plan for children, on the other hand, would follow the Kennedy-Corman bill's exclusion of cost-sharing.

The program could be expanded, if thought desirable, on a manageable basis each year for the first five years. Adding two years to the child eligibility level each year would mean that children under sixteen would be completely covered by the end of the program's first half-decade. This option leaves open whether at that time the child health insurance program should or should not be extended to the rest of the population. Over the implementation period (extending into the 1980s) the rest of the population, and most particularly the unemployed, aged, and working poor, would be relieved of the worry that medical expenses could bankrupt them. Medicare and Medicaid would be left in place as further protection. Because of this plan's incremental design, it may, in the near term, be a sensible and traditional way to introduce national health insurance amid current budgetary restraints.

Marmor's plan, outlined in Table 7–20, balances several of the concerns that have dominated the debate over NHI. First, a comprehensive health insurance program for preschool children could be relatively cheap and thus satisfy the criterion of fiscal feasibility. Medical care for children, as previously noted, costs less than that for any other comparable age group in the population: about one-sixth the expenditures for the elderly. Per capita payments of $200 a year per child under six would total about $4 billion; the cost of prenatal and postnatal care for approximately 3.2 million births per year would probably cost some $3 billion a year. Thus, something on the order of $7 billion annually would pay for Kennedy-Corman benefits for preschool children and their mothers.[k] Not only would the total

---

Statement to Health Subcommittee of the House Committee on Interstate and Foreign Commerce, Washington, D.C., June 16, 1976.

[j] A plan similar in its child-oriented features—The Maternal and Child Health Care Act—was introduced by Representative James H. Scheuer on June 10, 1976. Hearings were held on June 16, 1976, by the House Subcommittee on Health and the Environment. The plan proposes a program of comprehensive health care for all children from birth to age eighteen and for all pregnant women. The program would be administered by a three-person Maternal and Child Health Board within the Department of Health, Education and Welfare.

[k] The same amount ($7 billion) is now spent on medical care through the medical expense deduction and other tax breaks for health insurance. Note too that the estimated cost of the child plan is gross federal cost, not new spending on children.

Table 7–20.   Comprehensive Health Insurance for Preschoolers and Pregnant Women

BENEFITS	The benefit package would be inclusive: partly preventive in nature, including prenatal care for mothers, fertility benefits, dental care, such kinds of nutritional and well-baby care that seem to work, immunizations, setting broken bones, etc. Neonatal intensive care, renal dialysis, heart surgery would be included as would all the conventional minor acute care.
PROVIDER REIMBURSEMENT	The only form of payment would be capitation. The federal government would offer perhaps $200 per year per child, possibly adjusted for regional differences, to any qualified provider, individual or organization capable of providing these benefits. Providers would sign up children, just as GPs in Britain sign up families. Those wishing to buy care in the regular fee-for-service system would be free to do so but not with government subsidy. Women in pregnancy would be included and, in the case of teenagers, could enroll in their own names even though they are minors.
PATIENT COST-SHARING	No cost-sharing at the time of receiving care would be required, except perhaps for some nominal payment for drugs or other care where the serious possibility of overuse exists.
QUALITY REVIEW	A quality monitoring mechanism would be established, designed to reduce the likelihood that providers will provide too little care for the fixed per capita price.
FINANCING	Straight, general revenue financing, with the following tax adjustment: either reduction in the $750 exemption for children as partial payment for the benefit or half the tax credit for children at the median income as partial payment. Tax adjustments should provide approximately half the cost and should be adjusted as costs increase.
COST	At $200 per child per year on average, plus prenatal and postnatal care for an estimated 3.2 million births, $4 billion and $3 billion for an estimated $7 billion per year.
ADMINISTRATION	The child and maternal health insurance program would be administered by the local health boards specified in the Kennedy-Corman legislation. The setting of capitation rates and broad policy would fall to the National Health Security Board specified in the 1975 version of Kennedy-Corman. The catastrophic tax credit program would be the administrative responsibility of the Internal Revenue Service, managed by the division which implements the medical expense deductions under current tax law.
RESEARCH AND DEVELOPMENT	Some attempt should be made to link expenditures on research to reducing the need for the services covered by the children's program and producing technology for delivering those services more efficiently. Among the possibilities are: contraceptive research; funding of demonstrations of better manpower utilization; further research on prenatal care and well-baby care to determine effectiveness and to modify program benefits accordingly; a research and statistical effort comparable to Medicare's so that we can learn from doing.

initial cost of such a plan be modest, but the chances of an unpredictable inflationary surge are less with young children. At a time when concern about the size of the federal budget is so widespread, a reform alternative with limited federal costs has merit.

Second, a program for mothers and young children could be reimbursed on a capitation basis and thus expand a widely praised method of remunerating doctors. American doctors generally favor the traditional fee-for-service payment, but one can imagine far less medical objection to capitation if confined to obstetrical and pediatric care. We already have an existing pattern of prepaid lump-sum payments for obstetrical care, encouraged by the predictable character of the required medical services. The familiar nature of the required care for mothers and infants makes review of the quality and cost easier for this group than any other.

The serious problem of capitation is the possible discouragement of needed care. The annual lump-sum payment is an incentive either to keep patients well or to deprive them of expensive care. Deprivation is the alternative to prevention and efficient services. Of course, it is unethical, but widely understood standards for ordinary care make it easier to monitor whether a group of providers receiving capitation payments are underserving or abusing their patients. Pediatrics is an area in medicine with relatively clear standards of adequate care.

Third, the capitation program would enhance the likelihood that children would make appropriate use of preventive and routine acute care services. These services are the most important ones for most children and offer external benefits for all citizens. It is less likely that children would end up at the end of the queue for primary care services. In addition, incentives would exist to further the development of family practice and primary care, rather than to increase concentration in the hospital sector.

The Catastrophic Tax Credit Program. Comprehensive health insurance for preschoolers and pregnant women in the Marmor plan would be supported by a national catastrophic plan for all. A responsible national health insurance program should respond to the widespread fears of financial ruin from ill-health, fears which the arguments for a Kennedy-Corman plan for children do not address. A catastrophic protection program of tax credits addresses those fears and is a crucial ingredient in an over-all staged plan. It calls for the incorporation of that protection into a reformed tax policy for medical expenses amounting to tax expenditures estimated to be less than $3 billion (Karen Davis, personal communication).

Benefits. Comprehensiveness of covered services is important for any catastrophic program. That is, practically all medical care expenses should be eligible for tax credits, though the amount of the deductible, coinsurance, and maximum out-of-pocket liability could vary. One promising schedule, whose distribution of benefits by income levels is compared below with our current regressive tax deduction policy, has a deductible of 10 percent of taxable income and 50 percent coinsurance up to a maximum family expenditure of 20 percent of taxable income. Taxable income for this tax purpose would be more broadly defined than under current law. It is important to prevent incorporating loopholes into the plan, where the very definition of catastrophe depends upon the relative burden of illness expenses on family income.

These benefits, it should be emphasized, provide only minimal protection against burdensome medical expenses. The tax credit works like a catastrophic health insurance plan that requires families to pay up to 10 percent of their taxable income before the insurance benefits begin. By providing 50 cents for each dollar of further expense up to the maximum family liability, the plan shares expenses with those having high costs and places a ceiling on the family's medical liabilities short of financial disaster. Further, it does so equitably, so that at higher income levels benefits decline gradually (Table 7—21). And it is progressively financed, through foregone tax revenues—income tax revenues.

The payments of benefits would be integrated into the current tax cycle. That would mean annual adjustments for most, quarterly for those who chose to so report their income and expenses. The schedule shown in Table 7—21 illustrates how the tax credit for out-of-pocket expenses (including health insurance premiums) would affect families at different income levels. A family with an income of $5000 and ruinous expenses of $5000 would be entitled to a tax credit of $4000. The credit would decline for families with the same expenses but higher incomes, as the fourth column illustrates. For a $15,000 family with the same $5000 medical expenses, the tax credit would amount to $2000 for the year.

A credit against one's tax bill would work for those with incomes high enough for the IRS to tax. A credit in the form of a cash rebate would be paid in April for those, like pensioners on Social Security, who have little or no taxable income. Some critics of this plan fear that health providers might have problems getting prompt payment of their bills by the poor and the old. This plan would not directly address that difficulty. It is insurance protection for individuals, not protection against cash flow problems of hospitals, doctors, and nurs-

Table 7–21. Tax Credits Under the Marmor Plan and Tax Savings Under Current Personal Income Tax Medical Deductions

Adjusted Gross Income	Out-of-Pocket Medical Expenses			
	$500	$1000	$2000	$5000
	Amount of tax credit under proposed plan			
$5000	$ 0	$250	$1000	$4000
$10,000	0	0	500	3000
$15,000	0	0	250	2000
$20,000	0	0	0	1000
	Amount of reduced tax under current personal income tax provisions[a]			
$5000	$ 0	$ 0	$ 0	$ 0
$10,000	55	150	334	806
$15,000	33	141	361	957
$20,000	38	123	373	1093

[a] Based on family with four exemptions. Assumes families under $5000 income take the standard deduction. Also assumes other families have itemized deductions of $1500 plus medical expenses; $150 of the medical expense is assumed to be fully deductible as health insurance premiums, the remainder is subject to an exclusion of 3 percent of adjusted gross income. Calculations based on tax law in effect in 1974.

Source: Davis, 1975c.

ing homes. But the assurance that no patient would become destitute from medical expenses substantially underwrites the working poor and the medically impoverished and in that sense assists the providers. What is more, the possibility of using quarterly declarations and year-end tax adjustments might go a long way to allay their fears.

Objections. Such a balanced proposal is not exempt from criticisms. Most of them are common to all children's health insurance plans.

1. The plan might encourage a separate delivery system for children. Many rural areas cannot support two systems.

2. It takes money away from other higher priority needs. One cost estimate of the Marmor plan is $10 billion. This could fund 10,000 neighborhood health centers, 100,000 health centers staffed by two or three nurse practitioners, midwives, or physician assistants,

or annual children's allowances of $1000 each for the 10 million children below the poverty line.

3. There are few mechanisms for controlling costs in the system (save capitation methods of payment for children's services).

4. The plan omits cost-sharing on children's and maternity benefits and is thus likely to stimulate marginally beneficial use of services.

5. There is no greater likelihood of promoting HMOs under this plan than under currently unsuccessful schemes.

6. The plan will use the applicant's health experience to avoid bad risks, which will be left to public programs like Crippled Children's. Preventing "cream-skimming" is a classic problem with uniform capitation rates.

7. The plan will raise false hopes of cutting costs through nurse practitioners. Current experience suggests they spend more time with patients, locate in places where physicians will not, increase accessibility, but they do not cost less. Further, most capitation schemes place nurse practitioners under the control of physicians, a terrible problem in underdoctored rural areas.

8. The receiver of the capitation payment would be the single entry point into the medical system. Consumers would have to pay for care outside this point. But many people want to be able to go to hospital emergency rooms when they feel like it; to the community health center when they feel like it. Convenience, less waiting time for appointments, presumed higher quality, and second consultations account for this, but why do advocates of children's insurance through capitation think they can ignore this disposition?

Many of these criticisms identify problems one must alleviate. Some are counsels of perfection which are of little practical significance; still others are just wrong. But all touch on issues that the advocates of a national health insurance plan with benefits on the order of the Kennedy-Corman plan should confront.

Federalization of Medicaid

The second plan, advanced by Karen Davis, calls for the federalization of Medicaid (perconal communication). Such a plan would stabilize and improve the Medicaid system by extending a uniform, generous benefit package to eligible persons in all states. In addition, the plan would assure uniform eligibility criteria across states, presumably at a level comparable with the more generous current state guidelines (e.g., New York and California). Payment levels for services would be adjusted to reflect accurately the cost of services in various regions and residential areas.

There are several advantages to this plan. First, many children would become eligible for services who, according to current state formulas, are now excluded. These would include children from poor families who for various reasons are not eligible for AFDC, and near-poor children whose families are not otherwise covered by any form of insurance. The effect of this extended coverage would be to increase by nearly a third the number of children covered by Medicaid. Second, because the reimbursement of federal categorical programs such as neighborhood health centers and Children and Youth projects has been prohibited in many cases by the unwillingness of state authorities to participate in cost-sharing, it can be presumed that under a wholly federal plan such programs would be further subsidized. This may enhance the incentive to extend such programs into poverty areas. Third, the equity issue in regard to financial access is resolved on traditional income-related grounds rather than age-related ones, thus increasing the political attractiveness of the plan. The fourth, perhaps greatest advantage of such a plan is that it would require relatively little revision of the current public finance infrastructure.

Potential disadvantages of the plan also need to be carefully weighed. There is no assurance that preventive care services from traditional tax-based sources such as health departments or school health programs are going to be more willing to participate. Thus, the problems inherent in EPSDT are not likely to subside, and there is no adequate assurance that care sources for children will be consolidated. Moreover, much routine care may not be subsidized for any but the poor, and notch effects (sharp decreases in benefits as a result of moderate increases in income) may be great for children in families beyond the poverty income level.

A Federal Maternal and Child Health Service

The third scheme would establish a federal maternal and child health service, with direct federal provision of services via wholly subsidized comprehensive care programs. Such a service has long been advocated.[1] If set up on the model of the Public Health Service or the National Health Service Corps, it would probably prove less expensive than comprehensive coverage through a financing scheme. Although it would almost certainly strengthen the current pattern by which the poor child receives public services and the rich child private ones, it would be no worse in its equity consequences than a system of free care under NHI if nonfinancial barriers to access

[1] C. Arden Miller, address to Bicentennial Conference on Children, February 2, 1976.

among minorities and the poor remained as great as they are at present.

Income-Related Package for All, with Special Subsidy for Children's Primary Care

The fourth scheme could be regarded as a synthesis of the Marmor and Davis proposals. Under this plan, Medicaid would be federalized, or some other form of income-related eligibility for NHI benefits would be applied to the entire population. For children an additional component would be grafted onto the plan assuring free preventive, chronic, and acute care up to a certain ceiling for every child. In essence, this would be a plan with full capitation subsidy of children's primary care, as a component of a larger income-related insurance package for all age groups. The plan would have the effect of providing free those children's services with highest public benefit. For more complex and expensive care, it would treat children like other members of the population. Nonprimary care would be subsidized completely for the poor, but for others some cost-sharing would be required.

This proposal sounds at first like the reinvention of EPSDT, but there are two significant differences: it would extend benefits to all children, and it would include support for routine acute and chronic care as well as preventive care. The plan could be administered by a scheme of provider reimbursement like the current Medicaid billing system, or alternatively, every child under a certain age might receive a credit card or voucher entitling him or her to a finite number of free physician visits and medical services (up to a specified total cost). The plan might broadly define professionals and provider arrangements eligible for reimbursement. Such a system would provide no incentive to further separation of preventive and acute care, but would still permit reimbursement of the present dispersed system of provider arrangements.

Advantages. The financial advantages of primary care capitation for children are considerable.

1. It would enable public support of the major component of children's care without setting up additional incentives to hospital care or other care at the secondary and tertiary levels.
2. It would encourage providers to practice primary care.
3. If billing regulations were flexible enough to allow for the reimbursement of physician extenders, it might promote development of an entire system of nonphysician care for children's routine needs.

The cost would be much lower than the anticipated cost of a comprehensive care plan oriented to physicians in office-based practices.

4. It would also reduce problems of equity in extent of services between children and adults, offering children something short of completely free care while enabling a better allocation of funds for secondary and tertiary care to adults.

Disadvantages. First is the danger of separating still further primary care from other parts of the medical care system. The problem of EPSDT need not be recreated if financing of routine preventive, acute, and chronic care are drawn together. But there would need to be some assurance that sites of care for children would not be further proliferated without providing adequate linkage to backup facilities and higher levels of the medical care system. In addition, reimbursement schedules would need to be carefully designed to assure adequate physician participation.

DISCUSSION

Useful appraisal of any policy proposal involves more than calculating its merit on a single evaluative criterion. Judging national health insurance plans by what health benefits they would bring to children is too narrow a basis for gaining supporters. The fact that children have not been central to the NHI debate means the proposals under review in the preceding section have extraordinary political obstacles to overcome. Not only are children's health issues peripheral to national health insurance preoccupations, but their political representatives are weaker than those in the unions and in the senior citizen movements.

These differences in constituency influence are reflected in the institutional structure of Congress. Children, unlike workers and the elderly, are not the focus of a durable standing committee. Child advocates have found sympathetic spokespersons in Congress, and hearings called by former Senator Mondale of Minnesota have highlighted the medical and other problems of American families. But over all, there are relatively weak institutional mechanisms for regularly monitoring the problems of children.

The representation of children's interests is discussed in Chapters 8 and 9. The implications of the weaker child lobby are important for appraising the feasibility of NHI proposals directed at children (Steiner, 1976). Appeals to merit alone—whether of cost-effectiveness or the worthiness of children—will not be sufficient to make it likely that NHI will focus on children. Benefits for other politically salient constituencies are required to make any NHI plan that concentrates on children politically feasible.

The advocates of special programs for children must confront the problems of securing political support from constituencies relatively uninterested in the health of children.

Demonstrating that the costs of child programs would not foreclose options for others will not be enough to secure that needed support. The difficulty is not simply to deal with a zero-sum budgetary perspective that pits the elderly, for example, against the advocates of children. The problem is also to provide material benefits of interest to others (like catastrophic protection), budgetary advantages to those worried about the growth of federal expenditures (like the Congressional Budget Office), and political benefits to those who have long fought for health insurance on universalistic grounds (like Kennedy-Corman supporters). These considerations distinguish the balanced package of the Marmor proposal. Whether that balance is appropriate is one question, but that programs for children will have to widen their appeal beyond serving the most pressing needs of children is less open to question.

In widening their appeal, child advocates confront a major obstacle beyond the present congressional committee structure. When advocating programs for all children, they reveal a discrepancy between the few children who face the most serious problems and universalistic solutions. Most parents are not worried about how to pay for the relatively inexpensive childhood illnesses. The average member of the benefit constituency is not presumptively in need. This contrasts sharply with universal programs for the elderly like Social Security and Medicare. Though the elderly are heterogeneous, the overwhelming majority face less income and greater medical expenses. So universal programs for them rest on the presumptive needs of the present majority of the elderly, a fact not lost on their children, the future elderly. By contrast, universal programs for children, while in one sense benefiting all families with children as against the childless, are open to the charge of inefficiently targeting their benefits.

Yet, if the worst health problems beset poor children, nonetheless, programs for the poor alone have been burdened by programmatic and fiscal instability (Holahan, 1975). Proposals that are targeted on the poor must face being politically controversial. Universal plans, like Marmor's, must be prepared to show why the gains in administrative simplicity and programmatic stability outweigh the "inefficiency" their strategy necessarily embodies.

REFERENCES

Abel-Smith, B. *An International Study of Health Expenditure.* WHO Public Paper No. 32. Geneva: World Health Organization, 1967.

American Medical Association. "Statement on national health insurance by Max Parrot," *Hearings on National Health Insurance.* Committee on Ways and Means of the U.S. House of Representatives. Washington, D.C.: Government Printing Office, 1971.

American Medical Association. *Profiles of Medical Practice, 1974.* Chicago: American Medical Practice, 1974.

Andersen, R., et al. "The public's view of the crisis in medical care: an impetus for changing delivery systems?" *Econ Bus Bulletin* 24 (1971): 44–52.

Andreano, R., and Weisbrod, B. *American Health Policy: Perspectives and Choices.* Chicago: Rand McNally, 1974, p. 35.

Andreopoulous, S., ed. *National Health Insurance: Can We Learn from Canada?* New York: John Wiley and Sons, 1975.

Andreopoulous, S., ed. *Primary Care: Where Medicine Fails.* New York: John Wiley and Sons, 1975.

Beck, R.G. "Economic class and access to physician services under medical care insurance," *Int J Health Serv* 3 (1973): 341–355.

Council on Wage and Price Stability. *The Problem of Rising Health Care Costs,* No. 81. Washington, D.C.: The Bureau of National Affairs, Inc., 1976, p. x-4.

Davis, K. *The Effects of Medical Care Financing on Racial and Geographic Barriers to Medical Care,* xerox draft. Cambridge, Mass.: Harvard University, 1974.

Davis, K. "A decade of policy development in providing health care for low income families," (draft for *A Decade of Federal Anti-Poverty Policy: Achievements, Failures, and Lessons,* edited by R. Haverman. Madison: University of Wisconsin, Institute for Research on Poverty, 1977), xerox, 1975a.

Davis, K. *National Health Insurance: Benefits, Costs, and Consequences.* Washington, D.C.: The Brookings Institution, 1975b, p. 95.

Davis, K. *Tax Credits for Health Relief for the Working Class, Unemployed, and Disadvantaged,* revised version. Paper presented to the National Health Council Annual Forum, Orlando, Fla., 1975c.

Davis, K., and Carney, M.K. *Medical Care for Mothers and Children: The Title V Maternal and Child Health Program,* unpublished. Washington, D.C.: The Brookings Institution, 1974.

Enterline, P., et al. "The distribution of medical services before and after 'free' medical care: the Quebec experience," *N Engl J Med* 289 (1973): 1178.

Feldstein, M. "A new approach to national health insurance," *Public Interest* (Spring 1971): 93–105.

Friedman, E., and Kountz, S. "Impact of HR–1 on the therapy of end stage uremia," *N Engl J Med* 288 (1973): 1287.

Goldberg, V.P. "Some emergency problems of prepaid health plans in the Medi-Cal systems," *Policy Analysis* 1 (1975): 54–68.

Green, M., and Haggerty, R.J. *Ambulatory Pediatrics.* Philadelphia: W.B. Saunders, 1968.

Haggerty, R.J., Roghmann, J.J., and Pless, I.B. *Child Health and the Community.* New York: John Wiley and Sons, 1975.

Holahan, J. *Financing Health Care for the Poor.* Boston: D.C. Heath and Co., 1975.

Kasper, J., Andersen, R., and Brown, C. *The Financial Impact of Catastrophic Illness as Measured in the CHAS–NORC National Survey*, prepared for Health Services Research. Chicago: University of Chicago, Center for Health Administration Studies, 1975 (unpublished).

LeClair, M. "The Canadian health care system," in *National Health Insurance: Can We Learn from Canada?*, edited by Spyros Andreopoulous. New York: John Wiley and Sons, 1975, pp. 42, 56–57.

Lynch, D. *Declaration of Interdependence: Developing America's Health Policy.* Proceedings of the Twenty-fourth Annual National Health Forum. Philadelphia: National Health Council, 1976, p. 36.

Marmor, T. "The comprehensive health insurance plan of 1974," *Challenge* (November-December 1974): 44–46.

Marmor, T. "Welfare medicine: How success can be a failure: A review essay," *Yale Law Journal* 85 (1976): 1149–59.

Marmor, T., and Kudrle, R. *National Health Insurance Plans and Their Implications for Mental Health*, unpublished paper. Delivered at the Symposium on Political and Community Problems in Mental Health Care. DeKalb: Northern Illinois University, 1975.

Marmor, T., Heagy, T., and Hoffman, W. "National health insurance: some lessons from the Canadian experience," *J Health Policy, Politics and Law* 1 (1975): 447–66.

Marmor, T., Wittman, D., and Heagy, T. "Politics, public policy, and medical inflation," in *Health: A Victim or Cause of Inflation?*, edited by M. Zubkoff. New York: Milbank Memorial Fund, 1976.

Maxwell, R. *Health Care: The Growing Dilemma.* New York: McKinsey and Co., 1975.

Meany, G. "Statement of the AFL–CIO," *Hearings on National Health Insurance.* Committee on Ways and Means of the U.S. House of Representatives. Washington, D.C.: Government Printing Office, 1971, p. 239.

Meyer, M. *Catastrophic Illnesses and Catastrophic Health Insurance.* Washington, D.C.: The Heritage Foundation, Inc., 1974.

Meyer, M. "The national health insurance debate: shifts toward reality?" *J Health Policy, Politics and Law* 1 (1975): 13–17.

Mueller, M.S., and Gibson, R.M. "National health expenditures, fiscal year 1975," *Social Security Bulletin* 39 (February 1976): 17.

Nixon, R. "The nation's health care system," *Weekly Compilation of Presidential Documents* 28 (1969): 963.

"Our ailing medical system," *Fortune* 81 (1970): 78–99.

Regie de l'Assurance Maladie du Quebec. *Statistiques Annuelles.* Montreal: author, 1974.

Russell, L.B., et al. *Federal Health Spending, 1969–74.* Washington, D.C.: National Planning Association, 1974.

Simanics, J.G. "Medical care expenditures in seven countries," *Social Security Bulletin* 36 (March 1973): 39.

"The social security revolution," *Congressional Quarterly: Congress and the Nation,* Vol. 1. Washington, D.C.: Congressional Quarterly Service, 1965, p. 1225.

Steiner, G. *The Children's Cause.* Washington, D.C.: The Brookings Institution, 1976.

Stevens, Robert, and Stevens, Rosemary. *Welfare Medicine in America: A Case Study of Medicaid.* New York: The Free Press, 1974.

Strickland, S.P. *U.S. Health Care: What's Right and What's Wrong.* New York: Universe Books, 1972, pp. 43, 102.

United States Congress, House of Representatives, Committee on Ways and Means. *Basic Charts on Health Care.* Washington, D.C.: Government Printing Office, 1975, pp. 44–45.

United States Congress, House of Representatives, Committee on Ways and Means. *National Health Insurance, Panel Discussion.* Washington, D.C.: Government Printing Office, 1975b.

United States Department of Health, Education and Welfare, NCHS. *Current Estimates from the Health Interview Survey, U.S. 1972.* Vital and Health Statistics, Series 10, No. 85. Washington, D.C.: Government Printing Office, 1973.

United States Department of Health, Education and Welfare, Social Security Administration, Office of Research and Statistics. *Note No. 6.* Washington, D.C.: 13 May 1975.

United States, Executive Office of the President. *Budget of the United States Government, 1976: Special Analysis.* Washington, D.C.: Government Printing Office, 1975.

Waldman, S. *Benefits for Children Under National Health Insurance Proposals.* United States Department of Health, Education and Welfare Publication. Washington, D.C.: Government Printing Office, 1974.

Waldman, S. *National Health Insurance Proposals: Provisions of Bills Introduced in the 93d Congress of July, 1974.* DHEW Publication No. (SSA) 75–11920. Washington, D.C.: Government Printing Office, 1975.

Weber, G. *An Evaluation of an Expanded Public Role in the Health Care of Children,* unpublished draft. Health Policy Program, University of California at San Francisco, 1975.

Zubkoff, M. *Health: A Victim or Cause of Inflation?* New York: Milbank Memorial Fund, 1976.

Part III

Influencing Decisionmaking in the Health Sector

✳ *Chapter 8*

Children's Advocacy and Primary Health Care

Richard F. Tompkins[a]

Sometimes when I get home at night in Washington I feel as though I had been in a great traffic jam. The jam is moving toward the Hill where Congress sits in judgment on all the administrative agencies of the government. In that traffic jam are all kinds of vehicles. . . . There are all kinds of conveyances, for example, that the Army can put into the street—tanks, gun carriages, trucks. . . . There are the hayricks and the binders and the ploughs and all the other things that the Department of Agriculture manages to put into the streets . . . the handsome limousines in which the Department of Commerce rides . . . the barouches in which the Department of State rides in such dignity. It seems to me as I stand on the sidewalk watching it becomes more congested and more difficult, and then because the responsibility is mine and I must, I take a very firm hold on the handles of the baby carriage and I wheel it into the traffic (Grace Abbott, 1934).

Children cannot always articulate their own interests or make their own decisions; they have relatively limited capabilities, and even though these abilities increase substantially and fairly predictably throughout childhood, society is forced to find ways to make decisions for children. Children's advocacy is fundamentally an attempt to improve the lives of children. The advocacy effort may be directed either toward improving the outcomes of the decision or the process

[a]The author would like to thank the following individuals for thoughtful support and encouragement:

Judy Baumann, Liz Berger, Larry Brown, John Butler, Marian Edelman, Peter Edelman, Steve Finan, Nancy Leamond, Ted Marmor, Steve Minter, David Mundel, Mariam Noland, Henry Saltzman, Marcia Sorcinelli, Gil Steiner, Rachel Tompkins, Janet Ubel, Homer Wadsworth, Paul Ylvisaker.

193

through which the decision is made. Advocacy is "intervention on behalf of children in relation to those services and institutions that impinge on their lives" (Kahn et al., 1973).

During the late 1960s and early 1970s different enterprises have been conducted under the rubric of children's advocacy. They have been initiated or funded by both public and private sources at all levels: federal, state, and local. The quotation of Grace Abbott, with its vivid image of a woman guiding a baby carriage, competing with tanks, plows and limousines, captures much of the spirit of those who would call themselves advocates.

Earlier surveys of children's advocacy activities, most notably a national baseline survey conducted by Kahn et al., have attempted to define children's advocacy activities. After extensive field work, Kahn summarized their diversity:

> affirming new concepts of legal entitlements; offering needed services in areas where none existed; persisting in the provision of services when other more conventional programs dropped cases; assuring access to entitlements and help; mediating between children or families and institutions such as schools, health facilities, and courts; and facilitating self-organization among deprived community groups, adolescents, or parents of handicapped children (Kahn et al., 1973, p. 9).

Health care is an area where society has a considerable interest in good decisionmaking on behalf of children. On humanitarian grounds, society has a caretaker interest and responsibility. On economic grounds, society benefits from the healthy development of its children, who represent a resource pool. Society frequently must bear the consequences of certain disabilities or illnesses, including the cost of suboptimal productivity, unemployment, or custodial care resulting from poor health.

This chapter, an overview of children's advocacy efforts in the health sector, has four parts: first, a review of the basic characteristics of children's health status, the health care industry, and the political environment in which child health advocates must operate; second, a description of the required skills and possible tactics and organization of advocates; third, a description of some fruitful areas for advocates; and finally, suggestions for fostering advocacy talent.

CHILDREN'S HEALTH STATUS[b]

Children are relatively healthy. Even though they may get sick more often than adults, the care required is usually routine and the result

[b]This section was taken from Volume I of this series and "Health Needs of Children" by Barbara Starfield in Volume II. See also American Academy of Pediatrics, 1971; Birch, 1970; Kessner, 1973 and 1974; and Messenger, 1975.

of a self-limiting disease. Infectious disease has been limited or conquered and the problems of child health are in most cases problems of prevention and appropriate health-inducing behavior. Routine health measures, such as immunizations, are predictable and can be scheduled. For some low-income groups routine care is not fully accessible. Health status has suffered as a result. Examples of these problems of the poor include higher than necessary infant morbidity and mortality rates, inadequate immunization levels, preventable dental disease, a higher prevalence of infectious disease, and unnecessarily high morbidity and disability rates.

There are also a growing number of children with illnesses or problems fundamentally associated with poverty, degenerating environment, nutritional deficits, accidents, and psychocultural factors. While medical care can offer some therapy for these problems, long-range amelioration may be aided particularly by efforts to redistribute societal assets.

Further, the number of children with chronic disease problems is also increasing. These are children who might not have survived when medical technology and knowledge was less sophisticated. These and other complex acute cases, however, may require sophisticated and costly care, and while the technology and accessibility of this type of care has not expanded to the extent that it has for adults, it is growing.

Finally, the benefits of good health care and the disadvantages of poor care may not be apparent immediately and may in fact be most evident in later years, or throughout the life of the individual.

These child health status characteristics, important in their own right, have a significant effect on public attitudes toward developing effective health care policy for children. They contribute to the diffuse nature of child health interests.

CHARACTERISTICS OF THE HEALTH SECTOR

The health sector has certain industry characteristics that have important consequences for child health care decisionmaking. To begin with, this sector of the economy is predominantly adult-oriented. Another important characteristic is that health care consumers are relatively uninformed (Mushkin, 1974).

Much of the decisionmaking in our society is organized through our economic system, where consumers make choices and allocate their resources on the basis of a set of preferences. In theory this serves to direct resources to their most productive use. It does not, however, guarantee that resources are equitably distributed or that efficiency is obtained in markets that depart from the competitive model. The competitive model includes the assumption that consumers are informed. In the health sector it is difficult for the average consumer to make price and quality comparisons or to understand the relationship between technical inputs and desired outcomes. Relative consumer ignorance holds true for adults in their role as parents influencing decisionmaking for children, for children in their own right, and also in some cases for adolescents whose developmental capabilities are limited. Consumer ignorance can have a number of unfavorable effects. An example highly publicized in the national press illustrates the problem: two Alabama girls were sterilized when their mother consented to what she thought were routine contraceptive services (*New York Times*, 1 August, 1973). That the mother could be so uninformed about basic family planning information is an extreme example of how the consumer frequently provides little check against professional or bureaucratic discretion. While such abuses do not predominate, even a few examples suggest the need for concern.

Since the microeconomic assumption of an informed consumer infrequently applies, responsibility for decisionmaking has shifted principally to health care providers. Consumer ignorance in combination with the predominance of solo, fee-for-service medicine has allowed the individual physician monopoly control over his practice, over the hospital, and over his fees (Kessel, 1958; Newhouse, 1970). These facets of organization have led to weak or underdeveloped accountability structures. Accountability is handled on a case-by-case rather than systemwide basis. The general practitioner or family physician will be accountable for the care of a child only if that child reaches him initially and then returns voluntarily for treatment on a periodic basis. With the exception of malpractice litigation, procedural protections for the consumer of health care have primarily focused on state enforcement of minimum standards of hospital and personnel licensure. Malpractice protection for the consumer is most prevalent in costly cases of specific injury; thus, it is not a wholly suitable accountability mechanism for the routine care needs of children, nor in many cases for the growing layer of child health problems associated with socioeconomic status or cultural factors.

The health care system does not routinely produce information that enables the performance of the industry to be monitored (Wennberg and Gillelsohn, 1973). Without routine information on the performance of the health sector, the job of advocacy becomes more difficult. Data that focuses especially on children is even more sparse. Better information on child health status, finance, access, utilization and outcomes, as well as information on the clinical effectiveness of pediatric procedures, is needed.

Initial access to health care services for children and youth is seldom independent of parental discretion. This problem of split authority between parent and child is complicated by the fact that child health benefits are usually financed by parents or tied to parental characteristics such as employment status or welfare eligibility. For children, dependence on parents for financial access to health care may limit the access to, and response of, the health system.

Finally, several factors in the development of health care financing have had important implications for children. Health insurance coverage emerged historically in the United States to prevent the unfortunate financial consequences of catastrophic illness and to underpin hospital financing (Sommers, 1966). The focus on the financing of hospital care, statistically less important for children than for adults, has provided us with a system of private and public financing that does not generally provide first-dollar coverage for routine children's services, and that does not generally encourage periodic and comprehensive care (Chapters 6 and 7). Also, the financing of medical research has been closely tied to medical school and academic health center financing. The natural tendency of the medical researchers has been to focus on a few complex cases in tertiary care centers rather than routine needs of children.

How Well Does the Health Sector Serve Children?

Are the health care needs of children well satisfied relative to the performance that the health sector affords to other groups? Are the health care requirements of children well satisfied given available technology? Are the needs of poor children provided for on an equitable basis in comparison to nonpoor children? Available data is sparse and does not always answer these questions satisfactorily. Particularly disturbing is the information we do have which suggests income-related inequalities of utilization, financial access, and outcome which are far greater for children than for other groups.

In 1972 only 79 percent of preschoolers with annual family income less than $5000 visited a doctor. For preschoolers with annual family income greater than $15,000, 91.3 percent had one or more physician visits (Davis, 1975). Given the importance of physician services or their equivalent to the routine primary care needs of children, these income-related inequalities are especially disturbing. When the utilization of physician services is expressed as a ratio of poor to nonpoor rates, it is generally true that the income-related disparities are greater for children than for the population as a whole and for most other age cohorts. Davis, in an analysis of the impact of the Medicaid program, has noted that between 1964 and 1974 the trend of lower utilization by the poor was reversed. The poor overtook high-income persons in utilization of physician services. This general reversal of the trend did not apply for children, however, and although the differential between nonpoor and poor utilization decreased from 66 percent more visits for high-income children in 1964 to 16 percent more visits in 1974, the balance was still in favor of the nonpoor (Davis, 1976).

Inequalities in financial access are more difficult to measure. Some poor and most near-poor children are clearly at a relative disadvantage given that primary care or first-dollar services are most frequently financed through self-payment rather than through insurance. Where health care needs are equivalent, these expenditures will cause a greater burden for the poor and near-poor, because they consume a greater portion of family income. Davis has provided some information on financial access as measured by the percentage of the population covered by private hospital insurance. Since the poor are generally covered by Medicaid, the most important differences are to be found in the comparison of the insurance status of the near-poor to the high-income group. The percentage of children in families with incomes between $3000 and $4999 with private health insurance is 41.7; between $5000 and $9999, 77.3 percent. Both percentages are substantially lower than the 90.4 percent of children with family incomes over $15,000 who have private insurance (Davis, 1975). Of course, these statistics do not provide information on potentially significant differences in benefit packages for the poor, the near-poor, and the high-income groups.

Inequalities in utilization of prenatal care across ethnic groups has been extensively documented by Kessner in a study of infant death in New York City. He found that while 43.3 percent of white native-born women received adequate care, only 4.3 percent of black women did (Kessner, 1973). Much more discouraging, however, than income or socioeconomic related inequities in financial access and/or utilization is the evidence of significant inequities in outcomes. Perhaps the most powerful evidence to date is provided by Kessner. His New York City study documented that infants born to white native-born women had a death rate of 15.2 per 1000 while infants of black native born women had a death rate of 35.7 per 1000—almost two and a half times higher (Kessner, 1973).

Kessner, in a study of the quality of primary medical care, has documented substantial gaps between health care technology available and what is delivered. He concludes, for example, that substantial hearing loss occurs to children in all income levels although much of it is easily preventable (Kessner, 1974).

The above examples are sufficient to suggest that the delivery of health care to children, particularly poor children, can be improved. To effect change, however, one must be aware of the nature of the political environment in which change must occur.

Political Environments and Children's Needs

Many of the individuals and institutions engaged in children's advocacy activities, including those in the health sector, have attempted to intervene on behalf of children in the political processes. While there is a trend of thought which places issues of family and children "above politics," many, including Rodham, have aptly pointed out that this should not be the case (Rodham, 1973). Children are disadvantaged in political affairs because they lack the basic power to vote. Children have limited organizational capabilities and frequently must be represented by their parents or established groups organized to lobby, litigate and exhort on their behalf.

One factor confronting children's advocates who want to influence health policymakers and health politics is the diffuse nature of child health interests, which stems from the nature of children's health problems discussed previously.

Diffuse interests are those interests that provide less important benefits and costs to individuals whatever the aggregate levels of costs and benefits to society (Olson, 1965). Diffuse interests are neither exciting nor in many cases immediately pressing. Whether an interest is diffuse or concentrated, political theorists have noted, affects the way individuals and groups behave. The primary health care needs of children represent a diffuse interest for two reasons. First, primary health care needs represent relatively less urgent problems distributed over a large population. Second, the costs of inadequate primary health care are frequently cumulative over a long period and are not immediately obvious.

Olson, in a perceptive book on the theory of groups and organizations, has employed economic and political theory to explain the behavior of large groups whose individual members have common but diffuse interests. Olson's work is particularly helpful in understanding the effect that children's health status has on the potential formation of advocacy groups. His conclusion is that there is no presumption that large groups will organize to act in their common interest (Olson, 1965). He argues rather convincingly that only when groups are small, or when they are fortunate enough to have an independent source of selective incentives, will they organize or act to achieve their objectives (Olson, 1965).[c]

The group of parents and children with interests in primary care is quite large but generally unorganized. With the exception of the poor, who have a limited ability to provide financial resources for first-dollar health costs, the interests are very diffuse. Among the poor the interests of parents and children are more concentrated, but still relatively diffuse in comparison to the highly concentrated interests of such daily survival needs as housing, employment, welfare entitlements, and food. While the average American would be seriously disturbed by finding children whose lives and opportunities are limited by preventable and treatable conditions, the general concern of these individuals has not been developed into a broader national and political awareness. Thus, the political constituency for primary care improvements is difficult to mobilize. Similarly, the interests of parents and children with problems stemming from socioeconomic and psychocultural factors, while more concentrated, frequently appear diffuse primarily because the problems are hard to identify and because the costs of untreated problems are not immediately apparent.

While the interests of parents and children with acute problems that require sophisticated tertiary care are more concentrated, in many cases the need for these services is either not predictable, of a very low probability, or is currently widely covered by health insurance, thus making it difficult to organize constituencies around these health issues. On the other hand, the parents of children with certain chronic problems such as mental retardation, cystic fibrosis, physical handicaps, multiple sclerosis, sickle-cell anemia, hemophilia, etc., have formed strong organizations in their attempts to expand private and public support for the problems of their children. One effect of the distribution of child health problems is to create groups that focus concentrated energy and political attention toward the treatment of chronic problems, and at the same time to dissipate concern and attention for primary medical and health services.

Child health advocates concerned with directing attention toward primary health care needs must be aware of this existing imbalance of interests and of the consequences for their work in the political marketplace. A political market refers to institutional arrangements— relationships among organized pressure groups, voters, authoritative governmental agencies, and affected citizens. These markets determine what governments do. The balance of political markets depends partially on the interests represented in them and whether these inter-

[c]For an analysis applying these concepts in the health sector, see Marmor, 1976.

ests are concentrated or diffuse. It also depends on the individuals to be represented and their relative position in the political market. Children, because they cannot vote and must be represented by others, are already at a disadvantage. Further, in the health sector there have been conditions of strong private interests monopolizing the political marketplace (Alford, 1972).

Alford has characterized organized medicine as the dominant interest group "with their powers and resources safely embedded in law, custom, professional legitimacy, and the practices of many public and private organizations" (Alford, 1972, p. 132). In an example directly related to a child health program, Altenstetter has described the balance of political forces controlling the crippled children's program operating in Connecticut under Title V of the Social Security Act:

> Whenever federal action threatened the influence and authority of either public or private Connecticut groups, opposition was mobilized and conflicts developed. In most cases, these conflicts were resolved to the satisfaction of the group involved and particularly in favor of the medical interests. Accommodating private interests was a standard routine (Altenstetter, 1973, p. 59).

Examples of child health decisionmaking in imbalanced political markets abound. For example, most health insurance coverage offered for sale in Massachusetts prior to 1974 provided no coverage for infants from birth to the fourteenth day. It is during this high-risk period that the preponderance of severe physical and mental abnormalities are first discovered and treated. Lack of insurance for this high-risk group has shifted the burden of initial and, where needed, continuing treatment costs to the family or the state or both. Kagay (1975) described the political environment in Massachusetts when a number of bills were proposed to prohibit sale of insurance policies with gaps in newborn coverage. While the absolute amount of money involved in any one case is potentially quite high, the absolute number of cases is generally quite small. Thus, the perceived interests of parents are relatively diffuse. The interests of the state are somewhat more concentrated given the potential costs for medical and custodial care, but because these costs can be spread over the entire tax base, the interests of the state are not as concentrated as one might expect. The highly concentrated interests of the half-dozen insurance companies seeking to maintain maximum profits were reflected in heavy and costly last-minute lobbying efforts against the legislation directed at the members of the Ways and Means Committee.

Given the realities of professional dominance in the health sector, imbalanced political markets are the rule rather than the exception. This is also the case when health care decisionmaking is conducted in public arenas such as legislatures and public bureaucracies (Kotz, 1969; Mass. Advocacy Center, 1972 and 1974; Citizen's Board of Inquiry, 1968 and 1972; Shay, 1974; Redman, 1973). These realities have two implications for those concerned about improving the lot of children through political activity. First, because the environments are imbalanced, targets for change must be carefully selected. Second, strategies must be geared to the relative disadvantage imposed by the structure of the political markets.

To summarize, children as a class are not well served by the health sector relative to other groups; poor children receive benefits and bear costs unequal to the nonpoor; and there is an unnecessary gap between what our technology is capable of offering and what is actually provided. These facts, in combination with the understanding that child health decisions are frequently made in arenas where the interests of children are not well represented, and that children cannot always effectively articulate and pursue their own interests, strongly suggest that child health care decisionmaking can be improved. Children's advocacy offers opportunities for such improvement.

THE ADVOCATE: TACTICS AND ORGANIZATION

To be effective, the child advocate must be able to combine people, resources, and ideas in order to improve outcomes for children. Thus, the advocate is not unlike an entrepreneur. The advocate working in the health sector must possess or be able to deploy a variety of skills, including political, legal, legislative, systems management, negotiation, research, and analytical skills. The example of the advocacy efforts directed toward development and implementation of the Early and Periodic Screening, Diagnosis and Treatment Program (hereinafter EPSDT) provides a good context in which to discuss and understand advocacy tactics and organization.[d]

As a program specifically targeted on poor children and their primary health care needs, EPSDT is the largest and most ambitious federal child health program launched to date. EPSDT was initially developed as part of the extensive Social Security Amendments of

[d]The following review of EPSDT is based on Foltz, 1975. See also Comptroller General, 1975; Kirk et al., 1976; Meyer and Lingle, undated; USDHEW, 1966 and 1973; Shay, 1974.

1967. It represented a major new national strategy for financing preventive and continuing health care for poor children as part of the Medicaid program and, in addition, provided experience in the implementation of such a strategy through state financing and delivery mechanisms.

A year before EPSDT became law, the office of the Secretary of the Department of Health, Education and Welfare described and provided cost projections for three proposals for screening, diagnosis, and treatment of low-income children. As it turned out, none of the programs analyzed by HEW was sufficiently akin to the final version of the legislation for the analysis to be useful. There appeared to be little or no understanding of the trade-offs among cost, quality, and access to care, or of the considerable problems the EPSDT program, as part of the Medicaid system, would inherit. Since the EPSDT legislation was a minor part of a large-scale effort to amend the Social Security Act, little political or analytical attention was paid to it. Throughout the hearings and debate in the House, cost and responsibility for program administration were the primary concerns, with most comments coming from bureaucrats, health care providers, and professional associations. Only one witness in the Senate hearings made any reference to the child health measures involved in the amendments. While this may have been part of a strategy of the bill's supporters to sneak through the EPSDT program without arousing opposition to the effects of the program on cost and health care delivery, the strategy had an additional effect. It resulted in failure to mobilize or develop strong constituency support for the measure, even among the poor, a shortcoming still evident today which has hindered smooth and vigorous implementation.

The debate over EPSDT provides an example of how difficult it may be to blend medical expertise with advocacy skills. Some biomedical researchers have questioned the effectiveness of certain kinds of screening (Bernick, volume II). Some child advocates, however, view screening as an effective political tool for documenting systemwide health needs of children, and thus see the implementation of screening programs as an effective tactic leading to the ultimate extension of entitlements for children. In this issue there is a tension between professional judgment and strategies that are politically viable in the short and long term.

In the process of the development of EPSDT legislation, advocates played no highly visible part. Missing from the process were the advocacy efforts to develop information; synthesize research results and put the information into a format useful for decisionmakers and the public; describe and forecast the impact of decisions; and, finally, frame program development and evaulation strategies. The tactics associated with such efforts might have been many and varied: submission of model legislation; support for a particular HEW proposal and lobbying efforts directed toward Congress; participation as witnesses at congressional hearings; dissemination of information on the effects of the legislation by means of public hearings, press conferences, and other activities; development of a strong constituency of support.

Advocates played a greater public role in the effort to implement the legislation. The EPSDT program became law in January 1968, with an effective implementation date of July 1969. As part of Medicaid, EPSDT quickly assumed the two major political weaknesses of the Medicaid program. First, because it was a jointly financed program of the federal government and the states, considerable discretion was left to the states over the details of benefits, reimbursement, and other key administrative and policy issues. Thus, reluctant states found ways to resist or torpedo the program. Second, as part of a welfare system, the poor and their allies were the major constituents supporting the program. In the imbalanced federal and state legislative arenas where Medicaid decisionmaking is conducted, the poor constitute a relatively weak group. The imbalance in this case was exacerbated because the benefits of the EPSDT program, primary medical care, were quite diffuse and because the beneficiaries were children.

Responsibilities for administration of the program were lodged in the Department of Health, Education and Welfare and given to the Social and Rehabilitation Service (SRS). For several years the administration made no effort to develop regulations and guidelines for the implementation of the new law. This situation came to the attention of the Children's Defense Fund, which encouraged the early EPSDT-related advocacy efforts.

The Children's Defense Fund is headed by Marian Edelman, an extremely talented and versatile advocate. She developed and refined legal advocacy, political and bureaucratic monitoring skills as director of the NAACP Legal Defense and Education Fund in Mississippi and later as director of the Washington Research Project. In establishing the Children's Defense Fund, she assembled a group of lawyers, federal policy monitors, researchers and community liaison people interested in policies and practices affecting the lives of children. To get the EPSDT program moving, legal services attorneys representing the National Welfare Rights Organization negotiated with responsible officials of the federal bureaucracy. After realizing that this strategy was not working, a suit was brought on behalf of the National Welfare Rights Organization by the Children's Defense Fund and the National Health Law Program. These organizations, in asking whether or not the Department of Health, Education and Welfare would administer its program as the law dictated, provides a very good example of one important advocacy tactic: recourse to the legal system when bureaucrats fail to perform functions stipulated by law. This successful lawsuit was merely the first round in a continuing effort to minitor EPSDT implementation, encourage the bureaucracy through negotiation, and where necessary seek legal remedy.

The Children's Defense Fund and other groups monitored the progress of regulation development through participation in hearings, submission of comments, and continued discussions with responsible officials. However, even with these spurs from the advocacy groups, program regulations did not become effective until February 1972, over two and a half years after the program was to have been fully implemented, and four years after passage of the initial legislation.

While the combined strategy of program monitoring, litigation, and comments on rules and regulations by the Children's Defense Fund and their welfare rights allies had the effect of moving the program along, the delays were in large part due to its status as a part of the Medicaid program. From its inception the Medicaid program had run into serious difficulties, both at the federal and state levels (Stevens and Stevens, 1970 and 1974). Costs were much higher than anyone had predicted and political support for the program waned rapidly, particularly after state-level management abuses were widely documented in the press. Even with the issuance of guidelines and regulations, there were continuing problems with the administration of the program. At the federal level administrators failed to monitor the state EPSDT programs and to enforce compliance mechanisms built into the law, or even to use less formal means of influence and persuasion available to them. Federal research and development efforts were inadequate and delayed. The first key results were not available until the mid-1970s, six years after the required implementation date (USDHEW, 1974).

A number of the program's deficits were highly visible at the state level, and advocacy groups began work in several states to improve EPSDT implementation. In some cases program implementation at the state and local level needed the same sort of program monitoring that the Children's Defense Fund initiated at the federal level. New York City provides an example of an advocacy group attempting to stimulate implementation. Under the leadership of Henry Saltzman, a former Ford Foundation executive experienced in urban affairs, and with the support of a distinguished and powerful board, the Citizens' Committee for Children encouraged implementation of EPSDT legislation. Through the offices of the Citizens' Committee for Children, federal officials from the New York regional office, state and city Medicaid officials, as well as state and city public health officials were convened for the first time to consider the development of a strategy for an effective EPSDT implementation in New York City (Citizens' Committee for Children, 1976). At this first "summit" meeting, representatives of all levels of government agreed to form a "cabinet" which would be staffed by the Citizens' Committee for Children and which would have one high ranking official from each agency participating on a regular basis. The hope was that in this forum the complex problems of implementation could be discussed frankly, confidentially and could be successfully resolved. This coordinating strategy by an independent civic agency provided the arena within which public agencies could resolve issues of planning and implementation. It was developed because the size of the eligible population in New York City and the diversity of health care delivery system posed such monumental problems. These actions suggest the role as conveners that children's advocacy organizations can sometimes play. To a considerable extent, the ability to play this role was based on the board composition of the Citizens' Committee for Children. It is a powerful group of New York citizens, some with ties to the business, banking and legal communities, others with strong political bases and constituencies in political and social service organizations. The ability to play this convening role was also considerably enhanced by the administrative and bureaucratic savvy Saltzman brought to the children's advocacy environment from his experiences at the Ford Foundation and in New York City government.

In other states the attempts at negotiations with bureaucrats were unsuccessful. Lawyers at the Children's Defense Fund, working with lawyers in health-related OEO legal assistance backup centers at the University of Pennsylvania and the University of California at Los Angeles, provided the basic legal research, and in at least eleven states legal assistance and welfare groups brought suits against the states. Some suits were successful, either in stimulating a consent decree or in their final adjudication. Implementation of the court orders were enhanced where strong constituency groups backing the suits made their interests known through political processes. Where suits were brought without constituency involvement, especially where the judge was not an activist, the results from the suits were more limited.

The legal skills represented in the Children's Defense Fund and local legal aid societies are frequently necessary for the development of effective advocacy. As a starting point, knowledge of federal and state laws, regulations, and administrative procedures affecting child health considerations is fundamental. But it is not sufficient merely to know the laws and the regulations and procedures. Those who would use legal advocacy must also realize that recourse to legal remedy is a long and tedious affair and that a favorable decision does not always lead to the desired action on the part of public officials. Thus, it is important for those who use legal advocacy to have a knowledge of its use and limitations as a strategy for change.

In some cases where there is official ineptitude or malfeasance, investigative skills, including the ability to draw information from recalcitrant officials, are particularly important to advocacy monitoring tactics. The investigative process requires checking facts by consulting different sources. The investigator must have the persistence and skepticism to sift through a wide variety of oral information and written documentation. Developing sources of information is important. A sympathetic bureaucrat at a lower level may be willing to discuss "off the record" problems of program implementation or differences between executive policy and legislative intent. In addition to compiling data from such sources, the investigator must have the skills necessary to come to broad and correct conclusions from a few surface clues and then construct the evidence. These investigative skills may be possessed by reporters and certain researchers. Such investigative skills are the essence of the advocate who works outside an organization and attempts to affect its behavior or actions.[e]

In other states the provision of research and information services rather than legal advocacy was the tactic employed for improving implementation of EPSDT. The Institute for Governmental Services at the University of Massachusetts sponsored a thorough review of the Massachusetts EPSDT program. The review documented problems of implementation and quite clearly portrayed Massachusetts' inadequate systems for fully implementing and monitoring the program (Yarmolinsky, 1975). This academic report has had little effect to date on state policy. This is somewhat surprising in a state such as Massachusetts, with its several strong child advocacy organizations, including the Massachusetts Advocacy Center. The lack of impact of the report can perhaps be attributed to three factors. First, there was a new governor and state administration. Second, a statewide fiscal crisis shortly after release of the report focused attention on more pressing issues. Third, the researchers did not present their information in such a way that it was used by the advocacy networks that had been developed in the state, nor did they develop sufficiently

---

[e] Investigative journalists can play a particularly important role. For two examples of outstanding efforts in this area, see Hill, 1974, and Iglehart, 1974.

close relationships with these groups, such as the Massachusetts Advocacy Center.

In California, advocacy efforts on behalf of EPSDT were developed by the California Children's Lobby and carried forward by the extremely talented advocate Liz Berger (Berger, 1973). An economist by training, Berger had over twenty years of lobbying experience in the California state legislature and extensive contacts with leaders in government, professional, and political circles throughout the state. While earning a living lobbying for corporate clients, she had in recent years addressed her skills to the problems of children. Realizing the weakness of the constituency upon which the EPSDT program was based, Berger, in concert with legislative staffers and the Chairman of the Ways and Means Committee in the California legislature, developed a strategy to broaden the constituency of EPSDT. Assembly Bill 2068, the California Child Health and Disability Prevention Bill, provided some EPSDT benefits to all children in California. A.B. 2068 stipulated that these services be required for children prior to school entry and channeled administration through the county public health systems, either through the provision of direct services by the county or contracting for the services of private providers. The bill itself was passed principally due to the commitment of the Ways and Means Committee Chairman, Willie L. Brown, Jr., who was willing to hold up appropriations for improvements in the Governor's Mansion in exchange for Governor Reagan's commitment not to veto the program. The strategy depended on a committed and pragmatic legislator, an alert legislative staff, and a key lobbyist who understood the give-and-take of political activity.

The efforts of the California Children's Lobby did not end after successful passage of A.B. 2068. By providing expert witnesses from various provider groups and developing testimony of key citizen-witnesses from throughout the state, the California Children's Lobby had a significant effect on the benefit package and reimbursement structure (Berry, 1974). In achieving their goal of raising the level of reimbursement for Assembly Bill 2068, they were also able to piggyback raises in reimbursement for EPSDT services and thus make both programs more palatable to providers. In these efforts they relied on the self-interest of key provider groups and were able to orchestrate these in such a way that the self-interest was not totally inconsistent with the interests of program development. In these efforts the California Children's Lobby drew heavily on knowledge of the bureaucracy. Key here is understanding management, systems analysis, control, and economic analysis. Also important is the ability to diagnose the ebb and flow of power within organizations and the relationship between power and use of organizational incentives and disincentives. For example, in concentrating on reimbursement rates and benefits packages to be developed under Assembly Bill 2068, Berger realized the powerful incentives and disincentives that the state could offer to potential providers. In an effort to monitor the implementation of A.B. 2068, Berger and a number of other individuals have established the Children's Research Institute of California, a tax exempt, nonprofit organization that is able to receive foundation grants.

These examples show how, to be successful, an advocate must have a knowledge of political environments and processes, a knowledge that is instinctive, based on extensive experience rather than theoretical or academic understanding. The advocate must know when to court and when to condemn; when to negotiate firmly and when to yield. The advocate must understand the cycle of formal and informal political processes and also realize the attention span of key actors. Fundamental to successful operation is the advocate's ability to assess and identify the interests of various individuals and groups and to develop strategies and tactics that build on the positive aspects of their self-interest and at the same time minimize or neutralize those aspects detrimental to the interests of children.

Organization of Advocacy

A combination of the requisite skills of the advocate can occur in an individual advocate or in an advocate and affiliated professional staff, such as in the case of the Children's Defense Fund. Or it can be enhanced by a lay board, such as the Citizens' Committee for Children in New York City. It can even occur through loose coalitions of individuals, professionals, and lay groups, as has been the characteristic of the California Children's Lobby. The method of talent aggregation will vary according to circumstances, financial capabilities, and availability of talent. But, as Peter Edelman has noted in his analysis of the Massachusetts Advocacy Center, key to the process is leadership:

> Here, then is rule number one for citizen advocacy: someone must identify the problem and set the process for action in motion. Indeed, someone or small group has to stay with the effort throughout, or those whose interest, however genuine, is only a secondary priority will not stay involved long. There is a word for it: leadership (P. Edelman, 1973, p. 641).

The questions of organizational structure for children's advocacy programs are not new ones. In the 1960s both the federal government in its Mobilization for Youth programs and the Ford Foundation in its "Gray Area" programs attempted to improve outcomes for youth through a strategy of bureaucratic coordination and national planning. Marris and Rein (1967), in an analysis of these programs, found that they "failed for lack of imagination and adaptability" (p. 41) and concluded that "all the projects had great difficulty in reconciling systematic planning evaluation with political realism" (p. 119).

The conclusions of Marris and Rein weigh against endorsement of any advocacy structure that is too complex or bureaucratic. They call into question a model for advocacy developed by the Joint Commission on the Mental Health of Children. In its 1969 report, *Crisis in Child Mental Health: Challenge for the 1970's*, the Joint Commission proposed "the development of an advocacy system at every level of government to ensure effective implementation of . . . desired goals" (Joint Commission, 1969, p. 8). Specifically, the Joint Commission proposed a four-tiered organization for advocacy: at the national level, a Presidential Advisory Council on Children; at the state level, a State Child Development Agency; and at the local and area-wide levels Child Development Authorities with direct service responsibilities. Advocacy efforts based on this model incorrectly assume that the new decisionmaking structures will create a more, rather than less, balanced political market.

The examples of children's advocates operating to improve the EPSDT program, and the analysis of Marris and Rein, argue for an organizational structure for advocates which is:

> better realized by discrete political opportunism, than by attempting to induce a coalesence of power. Such a strategy does not create leadership, but unobtrusively supplies it, manipulating the existing structure. It demands no prior commitment, and threatens no jurisdiction. It does not predetermine the targets of reform, or theorize its plans, but exploits its chances. This flexibility makes it less vulnerable, more resilient under attack, and surest of its goals (Marris and Rein, 1967, p. 162).

The Citizens Board of Inquiry into Hunger and Malnutrition, the Massachusetts Advocacy Center, and the Citizens' Committee for Children in New York City have developed and successfully deployed models of small group advocacy organization. As Edelman has described:

> The model was fairly simple: elicit the interest of some key interest groups (UAW, the churches, and the civil rights/anti-poverty community), use that interest to attract a board of distinguished and representative citizens. They hold hearings and conduct staff inquiries, issue a searing report with maxi-

mum media coverage, and, finally, figure out how to get action on the reports (P. Edelman, 1973, p. 642).

A flexible organizational framework for advocates will make it possible for them to work with numerous allies in their efforts to improve health care for children. As public involvement in the financing and delivery of health care increases, allies in the public sector—state and federal executive, legislative, and judicial officials—become important possible allies. One important job of the advocate will be to assess where various officials stand on key children's issues, and how effective they are in the give-and-take of bureaucratic politics. In some cases, cooperation, collaboration, and assistance may be quite appropriate; in others, confrontation may be necessary.

Private health sector groups, such as medical professional societies, drug and equipment manufacturers, health insurers, partisan political groups, organizations of parents whose children have special needs, are also important allies. Many other groups that may have a less direct stake in the outcome of decisions that affect children should be considered potential allies of child health advocates. These include organized citizens groups focusing on health, welfare, education, and good government issues; legal advocacy organizations; academic and policy planning groups; and professional societies in welfare and education.

ISSUES FOR CHILDREN'S ADVOCATES

A child advocate must be able to identify problems that are amenable to solution through advocacy efforts. The advocate must bring these problems to the attention of key decisionmakers or, if the decisionmakers are unattentive or recalcitrant, the advocate must bring the issues before a broader public. Because political judgment and entrepreneurial acumen are the key ingredients, it is not possible to lay out a master plan for advocacy. Issues, strategies, and tactics will vary from state to state and will change with time, but one important general rule holds:

> Only certain kinds of issues can be addressed by small-group advocacy. The problem has to be small enough so that efforts for its solution do not turn into the naive pursuit of some all-encompassing agenda. The problem must be comprehensible to the public and capable of evoking the sort of strong emotion that attends the demonstration of a clear injustice. It must be manageable and packageable. And it must have specific remedies. . . . In the problem must be the victimization of children in specific ways, as opposed to things as global as mental health or quality education (P. Edelman, 1973, p. 641).

The author will risk describing a number of areas where fruitful advocacy might be accomplished on behalf of children in the years ahead.

Federal Policy Debates: Extending Health Entitlements to Children

Major new policy or program thrusts of federal or state governments provide fertile environments for advocacy. Perhaps the most prominent example of such an environment in the health sector is the continuing national health insurance (NHI) debate. The debate stems in part from an awareness that existing public and private programs inadequately serve the American population, and is principally over the extent to which financial access to health care will be offered as a right or entitlement to Americans. Depending on the ultimate form adopted, such a program can have a very important or relatively small impact on children.

Many characteristics of the health sector, described earlier, tend to weigh against the development of an NHI program responsive to all children. First, the historical trend in insurance has been to guarantee hospital finance and coverage against the costs of hospital care. This focus is not the predominant health need of children. Second, the desire for cost containment and resultant pressure against first-dollar coverage in any national health insurance plan may be viewed as inconsistent with financing the routine and continuing health care needs of children. Third, health insurance traditionally in the United States has been offered to children through their parents, whether through employment benefits or welfare entitlement. Fourth, routine maternal and child health care is essentially predictable and relatively low cost, thus making it difficult to justify its inclusion in an insurance package. Fifth, in areas where the federal government has intervened traditionally on behalf of children, the focus has been limited to programs for the poor. This has been true for both EPSDT as part of the Medicaid Program and also the Title V programs.

These general points have been compounded by another serious factor—the lack of substantial analysis. Prior to the work of Marmor (Chapter 7), little work had been done exploring the relationship between proposed national health insurance schemes and the needs and opportunities for improving services for children.

The EPSDT case study presented earlier suggests what child advocates can do to make the case for children in the national health insurance debate: (1) study existing public and private benefits, costs, and operations and suggest what improvements might be considered as part of a new national health finance scheme; (2) analyze existing national health insurance proposals for the impact they will have on child health problems and if necessary suggest new or modified proposals; (3) bring the issues to the attention of the public and key decisionmakers through analysis, public information, and, for nontax-exempt groups, through direct lobbying efforts; (4) if legislation passes, participate in the rulemaking process, articulating the interests of children; and (5) monitor program implementation.

While a national health insurance policy that is attuned to the special health care needs of children may be very important in improving financial access, advocates should also consider some of the nonfinancial aspects of NHI which may affect children. The distribution of primary care providers may be affected by decisions on national health insurance legislation or by such implementation details as the reimbursement rates afforded various specialty groups or geographic regions.

From the point of view of child advocates, another major question of the national health insurance debate may be evaluating the impact of such legislation on present federal financing and program efforts. In evaluating the Title V program, Davis (1974) presents evidence that the redistribution of primary care providers caused by the program subsidies can have an important effect on children by providing access to needed routine primary care. Advocates will have to play a role in structuring NHI legislation that takes such evidence into account.

Other federal policy debates, including the extent of subsidy for health care delivery programs such as neighborhood health centers, also can have important implications for children.

Monitoring Existing Programs and Administrative Mechanisms

Program monitoring is an important advocacy strategy. Removed from the pressures and disciplines of market forces, and adept at turning other public accountability strategies to their advantage, bureaucracies can quickly lapse into inefficiency or ineffectiveness.[f] Monitoring strategies can help point up situations where good intentions have gone bad, circumstances where bad intentions exist, and those surendipitous times when good intentions are achieved and should be rewarded and encouraged.

Monitoring activities can and frequently are conducted by citizens' groups, but they can also be encouraged through the procedural mechanisms developed in the public arena, including, for example: the development of decisionmaking processes that would require spe-

[f]For an excellent discussion of accountability mechanisms, see Rivlin, 1971.

cial analysis of the impact of alternative decisions on children; hearings or other public ventings; and stronger procedural precautions through which competing conceptions of the public interest might be resolved. In this type of arrangement, children's advocacy groups would have the primary role in efforts to monitor the performance of health service and financing institutions. A similar concept, the development of a Family Impact Statement for the legislative and administrative decisions of the federal government, has been proposed by then Senator Mondale.

Efforts to monitor those children's health and social services that attempt to overcome socioeconomic and psychocultural deprivation have been particularly useful. One of the earliest was the Citizen's Board of Inquiry into Hunger and Malnutrition (1968, 1972) in the United States which documented this unreasonable condition faced by too many American children. The Massachusetts Advocacy Center, one of the most sophisticated child advocacy organizations in the nation, has developed an outstanding track record in monitoring the implementation of state programs and policies designed to ameliorate health problems caused by socioeconomic and psychocultural factors, e.g., its efforts to improve the implementation of the Massachusetts state mental health program (Mass. Advocacy Center, 1972) and also the Massachusetts lead poison prevention program (Mass. Advocacy Center, 1974). The Citizens' Committee for Children in New York City (1974) employed a similar strategy in the area of school health. The Children's Foundation in Washington, D.C. has played an important role in monitoring federal nutrition programs (Children's Foundation, 1975).

The activities of Departments of Public Health and other state and local programs are important areas for probing and concern, as is the newly implemented Title XX of the federal Social Security Act which provides funds to the states for social service programs (Children's Defense Fund, 1975). Each state is required to develop a Title XX state plan. Since this plan can either reflect the interests of children or concentrate on other population groups to the exclusion of children, monitoring the development and implementation of Title XX plans can stimulate attention to the health-related social service needs of children. This can include the care of chronically ill children and their families as well as the care of children and families whose problems stem from the socioeconomic and phychocultural factors. These programs also might effectively be used to provide family support and other services for the acutely ill child in periods of crisis. Such efforts may be assisted by working with and developing coalitions of social welfare agencies and advocacy groups.

Regulatory environments in the health sector are becoming increasingly important. Recent federal planning legislation establishing regional Health Service Administrations (HSA) (PL 93–641) has increased the planning and regulatory powers at the local level. The enactment of the Professional Standards Review Organization (PSRO) has also created a new regulatory structure to control costs and to oversee the quality of health care (Bellin, 1969). These new agencies have been added to traditional federal regulatory efforts such as the Food and Drug Administration and to the traditional state public health regulatory work. Some states have added rate control and certificate-of-need commissions. Several national health insurance proposals stipulate increased regulatory activity at the state level (Posner, 1971a). Thus a myriad of regulatory activities exist or are being proposed. Regulatory mechanisms, as Wellford has noted, have been traditional targets for advocates:

> Because the forces of advocacy have been so unbalanced, the agencies which regulate . . . have more often subverted democracy than promoted it. . . . Victories which the public wins with the power of the ballot are often lost when they are interpreted by the regulatory bureaucracy (Wellford, 1972, p. xxii).

Regulatory agencies and state rate-making commissions are given rather extensive discretion, and with this discretion they can either further the interests of child health or effect policies that are neutral or even detrimental to children. Monitoring the processes, collecting information on how they impact children, and bringing this to the attention of the regulators and the public as well will be an increasingly important activity for children's advocates as more and more health care resources are allocated through regulatory agency processes.

A particularly serious threat to certain forms of monitoring through the legal system is the recent Supreme Court decision *Alyeska Pipeline Co.* v. *Wilderness Society*, which ruled that the federal courts do not have the authority to award attorney fees to citizens groups in cases where that group, acting as "private attorney general," has won a suit enforcing important public rights unless the statute under which the suit was brought specifically provides for such awards. Child advocacy organizations should encourage such provisions in all legislation affecting child health. Extension of freedom of information laws at the federal, state and local levels will also provide important levers for child advocates.

Child advocates have yet to focus their concern on state rate-making commissions. Yet these agencies fix the reimbursement rates for neighborhood health centers and other primary care settings and can provide incentives and disincentives for the use of alternative personnel such as pediatric nurse practitioners. The policies of these agencies affect the distribution of pediatric primary care services and facilitate either the creation or destruction of barriers to access.

One point is of key importance to child health advocates: regulatory environments almost always become imbalanced when the concentrated interests of the regulated industry are brought to bear. One disturbing example from the drug industry illustrates this point well and also provides a case of the importance of investigative journalism to children's advocacy. Pekkanen (1973) has documented the extensive overproduction of certain psychotropic drugs (amphetamines, barbiturates, and certain tranquilizers) and the very serious effect flooding the markets with these drugs has had on drug-abuse patterns for families and children. The interest of the drug manufacturers in maintaining the black market in these drugs was quite concentrated, primarily so that they would not ultimately lose the profit from the initial sales to Mexican and American druggists and wholesalers. The costs to parents and children ultimately caught up in drug-abuse, as well as the costs to society, were quite high, yet the interests diffuse. Pekkanen documents the struggle against the concentrated interests of the drug industry represented by the American Medical Association, the Pharmaceutical Manufacturers Association, and skillful Washington lawyer-lobbyists in the relatively imbalanced political markets characterized by Food and Drug Administration regulatory activity, and congressional investigatory and legislative processes. This is one example of how the behavior and actions of regulatory agencies can affect the health and welfare of children.

Restructuring Medical Care Decisionmaking Processes for Children

So far, we have looked at activities for advocates which are directed at improving the outcomes of decisionmaking. Whether these efforts are aimed at the establishment of new programs or the improvement of existing programs, their over-all goal is to affect directly the kinds and quality of health services for children. Another area of interest to advocates is the improvement of the decisionmaking process itself. Procedural reform may not affect immediately the improved delivery of goods and services to children, but the long-range goal of advocates working to improve decisionmaking processes is the same.

Harrison Wellford's definition of the public interest illustrates the immediate goal of procedural reform. "The public interest is not an absolute set of values to be dogmatically urged on whomever will listen. It is, instead, what emerges when all legitimate interests have a chance to compete and be heard on a particular issue" (Wellford, 1972, p. xxii). There are few areas where the distribution of rights and responsibilities for medical care decisionmaking are more complex than in the areas of acute perinatal care and human research and experimentation.

Rapidly advancing technology has made it possible to save the lives of many infants who previously might have died at birth. Weighing the interests of the child in such cases is a complex issue. An article by Duff and Campbell (1973) reports on forty-three severely defective babies who died when heroic measures were withheld. In these cases, parents and physicians agreed informally that the children's lives would have been devoid of "meaningful" human good. A well-publicized Maine case illustrates the possibility of a different outcome where a more formal setting for decisionmaking is utilized. The parents of a severely handicapped child were worried about the long-term problems of supporting the child. They asked the attending physician at the Maine Medical Center to halt life-sustaining measures and forego corrective surgery. The physician persuaded the hospital to seek an injunction against the parents, arguing that the deformities might well be correctable. A judge granted the injunction, ruling that the parents had no right to refuse permission for lifesaving surgery (Knox, 1974). The unusual aspect of the Maine case was the recourse to the courts, the shift from informal to formal process.

The years ahead may see significant shifts from informal to formal decisionmaking processes. As this occurs it may become increasingly important to ensure that the independent interests of the child are formally and effectively represented. In a call for such a shift in an analysis of the public policy issues raised by amniocentesis, Etzioni (1975) has noted medical research findings which suggested that if all mothers age thirty-five and older were screened during pregnancy and therapeutic abortion done in every instance where the technical indication of Down's syndrome occurred, the incidence of the condition would be halved. Deciding who should be tested involves balancing the small, but nontrivial risk to the pregnant women against the risk of bearing an afflicted child. In weighing the costs and benefits of amniocentesis for the detection of Down's syndrome, it is necessary to weigh the low incidence of the disease, the significant risk and the relatively high costs of the tests against the extremely high costs of institutional care for afflicted individuals. Answering who shall decide these issues is complex. While some of the more personal decisions might clearly fall within the domain of women independently or in concert with their husbands, there are many public policy issues for reflective advocates to consider. Whatever the answers to these questions, Etzioni clearly calls for formalized decisionmaking following rational public policy analysis.

Etzioni is not alone in calling for more formalization in health care decisionmaking. A number of groups, including the American Hospital Association, have urged the voluntary adoption of a patient bill of rights which formalizes certain procedural guarantees for patients. Adoption of a patient bill of rights has been considered in a number of state legislatures as part of malpractice reform legislation debates or as an independent issue. In almost all cases, there has been little health care provider support for the substitution of more formal procedures and protections for existing informal ones. In any event, as processes become more formal the tendency will be to shift power toward government, clearly at the expense of providers, and perhaps at the expense of children and parents. As more formal structures evolve, some attention will need to be given to providing input for and weighing the interests of the parent(s) and the child, especially in situations where those interests may be in conflict (Chapter 9). Careful attention must be given to structuring due process protections, and to assuring that the interests of the different parties are represented effectively (Rodham, 1973).

More formal processes also can improve the choices made in the area of human research and experimentation (Katz, 1972). Here, decisionmaking occurs in highly imbalanced political markets. The interests of the experimenters—professional advancement, compensation, self-esteem—are highly concentrated, a fact reflected in the heavy lobbying of the biomedical research interests following the issuance of recent HEW regulations on human research and experimentation. Marian Edelman of the Children's Defense Fund pinpoints the problem by:

> investigating the extent to which children, particularly institutionalized children, are used for medical experimentation without the provision of adequate informed consent procedures or other protections. It is an extremely interesting area. We have found it difficult for two reasons: first, medical research has been conducted largely in secrecy, without public knowledge or accountability, even while much of it is done with public funds; and second, doctors like lawyers and other professionals think that only they should regulate themselves—even in face of information showing substantial abuse (M. Edelman, 1974, p. 62).

The Children's Defense Fund participated in the rulemaking process on human research and experimentation at the Department of

Health, Education and Welfare. Their position paper urged prohibitions against research and experimentation on child subjects where there was potential risk to the subject (Children's Defense Fund, 1974). The argument was based on the assumption that most children do not have sufficient mental capacities to adequately evaluate the risks involved and provide truly informed consent. They also assume that the ability to provide such consent should not reside with the parent. This position is challenged by most medical researchers, who argue that the gains in infectious disease treatment, for example, could not have been achieved had this standard been applied during the last century.

Trade-offs frequently exist between the length of the research period, the precision of the results, and human risk. This point is well demonstrated by an example from a collaborative project on phenylketonuria (PKU), a childhood genetically related enzyme dificiency which leads to mental retardation if an infant is not treated with a special diet (NAS, 1975). While screening for PKU is fairly routine and diagnosis and treatment available, researchers are still uncertain at what age it is possible to remove a child from the restricted diet. Researchers have recently proposed to evaluate the effects of termination of the low-phenylalanine diet in a controlled study. The study design requires that when patients enrolled in the project reach six years of age, they are allocated either to a termination group (in which phenylalanine restriction will gradually end) or to a diet continuation group. The assumption is that such a random clinical trial will provide information on whether it is possible to terminate the diet at six years of age.

It is questionable whether a controlled experiment with a random assignment of subjects is necessary or desirable, given the risk of mental impairment. This is especially true when the possibility exists for a longitudinal study employing a quasi-experimental design and relying on the fact that some children for psychological reasons (cheating) or social reasons (family disorganization) will be inadvertently removed from the diet at varying ages. While some precision in results might be lost in such a quasi-experimental design, the potential risks to children may be much lower and certainly the responsibility of the researcher involved less severe.

The important point to stress again is that human research and experimentation decisionmaking occurs in highly imbalanced political markets. The interests of the experimenters are highly concentrated. The interests of potential subjects are more diffuse and less frequently heard in debate. Three principal checks apply against abuses. There is the presumption that the experimental subject will offer "informed consent" in a situation when a subject may be ill, tired, emotionally drained, poorly educated, or overawed by presumed medical expertise. While the interests of an actual subject are concentrated, it is reasonably clear that they are not necessarily powerful. The second check is provided by the peer-review committees at research institutions that consider the ethical aspects of proposed research. This review is dominated by individuals who have highly concentrated professional interests at stake. Its decisions are made without public scrutiny, and its actions are infrequently reviewed by institutional administrative or lay trustee oversight groups. The third check, ex post facto, lies in the courts through litigation. One clear requirement for child advocates is a more balanced political market for child human research and experimentation at the price of less freedom for investigators and possibly higher administrative costs. Advocates can and should seek procedural reform and greater substantive input on behalf of the interests of the child.

As advocates seek more formal processes, two problem areas should be noted. The first is the possible negative effects of putting decision-making solely into the hands of someone removed from the consequences of the decision. A judge may well act to preserve the life of a deformed child, yet the parents will bear the responsibility of raising the child. Second, the tendency may be to shift toward the government, clearly at the expense of the providers and perhaps at the expense of both children and parents. In both these cases, attention must be given to procedural protections for all concerned, so that Wellford's public interest—an environment where legitimate interests have a chance to compete equally—holds sway.

FOSTERING CHILDREN'S ADVOCACY IN THE HEALTH SECTOR

Developing Advocate-Entrepreneur Talent

At the present time, the primary constraint on children's advocacy activities is the identification, selection, and development of advocacy talent. There is a limited supply of child advocates. It is unusual to find individuals with the breadth and depth of skills necessary for good advocacy work, as well as the perseverance and high energy levels required.

The supply of advocacy talent, while generally limited, is even more severely constrained in the health sector. Basic career paths in the health and biomedical fields do not routinely provide challenges and opportunities to the advocate-entrepreneur. Entry to leadership positions in the health sector is most usually through biomedical research or skills in the art of medicine or other healing disciplines.

Health careers do not generally provide extensive training and background in organizational development, politics, policy research, the use of the media, and other areas. Thus, the health system itself does not usually generate advocates. These problems are compounded by other limitations. When people begin working in advocacy in the health sector, a number of forces tend to pull them away, principally because good advocacy skills are highly marketable in other areas and secondly because there are no career ladders or paths for advocates in the health sector.

Given these characteristics, one of the clear and necessary requirements for fostering advocacy is the process of identifying talent, nurturing it, and integrating that talent into the various networks of health sector and public decisionmaking.

The identification of talent can be a difficult and time-consuming process. Potential advocates may be found in a number of different places: the media, political or community organizations, academic or legal circles. Some, perhaps dissatisfied with the status quo and interested in expanding their own personal, social and political horizons, may come from the health sector. Others may come from children's advocacy efforts in other fields. Whatever the route, there is inevitably a requisite period of time during which the fledgling advocate must tackle a problem, refine existing advocacy skills, and acquire the necessary new skills and attitudes.

An apprenticeship or series of apprenticeships with distinguished child advocates is highly desirable. Where an apprenticeship is not possible, the opportunity to observe, to talk with, and to follow the work of other child advocates can be a useful but less desirable substitute for an apprenticeship.

There are of course other alternatives to a strategy that relies on the identification and nurturance of advocacy talent. One is a coordinating strategy, a strategy that attempts to put together key public and private actors of a given jurisdiction in an all-encompassing bureaucratic structure. The lessons of the Ford Foundation "Gray Areas" programs and of the federal proverty programs suggest that this strategy is of limited potential (Marris and Rein, 1967). In the political environments characterized by fiscal pluralism, coordinators have little leverage.

Financing Children's Advocacy

Another way to foster advocacy talent is to finance advocacy activities. Private philanthropy provides an excellent source of flexible financing for advocacy. The results of funding advocacy are less predictable than funding an established university-based researcher or a major community hospital; however, the foundation's traditional role, inspiring innovation, provides a strong justification for advocacy efforts.

In many respects, the attractiveness of advocacy strategies for philanthropy increases significantly as public responsibilities for financing health and social services grow. The resources of philanthropy can no longer finance directly the provision of health and social services, a role they once assumed. The financial involvement of the public sector in all spheres of American life has increased tremendously since the 1930s. Also, during the same period governmental expenditures for research and development have increased substantially, in many cases overshadowing the funds available through private philanthropy. Thus, a once pre-eminent role of foundations, developing experimental programs which if successful might be adopted and financed by the government, is now relatively less important.

Philanthropy today is most frequently reacting to public initiatives and public financing—providing last-dollar matching funds rather than first-dollar funds or venture capital. Robert Blendon of the Robert Wood Johnson Foundation has argued that what is needed is a new private policy for philanthropic giving which takes into account these new trends in public financing (Blendon, 1976). The key question is still one of leverage: How do you use limited but more flexible dollars to influence and improve the use of more significant funds? Perhaps the best answer lies in some of the advocacy functions. Certainly monitoring government performance has the potential for high leverage, both in strengthening the administration of existing programs and in providing analysis of alternative legislative approaches (Fleming, 1972). A monitoring strategy, coupled with a research and development effort closely attuned to public programs, can address questions or issues that it is not politically feasible to address with public resources. On another level private philanthropy following an advocacy strategy can provide the financial resources to allow individuals and organizations to articulate their own interests and compete more effectively in unbalanced environments. Such activities are critical to closing the gap between the promise and the reality of child health care in American society.

National foundations may have difficulty in assessing the situations of state and local advocacy environments, principally because of their lack of familiarity with the day-to-day politics, personalities, and community issues. The problem of assessment can lead to a tendency to hold back financial and other support to advocacy efforts until a track record has been established, thus limiting the supply of critical first-dollar support for advocates. This problem is serious, especially in light of the importance of discovering and nurturing fresh advocacy talent. With a program of small initial grants to promising but untried advocates in a variety of local and state situations may identify and encourage new talent, the costs to a national foundation in program officer time, administrative overhead, and travel expenses can be quite high in relationship to the size of the grants and the probability of success. These may be necessary costs for national foundations to assume, and surely the added knowledge of local environments can only add to the over-all effectiveness of national foundations. This might be a more logical task for community foundations or regional and local private foundations, groups which, on the whole, may be more knowledgeable of local conditions and talent. These foundations, unfortunately, may be less interested in assuming the delights and dilemmas caused by the repercussions of advocacy work. Also, pressure to fund established agencies rather than their critics or watchdogs may be significantly greater at the local and regional level, in part because foundation board members or their business associates frequently serve on the boards of the more established agencies, or because an advocacy strategy may press against governmental officials that foundation board members have personally supported.

Given their concern for innovation and their desire to maintain flexibility in their financing endeavors, foundations have limited staying power as a funding source. In many advocacy efforts, however, there is a span of attention which depends on the interests of key lay individuals, key staff advocates, and the cycle of issue-attention affecting the consideration of public questions, and these constraints may in fact be more limiting than the staying power of foundations. One children's advocacy organization, the Citizens' Committee for Children of New York City, has been able to develop a fairly long and consistent record through changes in leadership and issue interest. This has been accomplished, in part, by stringing together a series of foundation grants on a variety of children's issues, some related to the health sector, others not. Some fund-raising stability is needed; otherwise, fund-raising efforts can drain the energies of advocates, limit their effectiveness, or force them into other occupations. While some good arguments can be made for foundations providing general operating support, there is a delicate balance between offering some financial stability and encouraging an organization to be fat, lazy and unresponsive. Financing through corporations, board members, direct mail, membership, events, and sale of publications is possible.

Another shortcoming of foundations as an advocacy funding source stems from the tendency of national foundations to feel their job is done if someone else has supported one or two demonstration projects. For example, the Foundation for Child Development funded a series of projects for monitoring the development of the EPSDT program, including a statewide project in West Virginia, the efforts of the Citizens' Committee for Children in New York City, and the national efforts of the Children's Defense Fund (Foundation for Child Development, 1973–74). In discussions with a number of national foundations about their interest in children's health and their funding attitudes, the author encountered program officers who felt that these projects were sufficient to demonstrate the value of EPSDT advocacy efforts. They argued that public and community sources should continue financing these and other similar activities, if warranted. The assumption that other sources, possibly public sources, are willing to finance such advocacy activities is not well founded for reasons which will be discussed later. One important implication for funding must be drawn from the fact that advocacy work, while usually nonpartisan, is political in nature. Political strength lies partially in numbers. For advocacy strategies to be effective, both nationally and at the state level, they will in all likelihood have to include multiple approaches with strong national initiatives complimented by local endeavors.

One way that a philanthropic advocacy strategy may take on a multiplier effect is to work between the cracks to insure that publicly financed research and development efforts have the desired impact on public opinion and key decisionmakers. It is easy to point to an example: the work on EPSDT in Massachusetts conducted by the Institute for Governmental Studies at the University of Massachusetts was extensive and potentially quite useful; unfortunately, this work has had to date little impact on the Department of Public Welfare, the Massachusetts General Court, and public opinion. A small, well-placed foundation grant to the advocate-entrepreneurs at the Massachusetts Advocacy Center and/or at a local legal aid project could have had the effect of taking these ideas and issues and putting them before the legislature, the administration, the courts, and the public. Ultimately this might have yielded significant changes in programs and substantial benefits for children. Certainly such entrepreneurial strategy offers potential leverage on the effectiveness of considerable public research and development funds.

Foundations, in their more traditional research and demonstration efforts, can also be helpful to the cause of children's advocacy in the health sector. A basic strategy that any foundation might take is to assure that a given percentage of its efforts is devoted to children and children's issues. Thus, if a foundation's major thrust is in the health field, a certain percentage of its projects or its dollar volume might be directed toward children's issues. For example, if that foundation decides to fund a study of state regulatory cost and price control commissions in health care, in the process of negotiating that grant, the program officer might be attuned to insist that some of the data collection and analysis provide information that shows the impact of these regulatory activities on children. If the foundation sponsors a legislative staff seminar at the federal or state level, it might urge that a certain number of the sessions provide a platform for those investigators or practitioners with special insights on child health issues. If a foundation has a traditional program allowing reporters or journalists to spend a year in academia, it might arrange for some of these fellowships to be devoted especially to the study of child health. If the foundation sponsors seminars for judicial organizations, these sessions might provide background material and studies of the more difficult questions of the distribution of rights and responsibilities for medical care decisionmaking, areas where the courts may ultimately be required to make difficult and timely decisions under more pressing circumstances.

In one domain, direct legislative efforts and partisan politics, the use of tax-exempt philanthropic funds is proscribed (Caplin and Timbie, 1975). Thus, activities like the Massachusetts Children's Campaign, which entered the realm of partisan politics and attempted to influence electoral results and the legislative program of the California Children's Lobby, clearly cannot be supported by tax-exempt philanthropic funds. Financing for these activities may, however, come from membership dues and non-tax-exempt political contributions.

But not all the financial contribution to children's advocacy efforts in the health sector need be private. State and federal legislative bodies can do much more extensive work by financing and encouraging the legislative monitoring and oversight functions. Here, information gathering that focuses on children and periodically reviews the implementation of federal and state programs could pay high dividends and could be an important key to the process of developing public concern, support for effective program implementation, and new or redirected financial and program extensions. One concrete way that legislative bodies can encourage advocacy is to write legislation that allows advocates to recover legal fees when they have successfully brought class action suits against officials who fail to implement child-related legislation effectively.

It is probably impossible to expect that the executive branch officials will themselves welcome or encourage the activities of the advocate-entrepreneur. While some officials may have the confidence and the wisdom to fund their own watchdogs and critics and external allies, they are not always likely to be supported by their superiors in the bureaucracy and in political office. But one very clear contribution the public sector can make to advocacy efforts is a more targeted research and development program. This can occur in several ways. For example, more extensive efforts on research and development of child health problems, such as more effective routine care, chronic care, child-oriented tertiary care, and the problems associated with socioeconomic and cultural deficits, can be developed. This might call for a reallocation of national research and development efforts away from the more common diseases and problems of the adult and aging populations—heart, cancer, and stroke strategy—towards the issue of child health and development. Or for some adult problems, such as heart conditions and stroke, it may be possible to focus research efforts on the relationship between childhood conditions or life styles and the prevalence and incidence of these conditions in later life.

On another level, health care delivery research and development efforts could be more clearly focused on children, perhaps using children as a tracer to follow the impact of key federal financing and programmatic initiatives. Such efforts could be enhanced by placing higher priority on financing those investigators who have a clear track record and capability of marketing the results of their investigations in local, state, and national public opinion and decisionmaking arenas. Thus, considerations of funding would be based on some combination of the usefulness, timeliness, and quality of the research with the ability and track record of the investigator in communicating the results through various networks.

Governmental financing also has another constraint that private financing may not have. It is reasonable to expect accountability standards in government financing of research and development efforts that are more rigid than those imposed on philanthropic efforts. Private philanthropy can more appropriately take risks on programs where outcomes are harder to evaluate and benefits distributed over a longer period. Accountability standards and monitoring of these kinds of efforts cannot and should not be held up to the procedural standards of legislative and political accountability that governmental financing appropriately requires.

The 1976 Tax Reform Act modifies the basis under which nonprofit organizations can participate in the legislative process at the national, state, and local levels without losing their tax exemption or their ability to receive tax deductible contributions. The act allows public charities to continue to operate under the current vague test of "substantial" lobbying activity or to elect the new procedure. The new provisions place specific limits on the amounts which can be expected for traditional lobbying of legislatures and regulatory agencies and for grass roots lobbying, i.e., those attempts to influence the general public on legislative matters. Under the new provision, expenditures for lobbying can amount to 20 percent of the first $500,000 of the organization's expenditures in one tax year, plus 15 percent of the second $500,000, 10 percent of the third $500,000 and 5 percent of any expenditures over $1.5 million. Total expenditures cannot exceed $1.0 million in any tax year. The amount permitted for grass roots lobbying cannot exceed one-quarter of the total expenditures.

This new law clearly removes some of the uncertainty associated with most nonprofit organizations engaging in legislative activity. This is an important shift in an era where national health insurance may finally be debated seriously, where legislative amendments in EPSDT and Title V programs are clearly indicated, and where states have the unique opportunity to pioneer legislation responsive to the child health problems, poverty, degenerating environment, nutritional deficits, accidents and psychocultural factors. Judicious support of those advocacy organizations, both national and local in scope, for their legally allowable legislative activities offers the potential for substantial improvement in child health. To ignore or avoid this opportunity is to shortchange our children.

REFERENCES

Alford, R.R. "The political economy of health care: dynamics without change," *Politics and Society* 3 (1972): 127−64.

Altenstetter, C. *Federal Policy Goals Under the Crippled Children's Program and the Responses of the State of Connecticut, 1935−1969.* Working Paper No. 16, Health Policy Project, Yale University Medical School, 18 November 1973.

American Academy of Pediatrics. *Lengthening Shadows.* Evanston, Ill.: American Academy of Pediatrics, 1971.

Bellin, E.G. "Realpolitik on the health care arena: standard setting of professional services," *Am J Public Health* 59 (1969): 820.

Berger, E. *Out Lobbiest Tells Us 'How To' or an Instant Education in Political Effectiveness.* California Children's Lobby, 1973.

Berry, R. *Medical Screening of Children in California: An Evaluation of the Potential Impact of Chapter 1069 and Medi-screen.* Submitted to Willie Brown, California Assembly, xerox, 20 April 1973.

Birch, H.G., and Gussow, J.D. *Disadvantaged Children: Health, Nutrition, and School Failure.* New York: Harcourt, Brace and World, 1970.

Blendon, R.J. "Health panel: need to coordinate private-public funding," *Regional Reporter*, Council on Foundations, June 1976.

Caplin, M.M., and Timbie, R.E. "Legislative activities of public charities," *Law and Contemporary Problems* 29 (Autumn 1975): 183–210.

Children's Defense Fund. Letter to the Department of Health, Education and Welfare, 18 January 1974.

Children's Defense Fund. *Title XX: How to Look at your State's Plan for Social Services: A Child Advocate Checklist.* Mimeograph, 1 August 1975.

Children's Defense Fund. *Doctors and Dollars are Not Enough.* Washington, D.C.: author, 1976.

Children's Foundation. *Women and Children First . . . or Last: Comprehensive Report on the WIC Program and How It Works*, and *Whose Children: National Report on the Food Assistance Needs of Institutionalized Children.* Washington, D.C.: Children's Foundation, April 1975.

Citizen's Board of Inquiry into Hunger and Malnutrition in the United States. *Hunger U.S.A.* Boston: Beacon Press, 1968.

Citizen's Board of Inquiry into Hunger and Malnutrition in the United States. *Hunger U.S.A. Revisited.* Boston: Beacon Press, 1972.

Citizens' Committee for Children of New York. *Change is Overdue.* Report of the Task Force on School Health, New York: Citizens' Committee for Children, April 1974.

Citizens' Committee for Children of New York. *The Best Kept Secret in Town: EPSDT in New York City.* New York: Citizens' Committee for Children, August 1976.

Comptroller General of the United States. *Improvements Needed to Speed Implementation of Medicaid's Early and Periodic Screening, Diagnosis and Treatment Program.* Report to the Congress, MWD–75–13, 9 January 1975.

Davis, K. *National Health Insurance: Benefits, Costs and Consequences.* Washington, D.C.: The Brookings Institution, 1975.

Davis, K. "Medicaid payments and utilization of medical services by the poor," *Inquiry* 13 (1976): 122–35.

Davis, K., and Carney, M.K. *Medical Care for Mothers and Children: The Title V Maternal and Child Health Program.* Unpublished paper, The Brookings Institution, December 1974.

Duff, P.S., and Campbell, A.G.M. "Moral and ethical dilemma in the special-care nursery," *N Engl J Med* 289 (1973): 890–94.

Edelman, M. "An interview with Marian Edelman," *Harvard Educational Review* 44 (1974): 53–74.

Edelman, M. "Coming to the defense of children," *Carnegie Quarterly* 23 (1975): 1–4.

Edelman, P. "The Massachusetts Task Force reports: advocacy for children," *Harvard Educational Review* 43 (1973): 639–53.

Etzioni, A. "Public policy issues raised by a medical breakthrough," *Policy Analysis* 1 (1975): 69–76.

Fleming, H.C. "Riding herd on government programs," *Foundation News* 73 (1972): 5–9.

Foltz, A.M. "The development of ambiguous federal policy: Early and Periodic Screening, Diagnosis and Treatment," *Milbank Mem Fund Q* 53 (1975): 35–39.

Foundation for Child Development. *Annual Report.* New York, 1973.

Foundation for Child Development. *State of the Child: New York City.* New York: Foundation for Child Development, April 1976.

Hill, P. *ABC News Closeup on Children.* American Broadcasting Companies, xerox, 1974.

Iglehart, J.K. "Health report/HEW states' child care record may affect agency's insurance role," *Nat'l J Reports* (1974): 969–74.

Joint Commission on the Mental Health of Children. *Crisis in Child Mental Health: Challenge for the 1970's.* New York: Harper and Row, 1969.

Kagay, C. *The Massachusetts Newborn Health Insurance Proposal.* Harvard Child Health Project research paper, xerox, 1974.

Kahn, A.J., Kamerman, S.B., and McGowan, B.G. *Child Advocacy: Report of a National Baseline Study.* Washington, D.C.: Government Printing Office, 1973.

Katz, J. *Experimentation with Human Beings.* New York: Russell Sage Foundation, 1972.

Kessel, R. "Price discrimination in medicine," *J Law Econ* 1 (1958): 20–53.

Kessner, D.M., et al. *Infant Death: An Analysis by Maternal Risk and Health Care.* Washington, D.C.: Institute of Medicine, 1973.

Kessner, D.M., et al. *Assessment of Medical Care for Children.* Washington, D.C.: Institute of Medicine, 1974.

Kirk, T.R. et al. "EPSDT—one quarter million screenings in Michigan," *Am J Public Health* 66 (1976): 482–84.

Knox, R.A. "Defective newborns: life or death issue," *Boston Globe*, 10 March 1974.

Kotz, N. *Let Them Eat Promises: The Politics of Hunger in America.* Englewood Cliffs, N.J.: Prentice-Hall, 1969.

Marmor, T.R., et al. "The politics of medical inflation," *Journal of Health Politics, Policy and Law* 1 (1976): 69–84.

Marris, P., and Rein, M. *Dilemmas of Social Reform.* New York: Atherton Press, 1967.

Massachusetts Advocacy Center. *State of Danger: Childhood Lead Paint Poisoning in Massachusetts.* Boston: author, 1974.

Massachusetts Advocacy Center (formerly Task Force on Children Out of School). *Suffer the Children: The Politics of Mental Health in Massachusetts.* Boston: author, 1972.

Messenger, K.P. *Child Health in America.* Draft paper for Carnegie Council on Children, New Haven, June 1974.

Meyer, R., and Lingle, B. *Tracer Evaluation of Diagnosis and Treatment of EPSDT Referrals.* Phase I report of Program in Maternal and Child Health. University of Michigan, undated.

Mushkin, S.J. *Consumer Incentives for Health Care.* New York: Millbank Memorial Fund, 1974.

National Academy of Sciences. *Genetic Screening.* Washington, D.C.: National Academy of Sciences, 1975.

Newhouse, J.P. "A model of physician pricing," *Southern Econ J* 37 (1970): 174–83.

Olson, M. *The Logic of Collective Action.* Cambridge, Mass.: Harvard University Press, 1965.

Pekkanen, J. *The American Connection: Profiteering and Politicking in the 'Ethical' Drug Industry.* Chicago: Follett Publishing Company, 1973.

Posner, R.A. "Regulatory aspects of national health insurance plans," *University of Chicago Law Review* 39 (1971): 9.

Redman, C. *The Dance of Legislation.* New York: Simon and Schuster, 1973.

Rivlin, A. *Systematic Thinking for Social Action.* Washington, D.C.: The Brookings Institution, 1971.

Rodham, H. "Children under the law," *Harvard Education Review* 43 (1973): 487–514.

Shay, C.F. *Enforcement Problems in EPSDT.* Health Law Project study, University of California, August, 1975.

Sommers, H.M. *Doctors, Patients and Health Insurance.* Washington, D.C.: The Brookings Institution, 1966.

Steiner, G. *The Children's Cause.* Washington, D.C.: The Brookings Institution, 1976.

Stevens, R., and Stevens, R. "Medicaid: anatomy of a dilemma," *Law and Contemporary Problems* (1970): 348.

Stevens, R., and Stevens, R. *Welfare Medicine in America: A Case Study of Medicaid.* New York: Free Press, 1974.

USDHEW. *Maternal and Child Health Care Programs.* Washington, D.C., October 1966.

USDHEW. *Legislative History of Early and Periodic Screening, Diagnosis and Treatment Program for Children Under Medicaid.* Washington, D.C.: Government Printing Office, 1973.

USDHEW. *A Guide to Screening: EPSDT-Medicaid.* Washington, D.C.: Government Printing Office, 1974.

Wellford, H. *Sowing the Wind.* New York: Grossman Publishers, 1972.

Wennberg, J., and Gittelsohn, A. "Small area variations in health care delivery," *Science* 182 (1973): 1102–08.

Yarmolinsky, A., et al. *Health Policy Study.* Report of the Institute for Governmental Services. Boston: University of Massachusetts, 1975.

※ *Chapter 9*

Allocation of Child Medical
Care Decisionmaking Authority[a]

*Robert Bennett**

The law of child medical care decisionmaking contains
elements often at war with one another. A parent has a
"duty" to provide a child with medical care but is "free"
to withhold consent to it in cases where the care is obviously required. Public intervention is easily accepted in cases where neither
contagion nor near universality of the medical problem would seem
to require it, but quite wrenching in others where the medical justification is much stronger. Confusion abounds about the relevance of
parents' religious beliefs, the maturity of the child, presence of a
threat to life, and a host of other considerations.

Reform is already underway, mostly in the form of state legislative
changes. The law of children more generally is in a state of flux, and
the coming of national health insurance (NHI) may provide further
impetus for rethinking of the allocational rules. This chapter suggests
some guidelines for reform.

Some medical care decisions require difficult judgments, evaluation of risks or of personal considerations. For these the minor's
immaturity justifies some form of parental control. This may take
the form of a veto over all but the most sensitive irreversible personal
decisions. It may require total control of the weighing of medical
risks explained by the practitioner. Likewise, where parental cooperation will be necessary to proper treatment, the parent has an inter-

[a]In this chapter, case and statutory citations and the author's comments will
be carried by number, referring to an end-of-chapter list of "Notes and Cases
Cited." Books and articles will be carried in a separate references list.

est strong enough to justify at least diligent effort at consultation. The child's consent too should be necessary for irreversible personal decisions.

Some procedures are clearly required by a physical condition. Others are of unknown efficacy but harmless. The requirement of parental consent for either category is more a practical hindrance than an aid to practitioner, child, and parent. Lists of such uncontroversial procedures might appropriately be provided by governmental officials.

For those decisions requiring parental involvement it is appropriate to erect an arbitrary age dividing those children who require from those who do not require parental involvement. Anything else is unfair to the doctor. Indeed, if the law does not provide the practitioner with reasonable guidelines, he will undertake to do so himself. The law is predicated on the reconciliation of the interests of others. Without guidelines the practitioner will distort this reconciliation.

Mass public intervention in cases where medical risks and personal considerations are minimal should not dwell as much as it has on a requirement of parental consent. The requirement is probably ignored as much as it is heeded and serves no particularly strong interests of parent or child. If parental involvement is retained in such cases, it should probably take the form of a veto power rather than an affirmative requirement of consent. Particularized intervention, on the other hand, where the parent-child relationship is seriously affected, should be reserved for only the most serious of medical problems.

DECISIONMAKING AUTHORITY: LEGAL ELEMENTS

If the disparate areas of the present law which assign responsibility for child medical care decisionmaking have a common theme, it is parental authority. In each context this parental authority is limited, however, and neither its rationale nor the occasions for its curtailment are consistent across the different areas of the law.

Parental Consent: A "General Rule"

The common law of child medical care decisionmaking is a murky amalgam of tort, contract, and family law concepts. At common law any intentional touching of another's body without the latter's consent constitutes the tort of battery (Prosser, 1971). A surgical operation would be such a touching, and so would the most innocuous physical examination, as long as it involves physical contact [1].

Even an indirect contact, as where a doctor prescribes medication the patient later ingests or applies, would probably suffice (Prosser, 1971).

It was through the operation of the consent element that parents were originally given control over most medical care decisionmaking for their children. Consent by an adult to an intentional touching must be "informed consent." For medical care this means the consent must be based upon "adequate information about the therapy, the available alternatives and the collateral risks" (Waltz and Scheuneman, 1969, pp. 628–29). The child is generally considered incapable of giving informed consent, and often only the parent's approval can render an intentional touching of a child nontortious.

Some authorities approach the capacity of a child to consent to a touching by inquiry into the particular child's qualities of mind. The *Restatement of Torts* urges the following rule:

> If a person whose interest is invaded is at the time by reason of his youth ... incapable of understanding or appreciating the consequences of the invasion, the assent of such a person to the invasion is not effective as a consent thereto (Restatement, 1934, §59(1)) [2].

A few relatively recent court decisions approached the capacity of a child to consent to medical care on such an individualized basis [3]. For reasons difficult to fathom, however, most courts have treated medical, or at least surgical, care differently, enunciating a general rule that "unless there exists an emergency ... or other exceptional circumstances, a surgeon who performs an operation upon a minor without the consent of his parents or guardian, is guilty of a trespass and battery" [4]. Indeed it is often assumed that child consent is not only not sufficient, but not necessary. The parent, in this view, can order medical care over the minor's objection (Ellis, 1974) [5].

The rationales behind this aberrant approach are obscure. In the leading case of *Bonner* v. *Moran* [6] the rule was invoked "[i]n deference to common experience ... that many persons by reason of their youth, are incapable of intelligent decision ..." [7]. The same court drew further support from the rule "that a minor cannot be held liable on his personal contracts. ..."

In an interesting twist, the Michigan Supreme Court in *Bishop* v. *Shurly* [8] harked back to this same body of family law in insisting upon individualized attention to the minor's capacity. The court noted that parents are liable at common law for "necessaries" supplied to their children, and that children had full capacity to contract for such necessaries. Relying on these rules, the court assumed the minor could contract for the necessary of medical care, and thus felt he must be able to consent to it.

This conceptual confusion undoubtedly reflects judicial uncertainty. A requirement of parental consent responds to our perception of the minor's inferior capacity to deal with weighty decisions. In addition, once the decision is made about authority to decide, under our traditional fee-for-service financing system, the doctrine of necessaries results in a parent's being responsible for medical care rendered to a child with the proper authority. If the parents are to bear the economic burden of a decision, there is a certain justice to allowing them to make it. On the other hand, it seems fairly clear that much medical care was and, particularly in "free clinics" around the country, still is being administered at least to teenagers without parental consent (Hofman, 1973). Such behavior is commonly accepted as perfectly reasonable.

What emerges from these conflicting pressures is retention of the general rule but infrequent reliance on it to decide particular cases. The courts have developed a series of exceptions to the rule, and for older children at least, the exceptions simply ate up the rule when a court was faced with the prospect of practitioner liability for conduct viewed as natural and reasonable.

Common Law Exceptions

The reported cases suggest numerous grounds for refusing to apply the general rule of parental consent. In part these are genuine exceptions, well-defined and well justified subclasses of cases where the general rule is held inapplicable. In part, they consist more of a listing of factors upon which the courts rely in varying combinations to refuse to apply the general rule. And in large part they are formulations of a new rule which if openly acknowledged as such would radically restructure the law of child consent to medical care.

Emergencies are recognized as exceptions, not really to the parental consent requirement for children, but to the consent requirement for anyone. If a doctor performs an operation in a true emergency without obtaining consent, the courts find no battery, sometimes reasoning that the doctor was justified in assuming consent by the patient who will normally have been unconscious (Prosser, 1971). When the injured or ill person is a child, however, it appears that courts are more willing to invoke this emergency exception to protect the "life or health" of even conscious children [9]. It seems fairly clear, moreover, that the willingness of courts to find an "emergency" in a child case increases as the age of the conscious and consenting child increases [10].

The oldest child allowed to recover damages in a reported case after an operation to which he personally consented was fifteen years old [11]. Many minors over that age have been denied recovery [12]. This trend in the face of a general rule of parental consent has led many courts and commentators to find an exception to that general rule for "mature" minors or those capable of appreciating the nature and importance of the decision (Pilpel, 1972; Prosser, 1971) [13]. The courts in discussing this exception do not focus on whether the maturity or ability to understand must be present in fact or only reasonably appear to the practitioner to be present. Moreover, the maturity often is relied upon in combination with other factors in court decisions against practitioner liability [14].

Emancipation of a child is a concept inherited from Roman law to adjust a general subordination of children to their parents to a world where some children establish their independence early (Clark, 1968; Katz et al., 1973). In its purest form, if a child is found to be (or to have been) emancipated, he is deemed essentially to have all the legal capacity of a person over the age of majority (Clark, 1968). Emancipation was sometimes said to require the consent of the parent (Katz et al., 1973), but an unusually high degree of independence in fact enhances the chances of a finding of emancipation even without parental agreement (Family Planning, 1974; Parental Consent, 1975). Commonly accepted indications of such independence are marriage, economic independence, separate living arrangements, or abandonment by parents (Pilpel, 1972). A number of states provide for a statutory emancipation proceeding (Family Planning, 1974).

There are no cases specifically dealing with whether a fully emancipated minor is relieved from the parental consent requirement for medical care. But the law's treatment of "mature minors" makes it virtually certain that emancipated minors require no parental consent for medical care (Pilpel, 1972; Pilpel and Zuckerman, 1972) [15].

The emancipation concept has also been applied to children allowed some but not all of an adult's legal capacities. This selective emancipation, when invoked in a medical care situation, as one court has done, seems quite similar to the "exception" for mature minors or those able to appreciate the consequences of their decisions. The language of emancipation, however, might be thought to place more emphasis on acts of release of the child by his parents or on independence of child from parent in fact than on the child's judgment or appearance of maturity.

Courts and commentators have noted other factors as relevant to whether parental consent is necessary for administration of medical care to children. Prosser (1971) notes that the cases allowing teenagers to consent on their own behalf have all involved relatively inconsequential operations. In one leading case holding parental consent necessary, the court noted that the skin graft procedure in question was "so involved in its technique as to require a mature mind to understand precisely what the donor was offering to give" [16]. A more recent decision holding parental consent unnecessary placed explicit emphasis on the ease of understanding the procedure [17].

As a second factor, a few courts have discussed the medical advisability of the treatment. In 1970 the Kansas Supreme Court found parental consent to an operation on a child's finger unnecessary, noting "that the method of repair [of the finger] utilized was the approved surgical treatment and in the best interests of the patient" [18]. In an earlier case the Michigan Supreme Court supported its use of the emergency exception by noting the reasonableness of the doctor's judgment to proceed and the increased suffering that would result if doctors refused treatment whenever they were unable to obtain parental consent [19].

Other factors that courts have noted as important in determining whether parental consent is required include the unavailability or difficulty of locating the parents [20], the likelihood that the parents would have consented if notified [21], the consent of other adult relatives [22], and consultation with other doctors [23]. One court emphasized the fact that the laws of its state allowed minors of the age of the one involved to make other weighty decisions [24].

Finally, a leading case supporting the general rule may have rested not on the rule itself, but on the fact that the operation was performed for the benefit of someone other than the minor patient. *Bonner* v. *Moran* [25] involved a fifteen-year-old who was the oldest child in a reported case whose personal consent was not deemed sufficient to allow a doctor to proceed. The operation, a skin graft, had been performed with the express permission of an adult relative of the donor. Apparently most important in the court's thinking was that the skin graft had been carried on for the benefit of the child's cousin. All the exceptions to the parental consent requirement assumed, according to the court, that "the proposed operation is for the benefit of the child and is done with a purpose of saving his life or limb" [26]. Here, where the operation was "not for the benefit of the person operated on but for another," parental consent was strictly required [27].

Legislative Exceptions
In recent years state legislatures have become increasingly involved in the division between parent and child of the power to decide

medical care questions for the child. To a large extent this has consisted of engrafting exceptions for specific types of medical care onto the common law rule. The legislative approaches, however, have been many and varied.

Following the reduction of the voting age from twenty-one to eighteen in the Twenty-Sixth Amendment to the United States Constitution, several states have reduced the age of majority, most often to eighteen [28]. It seems clear that the capacity to consent to medical care is conferred on all those above the newly defined age. A number of states, including some that lowered the age of majority generally, have specifically lowered the age of consent for medical care. The state of Washington, for instance, lowered the age of majority to eighteen and then for good measure enumerated a number of decisions that persons could make for themselves at that age, including those "in regard to their own body . . . including surgical operations" [29]. A few states have chosen ages as low as fourteen or fifteen for such medical emancipation [30].

A number of states have codified variations of the common law exceptions for emergencies and for emancipated and mature minors [31]. Some states get at the emancipation notion by allowing those minors who have taken some step establishing independence from their parents to make their own medical care decisions. Among the steps mentioned in statutes are marriage, parenthood, pregnancy, and service in the armed forces [32]. A few states allow a minor "living separate and apart from his parents . . . and . . . managing his own financial affairs . . ." [33] to proceed without parental consent, though two states limit this to children fifteen or older [34].

Mississippi law provides the most striking codification of the mature minor exception, freeing from the parental consent requirement an "unemancipated minor of sufficient intelligence to understand and appreciate the consequences of the proposed surgical or medical treatment or procedures" [35]. In a remarkable and unique provision, Mississippi then subordinates the "mature" minor to the doctor, providing that minors able to consent may not "arbitrarily, obstinately or without reasonable medical justification" withhold consent to an operation recommended by a physician [36]. Some states address the "mature minor" problem from the physician's standpoint, allowing him to rely "in good faith upon the representation of the minor" that he is "a minor whose consent alone is effective to medical, dental and health services . . ." [37].

The legislatures have been even more active in adopting exceptions unrelated to the common law pattern. These have focused on specific diseases, conditions, or treatments and allow minors (sometimes with, sometimes without an age limit) to consent to the specific care or procedure. The most common of these provisions, now found almost universally, allows treatment of a minor for venereal disease without a parent's consent [38].

Increasingly common are statutes allowing minors to consent on their own behalf to medical care in connection with contraception or birth control [39]. Other statutory exemptions are for treatment for drug use [40] including alcohol in at least one state [41] and for donation of blood [42].

THE STATE AS DECISIONMAKER

In a variety of circumstances the state acts, not as allocator of child medical care decisionmaking responsibility among private individuals, but as the decisionmaker itself. The most important respect in which these interventions vary, however, is whether they focus initially upon some defined disease or condition on the one hand, or upon an individual child on the other.

Intervention Focusing on Disease or Condition

Immunizations. The most well-established public role in the substance of child medical care decisionmaking is the requirement of immunization against certain contagious diseases. Smallpox vaccinations have long been required for both children and adults [43]. Indeed these requirements are now being abandoned in some states as a result of the success in eliminating the disease to which they no doubt greatly contributed.

Compulsory school attendance laws are often used as the lever by which immunization requirements are enforced. A requirement of smallpox vaccination before a child may enter school has been common for over sixty years, and has been upheld as applied to most youngsters against a variety of legal attacks [44]. More recently immunizations against diphtheria, whooping cough, tetanus, measles, German measles, and polio and tests for tuberculosis have been required by a number of states as a prerequisite to attendance at school [45].

At least five states appear to allow parental objection on any basis [46]. Many allow an exception when immunization is medically contraindicated [47] and the United States Supreme Court has indicated that exemption on medical grounds may be constitutionally required [48]. Several provide for an exemption on religious grounds [49]. Arizona alone requires an affirmative indication of parental consent for immunization [50].

School Screening and Testing. Schools are also increasingly becoming the site (and school attendance laws providing the leverage) for medical screening procedures. Nearly all states condition school enrollment or attendance on such screening [51]. In some a certificate from a family physician may suffice in lieu of a school examination. In some screening is to be done by school or public health officials [52].

The range of required procedures is broad, and in some instances the measures are not really compulsory. Two states screen only for sickle-cell anemia [53]. Three require only vision and hearing screening [54]. The screening examinations in the other states are more extensive, including, for example, checking for "defects of the feet" in Massachusetts [55].

Almost half the states have no specific statutory provision for parental objection to these screening procedures [56]. A number appear to allow parental objection on any basis [57], while a larger number restrict objections to religious reasons and require that they be in writing [58]. California, alone among the states, statutorily requires that parents be notified at the beginning of the school year of the right to object to the screening procedures [59]. Ohio specifically provides that parental consent is necessary for any postscreening treatment [60]. New Hampshire, Rhode Island, New York, and West Virginia, on the other hand, provide that in some circumstances necessary care is to be administered, apparently regardless of parental willingness [61].

Newborn Testing and Screening. Many states also mandate procedures for newborn infants. The most common is a requirement of eyedrops within an hour or two of birth to prevent ophthalmia neonatorum [62]. Apparently only Indiana, New Jersey and North Dakota require diagnosis of the disease before administration of the drops [63]. A minority of states requiring drops defer to parental objection, four on any basis [64], five only on religious grounds [65]. The others with the requirement make no explicit provision for parental objection.

A more recent but now quite common requirement for newborn infants is a test for phenylketonuria (PKU). PKU is a genetically detectable condition which if not treated often leads to severe mental retardation. The condition is quite rare, occurring in about 5.4 infants per 100,000 screened, and it is noncontagious. It is thus somewhat surprising that about 90 percent of all newborn infants in the country are screened for PKU (National Academy of Sciences, 1975). A large number of these are screened in states with laws or regulations mandating testing and making no provision for parental objection on any ground [66].

A number of states do allow parental objection, either on any ground [67], or more commonly for religious reasons [68]. Even in these states, however, it appears that parents are often not informed of the right to object and often learn of the test, if they learn of it at all, only after it has been conducted (National Academy of Sciences, 1975).

Fluoridation of Public Water Supplies. Another prevalent public medical intervention directed at a noncontagious child health problem is fluoridation of public waters. The purpose of fluoridation is to retard tooth decay, particularly for children between six and fourteen years of age [69]. Fluoridation has generated controversy, including a large number of reported court decisions, and thus has provided an extensive body of law on compulsory public medical intervention.

Two states, Connecticut and Ohio, require fluoridation of public water supplies [70]. A number of others deal statutorily with the subject [71]. However, fluoridation has been undertaken—and the power to do so has been upheld—in many communities where the state legislature has remained silent on the question [72].

The large majority of courts to address the problem has upheld the public power to fluoridate the water supply [73]. None found merit to the claim that nontoxic levels of fluoridation unconstitutionally infringed the interests of children because the measures were compulsory or of adults because they were intended to aid children [74]. They uniformly rejected the repeated assertion that compulsory public intervention was permissible only for contagious diseases [75].

The rationales of the court decisions vary. They generally view health as a particularly good reason for public intervention [76], and some find special justification for protection of the health of children generally or of poor children who it is assumed will be less likely to obtain fluoride treatment by voluntary means [77]. In differing degrees, they have placed emphasis upon the seriousness and widespread nature of tooth decay [78], the economies of scale in administering fluoride by treating public water supplies [79], the fact that dangers accompanying mass fluoridation, though real, are minor [80], the unreliability of individual application of fluoride or a substitute [81], and dangers accompanying such individual application.

Communicable Diseases. Finally, almost all states require that certain communicable diseases when discovered be treated and sometimes quarantined. The most common are tuberculosis and venereal disease [82]. The requirements do not focus on children, but they are surely intended to be applicable to them. They contain no provision for parental consent, and thus represent a form of state-mandated treatment of children for specific diseases.

Intervention Focusing on the Child

Each state has some form of statutory proceeding by which a child can be found "neglected" or "dependent" and the parent or guardian deprived of custody (Wald, 1975; Areen, 1975). Sometimes the statute specifically mentions medical inattention or need for medical care as indicative of or constituting neglect. Pennsylvania includes as a definition of a "neglected child" one "whose parent . . . neglects or refuses . . . to provide proper or necessary medical or surgical care, or other care necessary for his or her health, morals or well-being" [83]. Other statutes contain much more general definitions of neglected children, but typically these can easily be read to include those suffering from medical inattention (Wald, 1975; Paulsen, 1966) [84]. California, for instance, includes as a neglected child one "in need of proper and effective parental care or control" [85].

It is difficult to specify what magnitude of medical problem will justify this court intervention. With rare exceptions [86] courts use language as broad as that of the statutes to indicate when intervention will be appropriate. The Illinois Supreme Court used particularly extravagant language: "Neglect . . . is the failure to exercise the care that the circumstances justly demand" [87]. Despite this broad language, when the cases reach appellate courts, intervention is usually limited to situations where the medical inattention poses a serious and rather immediate threat to the life of the child [88]. When medical intervention against the wishes of the parent is authorized in reported court decisions in non-life-threatening situations, other complicating factors are usually present. The parents' objection is not always clear cut, or one parent may approve [89]. More important, however, medical neglect or the need for medical care may be only part of a more complex pattern serving as a justification for public intervention [90].

Usually the child's views are not mentioned, apparently because not known or not deemed relevant. In a significant exception to this pattern the Supreme Court of Pennsylvania remanded for consideration of a fourteen-year-old's views on whether an operation should be performed to correct a non-life-threatening curvature of his spine, when the child's parent refused permission for necessary blood transfusions [91]. On remand the child opposed the operation, and the supreme court affirmed the lower court's refusal to order it [92]. The case thus clearly stands for the relevance of at least a teenage child's view, but in neither opinion did the Supreme Court of Pennsylvania indicate that such a view would be determinative.

A final consideration occasionally entering into a court's decisional calculus is whether the condition will remain remediable when the child reaches the age of majority. In a leading New York case, the court placed explicit emphasis upon the later ability of the child to undertake the operation [93]. The life threatening cases are, by definition, those for which time may well foreclose the decision to proceed.

The limited circumstances in which judges publish opinions ordering medical intervention over the parents' objections should not lead to the conclusion that the broad statutory and case language defining permissible circumstances for intervention is paid no heed. To the contrary, many commentators have noted that much more medical intervention takes place than ever reaches the pages of law reports (Wald, 1975; Comment, 1955; Council of Judges, 1968). Interviews with those familiar with neglect and dependency proceedings confirm that a great deal of medical intervention is based on neglect. Sometimes the intervention is formalized in court proceedings, but even more frequently it is not. A large proportion of it is in non-life-threatening situations.

Recent Constitutional Developments
The challenges to state authority to immunize and to fluoridate water have yielded constitutional decisions broadly affirming state authority. Until recently parental control vis-à-vis the child went largely unchallenged on constitutional grounds. The national controversy surrounding abortion, however, has now yielded a series of decisions dealing with the parent-child conflict on a constitutional plane [94]. In 1976 the United States Supreme Court struck down a Missouri requirement of parental consent to abortion unless "necessary in order to preserve the life" of the pregnant minor [95]. The 1975 decision of the Washington Supreme Court in State v. Koome, which reached a similar conclusion, is particularly illuminating because of its discussion of the allocation of child medical care decision-making authority in terms of the interests and roles of those involved [96].

The pregnant minor in the Koome case was sixteen years old and unmarried. She was a ward of the juvenile court, and neither her court appointed guardian, Catholic Children's Services, nor her parents would consent to an abortion she desired. Dr. Koome performed the abortion anyway and was prosecuted under a Washington criminal statute allowing termination of a pregnancy of a woman "if married and residing with her husband or unmarried and under the age of eighteen years, [only] with the prior consent of her husband or legal guardian respectively . . ." [97].

The state advanced various arguments to justify its invasion of the minor woman's right to privacy. First it pointed to the possibility of juvenile court intervention if parent or guardian was arbitrary. Washington is a state, however, that has made it particularly clear that court intervention in medical decisions should be rare [98]. The court saw juvenile court intervention as cumbersome when available, available primarily in life-threatening situations, and hence of little solace to an aggrieved minor [99].

Next the state attempted to justify the parental consent requirement as serving interests in " 'support of the family unit and parental authority' " and "an adequately reflective and informed decision on the part of the minor woman" [100]. The court acknowledged "the family structure" as "fundamental" and "parental prerogatives" as entitled to "considerable legal deference," but saw use of the criminal law as "both futile and manifestly unwise" when a minor had become pregnant and was on the verge of parenthood herself [101].

Likewise the court acknowledged the legitimacy of assuring reflective and informed decisionmaking, but questioned whether parental decisionmaking, possibly "colored by personal religious belief, whim, or even hostility to . . . [the child's] best interests" [102] could always add appreciably to physician-patient decisionmaking, given the physician's professional responsibilities and common law duty adequately to inform the patient. The court suggested that a requirement of "parental *consultation* might be permissible, but could not allow the state's " 'conclusive presumption' that the parents' judgment is better than the pregnant woman's" [103].

The *Koome* case also provided an interesting discussion of the distinctions highlighted by the statute between those over eighteen and those under, those married and those unmarried, and between abortion and other medical care decisions. Age distinctions, the court acknowledged, are inevitably arbitrary because the capacities for independent choice they are intended to reflect come incrementally, not suddenly.

> Parental authority wanes gradually as a child matures; it does not suddenly disappear at adulthood. Similarly, the ability to competently make an important decision, such as to have an abortion, develops slowly and at different rates in different individuals [104].

Nonetheless the court saw arbitrary age distinctions as in general "permissible, perhaps even where important rights are affected, because . . . inevitable" [105]. In the case before it, the court viewed an age cut-off as less justified. The biological "age of fertility provides a practical minimum age requirement for consent to abortion, reducing the need for a legal one" [106].

The court also questioned marriage as sufficiently indicative of mature judgment to justify the statute's distinction between married and unmarried women, requiring the latter but not the former to obtain parental consent to an abortion. Indeed the court noted that the distinction "encourages pregnant minors, whose parents withhold consent, to marry solely in order to terminate an unwanted pregnancy" [107].

And finally the court saw little merit in distinguishing abortion from other medical care decisions for parental consent purposes. The opinion rather exaggerated the minor's legal independence in medical care decisionmaking generally: "A doctor competently performing any other type of surgery on a consenting minor runs virtually no risk of even civil liability because of the absence of parental consent" [108]. But on the assumption that the minor had such independence generally, the court could see no basis for a strict parental consent requirement for an abortion decision which the United States Supreme Court had earlier characterized as "inherently, and primarily, a medical decision" [109].

DECISIONMAKING AUTHORITY RECONSIDERED: AN INTEREST ANALYSIS

The Washington Supreme Court surely exaggerated when it said that "a doctor competently performing any . . . surgery [besides abortion] on a consenting minor runs virtually no risk of even civil liability because of the absence of parental consent." It would be more accurate to say that a lawyer representing a doctor who has competently performed an operation on a minor without parental consent has a good shot, after much litigation effort and expense, at convincing an open-minded court that his client should not be held liable if the patient suffers injury. Any scarcity of cases holding doctors liable for procedures conducted on minors without parental consent probably reflects doctor unwillingness to undertake such procedures, the absence of injury in most treatments, and the fact that parents expect less deference than the law allows them. Certainly little credit is due to common law court decisions.

It is remarkable how out of touch with reality is the law on this subject. When doctors do proceed without parental consent, the law seldom finds them to have acted improperly. But in states where courts have shown themselves receptive to consent by a mature minor on his own behalf, there is reason to believe that doctors strictly insist on parental consent anyway, or dispense with it in the belief they are violating the law.

Ohio, as we have seen, is a state with a major court decision allowing mature minors to consent for themselves [110]. Yet in interviews with a number of Cleveland doctors and hospital personnel, I found a unanimous impression that the law forbade medical touchings of a minor without parental consent, with only narrowly defined exceptions. A 1974 memorandum of the Cuyahoga County Hospital and the Cleveland Metropolitan General Hospital reinforces this impression. It states: "In all cases other than drugs or venereal disease involving minors, we are legally required to obtain written consent from parent or legal guardian." Besides the exceptions for drug problems and venereal disease, the memorandum suggests the availability of an emergency exception. It also deals with the possibility of consent by a minor female to procedures necessary for child delivery if her parent or guardian is unavailable. It allows any married woman to consent on her own behalf and a mother of any age to consent to circumcision of her male child [111]. The memorandum is almost totally oblivious to the Ohio decision recognizing that a minor may be sufficiently mature to consent on his own behalf [112].

Such disparity between the law and the actual practice of doctors and hospitals should provide a warning. The recent statutory activity also suggests that something may be amiss with the common law approach. That statutory ferment also makes it easier to evaluate the broader problem largely free of the analytical framework provided by the common law. Reform then may more freely be based on an evaluation of the interests of the parties most directly affected by the rules of child medical care decisionmaking authority—the child, the parents, the practitioner and the state.

Interests of the Child

The child is at the center of the dilemma. It is his health and body which are involved, and hence his interest which should be given greatest weight in any balance of interests. The norm in our culture is to allow adults largely free rein in weighing their medical interests. For the child, however, the decisionmaking role is assigned to others.

The most important reason is the child's diminished capacities. Undoubtedly there is an age below which no child is qualified to make any medical decision for himself. The newborn infant cannot even communicate about whether to be circumcised or have a PKU test. Even as the ability to communicate develops, the young child requires a surrogate decisionmaker. The "childish" negative reaction to unpleasant procedures—bad tasting medicine, injections, stitches for a wound, or just a visit to the dentist—is almost universally perceived as wrong by the adult world and perhaps even by children. Left to their own devices, most children would likely ignore doctors through ignorance or indifference. Once in the practitioner's domain, the child has the additional burden that he knows little about his physical problems or medical history. What he does know he may find hard to express.

During the preschool years the question of whether medical care should be sought at the behest of an adult other than parent occasionally arises, probably most frequently in emergencies. From the time a child develops a life outside the home environment, perhaps starting with entry into school, the possibility of child initiative in seeking medical care for himself or resistance to it if sought on his behalf becomes more and more real.

From school age, five or six, until eighteen, the usual age of majority, an intricate weave of complexities emerges. The child's intellectual capacities and his likelihood of seeking medical care on his own if the law were to interpose no obstacle increase gradually, and at different rates for different individuals. In general, beginning with adolescence, the ability "to anticipate and evaluate future consequences" so important to many medical care decisions begins to develop (State Intrusion, 1974). Some commentators would put the age of capacity for fully independent judgment at sixteen to eighteen (State Intrusion, 1974, 1395–96). In his dissent in *Wisconsin* v. *Yoder* Justice Douglas placed at fourteen the age psychologists and sociologists substantially agree "that the . . . [child's] moral and intellectual maturity . . . approaches that of the adult" [113]. Capacity fed by experience, however, keeps developing or at least changing, respecting neither the law's age of majority nor any other arbitrary age cut-off for any or all individuals.

The inappropriate reactions of the young child are generally negative. As the growing child becomes more independent of his family he grasps the potential of medical science. The possibility of unwise child refusal of medical care is then joined by the possibility of unwise child request for medical care.

Allocation of medical care decisionmaking authority also becomes part of the age-old struggle for authority between parent and growing child. If one concludes that parental authority in general is in the child's interest, the law might opt for parental authority over medical care decisions not because the child is incapacitated or the parent particularly capable but because subordination to parents or family cohesiveness serves other developmental purposes (Areen, 1975; Parental Consent, 1975).

Growing children increasingly find themselves in differing situations with regard to the availability of the parental surrogate decisionmaker. While most children may remain in the parental fold through their teenage years and even communicate well with their parents, many do not. A recent report of the Senate Judiciary Committee indicates that "over a million children leave home without parental consent each year" and that in New York City "43 percent . . . are in the eleven to fourteen age category" (Senate Committee, 1974). It seems certain that many more, while living with their parents, do not have the kind of continuing attention by parents to medical questions which is accepted as the middle-class norm. And even among those children at home under their parents' attentive eyes, parental decisionmaking may be impaired for at least some medical questions because the child is unwilling to communicate about a problem (Pilpel, 1972).

Uncontroversial Procedures. As the child's capacities grow, the differences among medical procedures take on added significance. A medical procedure may be quite uncontroversial in that it is harmless and widely accepted as efficacious for the discovery, prevention, cure, or amelioration of disease or clear disability. An external physical examination when signs of illness are present is one example. But so are tests of many sorts and administration of medicines whose effectiveness and safety are widely accepted. Some of the publicly required procedures for children are uncontroversial: eyedrops, PKU tests, seeing and hearing tests, fluoridation of water. Indeed, it seems likely that the large majority of primary care procedures conducted on children are quite uncontroversial in this sense. It is true that a growing body of medical opinion questions the efficaciousness of some widely accepted procedures. For present purposes I would classify such procedures as uncontroversial as long as the risks attendant to them are minimal.

But a large class of medical procedures, although medically uncontroversial, have important physical consequences for the patient so that his involvement in the decision is important, not so much because it helps him make the decision but because it helps him live with it once made [114]. Amputation of a limb or any painful operation, a requirement of sustained inactivity, and ingestion of debilitating medicines when clearly required medically are examples.

For these medically uncontroversial decisions an adult patient seldom has anything to add to the decisionmaking process save agreement itself. The medical practitioner is the real decisionmaker. For the medically uncontroversial decision for a child, the serious problems are getting the child to the medical practitioner and obtaining his cooperation, not obtaining some form of appropriate consent by another once he is there.

Controversial Procedures.   On the other hand, a procedure may be medically controversial. Its efficaciousness or harmlessness may be a good deal less than certain or it may have mixed good and bad results where the place to strike the balance is not medically so clear. Finally, a procedure, whether medically controversial or not, may be personally controversial. Where there are religious objections to any or all procedures, for the person involved the procedure is personally controversial. For most people, however, personally controversial decisions are those where disease or disability is not involved, but where a doctor's art can further some other personal goal. A cosmetic change, a sex change, abortion of a fetus, and access to birth control devices or tranquilizers are prominent examples.

Children share with us all an interest in the integrity of their bodies. The degree of this interest, however, varies enormously. In the United States Supreme Court's original abortion decision, some of those challenging the states' restrictions asserted "an unlimited right to do with one's body as one pleases," but this the Court "refused to recognize" [115]. So surely the individual's interest in a medical care decision diminishes as the medical considerations dominate and provide a clear answer. Even for such procedures, the law requires the consent of an adult able to give or withhold it before a doctor may proceed. In assaying the degree of personal interest in a decision, however, it would seem that as the decision becomes medically or personally controversial the individual's interest in making it for himself increases, and particularly if the individual would shun rather than welcome a serious invasion of bodily integrity.

The medically or personally controversial decisions are not all equally controversial. The strength of the individual's interest in making the decision will vary along a number of dimensions, including the degree to which the medical judgment is clear, the short-term pain, discomfort, and physical invasion associated with the decision; and most important, the long-term nonhealth consequences of the decision. An extreme example of the last is the abortion decision, where the long-term nonhealth consequences of a decision not to abort are overwhelming [116], and of one to abort are very significant. When these elements loom large, and particularly where a given decision is irreversible but the opposite decision is not, the usefulness of a surrogate becomes clearest, but the individual's interest in making the controversial decision for himself, even if he is a child, reaches its peak [117].

Interests of the Parent

The principal role of the parent is as surrogate decisionmaker for the child. Our typical nuclear family structure is not found in all human society, but it is so pervasive in ours that it is obvious to turn to it for an alternate decisionmaker when a child is deemed disabled from making a decision [118]. The nuclear family laden with parental obligations and parental authority is so fundamental an institution that parents expect, and are accorded, rights with regard to children quite apart from their roles as surrogate decisionmakers. Before turning to the perplexing topic of the parent's substantive interest, however, it is important to note that appropriateness of the parent as surrogate decisionmaker is largely limited to what I have called medically or personally controversial decisions. Much of medical care decisionmaking involves technical judgments for which most parents are almost totally ill equipped. They rely upon doctors and other experts for such decisions for themselves and probably even more so for their children. Once they make decisions to seek medical advice for their children, as a practical matter their own decisionmaking role becomes minimal. Indeed the law articulates for them a general duty to provide adequate medical care for their children which probably includes most of what I call medically and personally uncontroversial care, if as a practical matter it is available.

The importance of the parents' role as surrogate decisionmaker diminishes as the age, ability, and independence of the child increases. Probably many parents gradually accede to their children's wishes about medical care, as about other things, as the child matures. The common law exception to the parental consent requirement for mature minors or those able to appreciate the nature of a decision mirrors this assumption. The exception for emancipated minors suggests further that when children have achieved independence from their parents in other respects, parental authority over medical care judgments is increasingly difficult to maintain, whether or not the decision is one ideally made by the parent. Any gain in wisdom of the decision that might result from parental decisionmaking is outweighed by the changed expectations of parent and emancipated child.

One consideration seldom addressed explicitly is that a parent may have a conflict of interest in making a medical care decision for a child [119]. Under the prevalent fee-for-service system the parent generally bears the financial burden of seeking medical care for his child [120]. He thus may have a bias against such care, as he may against expensive forms of medical care. This conflict will presumably be removed or lessened to the extent the government assumes medical care costs under some form of national health insurance. In any case, it is offset in part by legal and moral duties to provide care, and similar conflicts are so integral a part of the parent-child relationship that this one seems impossible to eliminate or ameliorate very much by any other means.

Other forms of conflict are more troublesome. Increasingly parents are being presented with choices of whether to aid one child at the expense of another, as by the donation of a kidney. In such cases, a judge is often asked to intercede because the parent's conflict of interest makes him an inappropriate decisionmaker (Baron et al., 1975) [121]. In the reported cases, the judge searches for some benefit to the would-be patient before ratifying a parental decision to proceed.

The cases where parents have strongly held religious views might also be viewed as posing conflicts of interest [122]. The parent is then acting as decisionmaker by weighing his own religious interests against the child's health. The problem with this view of the matter is that all parents have views about child rearing which color their judgments. If religious beliefs are felt to present conflicts of interest, so might any view which is deemed by someone else to interfere with a rational assessment of the child's interest. Moreover, religious views, unlike other views on child rearing, are accorded specific constitutional protection and thus might be thought relatively immune from consideration as a basis for diminishing the parental role.

Especially in light of this constitutional protection, it is striking how uniform the courts have been in overriding parents' religiously based objections to clearly required medical care [123]. These cases usually involve the extreme choice of life or death, but I suspect that courts have found solution somewhat easier because the parents' religious views so starkly interfere with their primary role as surrogate decisionmaker for the child. Certain of the recent cases on abortions for minor children have relied in part on this parental conflict of interests [124].

The parent's role as surrogate decisionmaker is further confused by his substantive interest in his relationship with the child. The legitimacy and nature of such a substantive interest is productive of debate and confusion (Wald 1975). In particular the question of whether parents have a "property right to their children" has received more discussion than it is worth. The property right notion survives from a day when children were of economic value, and a parent's right to his child's wages, still given lip service today (Clark, 1968), was a right of importance. Whether a parent has a "property right" in his children today is nothing more nor less than a matter of definition. It is reasonably clear that a parent has certain interests in regard to his children which the state will respect and protect against interference by others. If this be a property right, then the parent's right in his child survives. If a property right denotes something approaching complete dominion, however, then whatever may be said of its history, parents today enjoy no such "right" in their children.

Much that is said on the law of children would seem to deny the existence of a parental substantive interest. The most frequently encountered standard in dealing with children is their "best interests," which seems to suggest that theirs and not their parents' interests are to be taken into account. This notion is fed by cases awarding primary custody of a child to one parent where the two parents are separating and each is seeking custody. On the assumption that the interests of the two parents are of equal weight it is plausible literally to search only for the "best" interests of the child [125]. This does not mean, however, that it is either appropriate or feasible to consider only the child in cases where two parental interests are not so neatly cancelled out. The "best interests" standard in such contexts is awkward and misleading [126]. A child cannot be declared neglected and taken from his parents, for instance, "merely because his condition might be improved by changing his parents" (Mnookin, 1973) [127]. Even when parents are in dispute over custody of the child, the parent not awarded custody is usually given some rights of visitation without any searching inquiry into whether that would optimally serve the interests of the child [128].

Perhaps the clearest indication of some such substantive parental interest is *Stanley* v. *Illinois* [129]. In *Stanley* the father of an illegitimate child sought custody after the death of the mother with whom the child had been living. The state law gave the father of an illegitimate child no right of custody, but the United States Supreme Court held that he was entitled to a hearing on his fitness before custody could be awarded to someone else. The Court found "Stanley's interest in retaining custody of his children is cognizable and substantial" [130]. The controversy in *Stanley* arose only because the child was illegitimate. The unstated assumption of both sides was that parents of legitimate children have an "important" interest in their relationship with their children [131].

The contours of this parental right are much more difficult to ascertain than its existence. In his classic article, Roscoe Pound said:

> Parents may and do claim not merely the society of their children, as ministering a social pleasure, but the custody and control of them, especially while they are of tender years, and the power to dictate their training, prescribe their education and form their religious opinions. (Pound, 1916, p. 181).

Court cases reflect many of these elements of parental interest, but they are so often hedged in by qualifications in the interests of children or others that they are difficult to define much more precisely. Indeed, until the recent emergence of children as independent legal actors [132], the courts listened to parents alone and seldom had occasion to articulate whether the interests they were evaluating were those of parent or child.

It is clear, however, that the state can and does limit the substantive parental interest in major ways. Probably the most dramatic of these is the compulsory education requirement. Through these laws the state severely limits the power of parents to "prescribe . . . education" and at the same time takes a large portion of the child's time from parental discretion. While the courts have recently placed some procedural restrictions on the ways the public school system may proceed in carrying out the educational task, the state has wide leeway in prescribing a curriculum even for private school systems [133].

Neither commentators nor courts have spoken of any parental interest in the integrity of a child's body. Parents have a privilege to administer corporal punishment to a child as long as it does not reach the level of "abuse" (Paulsen, 1966). This almost surely is an adjunct of the parent's authority to act in the child's interest, not the parent's own. Battery of a child by a person other than the parent is invasion solely of the child's interests, unless as a collateral matter some protected interest of the parent is affected. The power of corporal punishment seems well accepted as an adjunct of the public school system [134], though recent court decisions have begun to accord procedural rights to students before corporal punishment may be administered [135].

It thus seems fairly clear that administration of medical care does not usually invade a separable substantive interest of the parent. At the same time, if as a consequence of administration of medical care, the ongoing relationship of parent and child is ruptured or substantially distorted, then a parent's interest in the "social pleasure," "custody," and "control" of the child would be invaded. In two old cases the schools had been found to go too far when they required students to be at home studying between 7:00 and 9:00 P.M. or to wear uniforms at home [136]. Similarly, any procedure requiring hospitalization or parental supervision of a child would interfere to a degree with this parental interest in the relationship.

Interests of the State

The state also acts in a dual capacity with regard to the child, as a surrogate decisionmaker and in furtherance of a collective interest of society. While it is possible to isolate examples of state action in these separate roles, the roles often become confused.

When the state interferes directly in the life of a family, as in finding of neglect, it seems reasonably clear that the state is displacing the parent in his role of surrogate decisionmaker but usually doing nothing more. The decision should at the least be uncontroversial and be prompted by a serious health problem. In reported cases the courts usually defer to parental decisions on medically controversial decisions [137].

At the other extreme, society has an obvious interest in arresting the spread of contagion which has struck a child quite apart from the effect on the child himself. State intervention is justified because the decision of whether to seek treatment has effects external to the decisionmaker—"externalities" or "neighborhood" effects.

The possibility of contagion is an extreme case of externalities in medical care decisions. Very few decisions of any sort are free of all externalities. It is plausible to argue that an uneducated child harmfully affects others around him. Likewise a sick but not contagious child has effects on his parents and directly or indirectly on others in the society. As the society accepts economic responsibility for the poor and helpless, actions by children that make their futures less secure tend to impose externalities on public finances. If national health insurance becomes a reality, this external effect of medical care decisions will be felt earlier and more frequently.

Other commonly accepted justifications for state intervention are inadequate information by private decisionmakers and related concerns of efficiency. If private decisionmakers lack adequate information about costs and benefits of a medical care decision, but would be overwhelmingly likely to make a certain decision if they had the information, the state might provide that information or simply impose the decision. Even if the presumed private reaction to information is not clear cut, public action may be less expensive than multiple private actions, in solely monetary terms or in terms that take into account costs in time and effort. Both of these justifications are advanced in support of fluoridation decisions or PKU testing.

There are those who do not insist on one of these justifications for state intervention. Courts sometimes talk of a public interest in the society of the future [138], and a societal interest in assuring a minimum of education or housing or health or nutrition is commonly asserted quite apart from concerns of neighborhood effects or efficiency or an inadequately informed citizenry (Pound, 1916). In the original abortion decision, the Supreme Court found a state interest in the health of the mother allowing the state to regulate abortions starting with the second trimester of pregnancy [139]. Some such purely "paternalistic" motivation may explain intervention on behalf of neglected children, but it is an even more important element when children are given eye and ear testing as a prerequisite to school attendance or in the compulsory school system itself.

When state intervention occurs, it is seldom accompanied by any detailed inquiry into external effects or efficiencies, and hence the motivation is difficult to trace. It does seem possible to conclude, however, that as serious external effects or the efficiency of public action increases, so does the case for public intervention. In addition, there is an inevitable tradeoff between state authority and private autonomy. As the medical judgment becomes less controversial, the private interest in making the decision recedes, and the case against public intervention is weakened.

Public intervention will usually be for noncontroversial procedures. As I indicated earlier, there is probably a constitutional requirement that medically contraindicated procedures not be coercively performed. The usual problem with public intervention is not that it presents medical danger for the child but that it may interfere with parent and child interests in their relationship.

With this in mind the form of public intervention becomes as significant as its substance. Compulsory medical testing in public schools, fluoridation, and PKU testing are forms of public intervention that interfere minimally with the parent-child relationship. The intervention is largely hidden from the parent and both medically and personally uncontroversial. In none of the cases is there any rupture or significant distortion of the ongoing relationship.

A much more remarkable form of public intervention is the compulsory schooling requirement where the parent-child relationship is severely ruptured. Probably the wide acceptance of compulsory schooling can only be explained by the economic and child-rearing functions it has come to serve.

At the other extreme is public intervention through neglect proceedings which may drastically, abruptly, and offensively rupture the parent-child relationship. It is clear that this form of intervention requires much greater justification than a more passive and universal one, and it is little wonder that courts in reported decisions usually limit such intervention in medical cases to life or death situations.

The Medical Practitioner's Interests

If the doctor or other medical practitioner has a substantive interest in child medical care decisionmaking, it is to see that good care is administered. The courts have occasionally suggested some such professional interest [140].

For the most part, however, the practitioner plays a decisionmaking role, very large in medically uncontroversial decisions, but quite important in medically and even personally controversial decisions. In performing this role the practitioner has great strengths, some weaknesses, and an abiding interest in the form of the governing legal rules.

The doctor's strengths are his expert training and knowledge and his professional responsibility. They have combined to make him and his satellite practitioners the de facto decisionmakers in most child medical care decisions once they become involved.

The doctor's weaknesses are too often overlooked. Under our current fee-for-service system of financing medical care the practitioner has an economic conflict of interest in virtually every decision he makes. His economic incentive is to favor expensive treatment and extensive care. If doctors are reimbursed under national health insurance on a piecework basis this conflict of interest may become even more serious. At the present time the parent with whom the doctor must deal acts to some degree to check the doctor's desire for more and more expensive care. The parent's incentive to act in this way would be reduced or eliminated if the government reimbursed for care administered. It is an open question whether government can act effectively as a check on medically unnecessary care. If national health insurance were to reimburse on a capitation basis, on the other hand, the doctor's incentive would be to provide less and less expensive care.

The doctor may have other, sometimes more serious, conflicts of interest. An intern or other young doctor still feeling he is learning may favor treatment to enhance his understanding of a disease or condition. A doctor engaged in research may have incentives to favor or disfavor treatment to enhance his research goals. In these and perhaps other noneconomic ways professional considerations may get in the way of medical judgments.

A doctor may also tend to treat too many problems on a technical basis. He may be reluctant to acknowledge that personal considerations appropriately play a role in many medical care decisions. And he may feel that medically controversial judgments are for him rather than the patient.

In fulfilling his decisionmaking role the medical care practitioner has an interest in receiving reasonably clear directions on what is lawful. Beyond clarity, his professional interest in providing medically uncontroversial care gives him an interest in limiting the nonmedical restrictions on his freedom of action.

A PRESCRIPTION FOR THE LAW OF CHILD
MEDICAL CARE DECISIONMAKING

Much of the law of child medical care decisionmaking reflects the pervasive tension in the law between the necessity to generalize and the desire to particularize. The use of the law of battery suggests an interest in bodily integrity which either is invaded or not. The requirement of parental consent suggests an ability to evaluate an invasion of that interest which a person possesses or does not. Obviously neither of those sharp distinctions reflects reality, and it is not-surprising to find exceptions to the general rule. The law's generalizations are under assault from life's variations.

The emphasis on battery and the requirement of informed consent have proved unusually resistant to the common sense with which life usually leavens the common law. The principal reason probably is that the proper legal status of children here as elsewhere remains elusive. A second reason perhaps is that the battery and consent emphases are so foreign to the interest and roles that the law should here be serving that the common law needs radical restructuring rather than the gradual adjustment by which it usually molds itself to the interest it serves. One type of PKU test, for instance, is performed on a baby's wet diaper. Another requires a blood sample. The latter is a battery, which the former is not, though the interests of parent, child, practitioner, and the state in a test are essentially independent of this legal difference.

My review of the interests and roles of the four actors in child medical care decisions reveals that the common law to date has served none of them very well. The interest most nearly served by a requirement of parental consent would be the medical practitioner's. The law owes him a high degree of predictability. A universal requirement of parental consent would provide it by telling him he cannot touch a person under the age of majority. At the same time such a requirement would often interfere with his interest in dispensing needed care. In any case the law has been unable to provide the practitioner with the certainty he craves, because the interests of others have created pressures for exceptions to the parental consent requirement. The exceptions—for emergencies, for mature and emancipated minors—if available in the jurisdiction give the practitioner little guidance in specific cases. The other factors that the courts occasionally find relevant are so diffuse and unpredictable as to leave the practitioner entirely at sea.

The practitioner's response has been to reintroduce predictability by insisting on parental consent anyway (Parental Consent, 1975), thus frustrating those interests to which the law was responding when it erected its exceptions. It is the almost universal understanding among medical care personnel that the law forbids them to touch anyone under the age of majority without parental consent. They usually recognize only limited exceptions, such as those for emergencies, as well as the increasing number of statutory exceptions. And this is so even in a state like Ohio where it represents a substantial misunderstanding of the common law rules.

The parent's interest in decisionmaking authority and in the "social pleasure" of his child might also be thought to be served by a parental consent requirement. For what I have called uncontroversial decisions, however, this interest is only minimally at stake, if at all. The parent labors under a legal obligation to provide such care to the child; in a general way the law has already taken the substance of such decisions from the parent's discretion. To be sure, preserving the form of parental decisionmaking might enhance parental authority generally. Most uncontroversial decisions, however, will be made with parental involvement regardless of the law's requirements. Parental financing assures this now, but even under national health insurance the nuclear family with parents in charge would remain a basic decisionmaking institution. It is when parental authority is already interrupted by a child's attendance at school, care by other adults, or independence from parents—or in the presence of some emergency—that the questions of uncontroversial decisionmaking without parents will arise. In such cases the incremental jeopardy to parental interests from dispensing with the requirement usually would be minimal.

In some cases of uncontroversial decisions parental interest will more clearly be at stake. Parental cooperation may be necessary for treatment. The home life of the child may be interrupted or distorted. Again in such cases the parents will usually be involved in the decisionmaking because that is the way most families operate apart from the law's requirements. If the parent is not present at the outset, moreover, good medical practice in such cases surely requires diligent effort by the practitioner to involve him. If these nonlegal facts of life have not produced parental decisionmaking, and the medically indicated course is clear, the parental interest in involvement should give way to the child's interest in good care.

The child also arguably has interests served by the requirement of parental consent. These are his specific interests in correct decisions and his more general interest in a regime of parental authority. Again, however, for medically and personally uncontroversial decisions these child interests are served only minimally by the requirement. Indeed, the child interest in correct decision is often undermined by the parental consent requirement. Medically uncontroversial care is all too frequently delayed and made more costly while practitioners, relatives, police, neighbors, and others search for temporarily unavailable parents. The interest is frustrated altogether for thousands of youngsters who seek no care because of the parental consent requirement.

There usually will be no societal interest at stake apart from the interests of the other actors. In certain instances, however, it seems that the requirement of parental consent undermines independent state interests by inhibiting a child from seeking treatment. Thus, the statutory exceptions for venereal disease were surely intended to remove inhibitions on children obtaining treatment and were justified by society's interest in arresting the spread of the diseases. Exceptions for abortions and birth control devices might be justified in part by the interest of society in avoiding the externalities caused by children who desire such treatment but are deterred from seeking it due to unwillingness to involve their parents.

It is thus painfully clear that for uncontroversial care the parental consent requirement is often useless or counterproductive. One should not, however, replace one unrealistic generalization with another. There are numerous medical procedures which doctors should not perform without parental consent, or at least not without a diligent effort at parental involvement. Where the procedure or test is medically or personally controversial, the child's interest in correct decisions is usually served by involvement of a surrogate decisionmaker sensitive to the child's needs. Where the parent-child relationship will be interrupted or distorted by the procedure, parental and child interests in the relationship are affected. And where the procedure is aided by parental cooperation, both child and doctor will be served by parental involvement.

Even in such cases, however, there will be times when a requirement of parental consent does more harm than good. If a parent has a serious conflict of interest, as in the sibling transplant cases or instances where overriding religious beliefs dominate judgment, it is questionable whether he should be allowed alone to weigh the medical and personal considerations on behalf of the child. When the parent favors treatment, perhaps the present procedure of requiring a judicial order is the best that can be done under difficult circumstances. When the parent resists treatment, usually for religious reasons, the law is already ambivalent. Parents have a duty of care, and if they grossly abuse it their religious objections stand as no excuse [141]. If they have not sufficiently inculcated their religious objections in a child who finds his way to a doctor and receives medically satisfactory treatment, the law could do worse than allowing the matter to rest there.

In other cases, the minor may not want to confide in his parents or after consultation may wish to proceed over their objection. Then the case for allowing him to proceed is strong if the reason for consultation is solely the effect on the parent-child relationship and not the controversial nature of the decision. If the decision is uncontroversial and the doctor is satisfied that he can substitute in a medically acceptable way for any parental cooperation, he should be allowed to proceed with only child consent after parent consultation or good-faith attempt to convince the child to allow consultation. In such cases, the child's medical interest is pitted against the parent's interest in not having a relatively mild interference with the relationship by nongovernmental actors, child and practitioner. In particular this doctor-child decisionmaking is greatly to be preferred to state rupture of the parent-child relationship, which may on occasion be the alternative.

The difficult questions that remain are when the problem is medically or personally controversial and the child is at odds with the parents, either wishing to proceed with a procedure or resisting one. It is in those rare cases that the question of whether parent or child should resolve difficult medically related problems on behalf of the child is posed in its starkest form. Should a child wear glasses or contact lenses, obtain an abortion, change sexes, have a breast enlarged or nose reshaped, take medication with mixed effects, or undertake a risky operation? Here, until developments in psychology tell us more about children's judgment, the dangers for a child from a wrong decision seem often to justify a requirement of parental consent. And a doctor's requirement of reasonable guidelines justifies a flat age cut-off with liability only for an unreasonable mistake as to the child's age.

It is these cases of controversial decisions where a requirement of parental consent is not only plausible but sensible. The present requirement is applicable much more broadly. It is so perverse that it actually undermines on occasion the important child interests to be served by parental consent to controversial care.

At present hospitals and doctors often obtain the required consent through use of a written form. In at least one Ohio hospital this form is deemed valid by the doctors and administrators for a full year, apparently for any treatment. The form of consent is preserved, while depriving the child of advice tailored to specific questions that may arise.

What is the "right" age? I leave the determination of the cut-off age to courts, legislators, and those expert in child development. It is probably as important to pick some plausible age, which after all will only at best be a statistical approximation as to search for the "right" age. The standard of a child who is capable of giving "informed consent" seems to me quite useless for the normal range of children. It provides little guidance to a doctor and will recede into irrelevance if a case should ever reach a jury. The impression of the jury or judge will be dominated by the appearance of the child at the time of trial, and this very likely will be several years after the procedure was performed. Whether the child has matured as they do rapidly at the ages we are considering, or has deteriorated due to the procedure, the fact-finder will be severely disabled in judging whether he was mature enough to have given "informed consent" at a time then well past [142]. The proper time for "informed consent" is when practitioner deals with parent about a medically controversial decision. On such occasions both the information and the consent are of real significance.

Several difficulties remain. Some decisions are effectively irreversible; others are not, although the line between the two will not always be clear. A parent probably should not be allowed over the child's objection to make a clearly irreversible decision for a child who is nearing the age cutoff. In addition, some decisions are so important to a child that he arguably should be allowed to make them for himself as he approaches the age cutoff. The argument for child autonomy gains persuasiveness when, as in the abortion or birth control cases, the matter is a highly personal one involving (especially in the case of abortion) the interest in physical integrity, it has obvious implications for the child after becoming an adult, parental judgment is likely to be clouded, reasoned communication between parent and child is likely to be difficult, a plausible cutoff age is provided by nature, and the externalities likely to result from requiring parental consent are far greater than those of the likely child decision [143].

The practical consequences of such a restructured law are many, but it is important to note that most doctor treatment of children would be carried on then as now with the parent's agreement, indeed at the parent's initiative. Emergency treatment could be administered without the frantic search for parents or agonizing about whether the law would classify the situation as an "emergency." As children began to act independently, practitioners could administer routine examinations and tests and prescribe routine or other uncontroversial care without parental consent and seldom arousing parental objection.

Practitioners with conflicts of interest are also of concern. If national health insurance provided third-party payment for uncontroversial care administered without parental consent, a doctor would have an economic interest in finding such care necessary. The doctor already has such an incentive, however, and the effectiveness of the parental check is uncertain. National health insurance will likely be accompanied by expanded forms of the utilization and professional standards review required under present law for Medicaid and Medicare payments (Havighurst and Blumstein, 1975) [144]. Alternatively, some have suggested a capitation form of payment under NHI by which medical personnel would be reimbursed at a set rate for each child and would be responsible for administering all necessary care for that child. This would reverse the practitioner's incentives and would itself require some review of practitioner action. But problems of incentives inhere in any form of third-party payment. In the case of child medical care decisions the problem at least is ameliorated slightly by the fact that one third-party payer, the government, is being substituted for another, the parent.

The doctor with research incentives presents problems that must receive attention even if the parental consent requirement is retained, precisely because parents so often defer to doctors. In addition the "parent" in many cases is an institution, with more mixed incentives than a natural parent. Perhaps all medical experiments on children which do not benefit them should be banned. At the very least the doctor conflict should be dealt with by requiring that child consent or parental consent, whichever is appropriate, be obtained after explanation by a practitioner with absolutely no interest in the research. Under the suggested standards, parental consent, not child consent, would be required unless the procedure was medically uncontroversial. This would always require at least that it be directly responsive to the child's medical problem or harmless.

The principal difficulty with the suggested standards is in drawing the line between controversial and uncontroversial care. If the doctor draws the line, it will be argued that he will have an incentive to call controversial care uncontroversial to maximize his own freedom of action. The vulnerable child would be less able to resist the practitioner's advice than would his parent, and incorrect decisions would be made. The standards might thus be one step in the direction pointed by the Mississippi legislature of not allowing a child to resist a medical recommendation of a licensed physician "without reasonable medical justification."

The seriousness of this objection depends in part on the method of categorization adopted. If national health insurance is adopted, the federal agency or state officials charged with administration might prepare a list of medically uncontroversial procedures, of irreversible procedures, of procedures requiring parental assistance, and of compellingly personal procedures [145]. While such lists would draw on medical expertise, final authority would reside in government officials charged with safeguarding parent and child interests and with holding down costs. Such authority would work to restrict those procedures that could be administered without parental consent.

If no such lists of procedures were governmentally provided, hospital and doctor groups would probably provide guidelines. A doctor would remain liable for negligence in deciding whether a procedure was medically or personally controversial, whether it required parental cooperation or disruption of home life, or whether the decisionmaking process would benefit from parental information. These judgments, unlike those the practitioner is called upon to make under present law, at least draw heavily upon his medical expertise. The practitioner is more likely to err on the side of parental involvement than noninvolvement if liability may ensue for erroneous noninvolvement. At least, experience under present law suggests this. But even if the suggested standards give some additional undesirable authority to medical professionals, this loss must be weighed against the gain in medical care to many children now impeded from seeking and receiving it by the parental consent requirement.

Public Intervention

This review of the interest and roles of the four medical care decisionmakers also provides some guidance for public intervention, particularly on a mass scale. Such mass intervention should be limited to uncontroversial care or testing, because the state can never on a mass basis provide sensitive attention to medically or personally controversial decisions. Intervention is most justified when there are serious externalities to an incorrect decision, but often seems justified as well when parents on a large scale demonstrably fail as surrogate decision-makers. If the intervention does not disrupt or distort the parent-child relationship, mass intervention is usually readily accepted, even, as in the case of PKU testing, where the medical condition guarded against is a rare one. In particular, if it can be administered at the hospitals or schools, it seems likely to be accepted as an adjunct of well-established public intervention between parent and child.

Some state laws on mass public intervention retain a requirement of parental consent or allow a parental veto, sometimes for religious, sometimes for any reason. The hold of common law concepts becomes almost ludicrous where, as in Colorado, hearing, vision, and breathing are to be tested by teachers but without touching the child [146]. If problems of practitioner liability for negligence are dealt with satisfactorily, a requirement of parental consent is no more justified for sensible mass public interventions than in the case of individual privately administered care. If a rare case of harm seems inevitable with mass procedures, that really does not differentiate them from multiple private procedures. Society might well compensate monetarily for these harms. A requirement of parental consent, however, seems likely to stand in the way of sensible procedures more than it will forestall such harm. Public resources should be devoted to evaluating the worth of procedures, not to obtaining a rote form of consent. If a parental veto is retained, however, because the medical justification is not thought sufficient to justify the affront to parental authority, caution should at least be exercised in borrowing the parental consent requirement intact from the common law. Opportunity for a parental veto after notice more than satisfies legitimate parental concern, while an affirmative requirement of consent may stand in the way of many children receiving uncontroversial and advisable care and testing.

Individualized public intervention is much more troublesome. It represents a serious state interference with parent and child interests in a regime of parental authority, and is therefore justified only when the child medical interest at stake is clear and quite substantial. It should probably be limited to compelling cases of uncontroversial care. It must be recognized, moreover, that the poor and powerless are subjected to the bulk of this intervention. Much of it takes place in the informal give and take of discretionary public decisionmaking which plays such a major role in the lives of the poor (Davis, 1969;

tenBroek, 1965). There is thus reason to confine such intervention in the interest of individual freedom as well as to allow it in the interest of child health. If mass public intervention can substitute in part for individualized intervention by finding and treating troublesome conditions early, it will have found strong additional justification.

NOTES AND CASES CITED

1. I will not deal with the related but separable problem of psychological treatment of minors. The subject has recently been explored extensively in Ellis, Volunteering Children: Parental Commitment of Minors to Mental Institutions, 62 Calif. L. Rev. 840 (1974). See also Note, Counseling the Counselors: Legal Implications of Counseling Minors without Parental Consent, 31 Md. L. Rev. 332 (1971). Even treatment of physical ills may not require physical contact, but medical practitioners appear to deal with all medical treatment as governed by the consent requirement of the law of battery.

2. The Restatement provides a body of expert opinion of what the law is and should be. It usually tracks the case law quite closely, but has only such independent force as its inherent persuasiveness commands.

3. See Younts v. St. Francis Hosp. 205 Kan. 929, 469 P.2d 330 (1970); Lacey v. Laird, 166 Ohio St. 12, 139 N.E.2d 25 (1956), noted in 10 Vand L. Rev. 619 (1957) and 9 Case West. Res. L. Rev. 101 (1957); Smith v. Seibly, 72 Wash. 2d 16, 431 P.2d 719 (1967).

4. Lacey v. Laird, 166 Ohio St. 12, 19, 139 N.E.2d 25, 30 (1956) (concurring opinion).

5. See, e.g., Friedrichsen v. Niemotka, 71 N.J. Super 398, 177 A.2d 58 (1962); Weston's Adm'x v. Hospital of St. Vincent of Paul, 131 Va. 587, 107 S.E. 785 (1921); In re Smith, 16 Md. App. 209, 295 A.2d 238 (Ct. Spec. App. 1972); Ellis, Volunteering Children: Parental Commitment of Minors to Mental Institutions, 62 Calif. L. Rev. 840, 855 (1974).

6. 126 F.2d 121 (D.C. Cir. 1941).

7. Id. at 122.

8. 237 Mich. 76, 211 N.W. 75 (1926).

9. See Sullivan v. Montgomery, 155 Misc. 448, 449–50, 279 N.Y.S. 575, 576–78 (City Ct. 1935); Wells v. McGehee, 39 So. 2d 196 (La. App. 1949); Yackovach v. Yocum, 212 Iowa 914, 237 N.W. 444 (1931). But see Rogers v. Sells, 178 Okla. 103, 61 P.2d 1018 (1936).

10. Compare Sullivan v. Montgomery, 155 Misc. 448, 279 N.Y.S. 575 (City Ct. 1935) with Rogers v. Sells, 178 Okla. 103, 61 P.2d 1018 (1936). But cf. Wells v. McGehee, 39 So. 2d 196 (La. App. 1949).

11. Bonner v. Moran, 126 F.2d 121 (D.C. Cir. 1941).

12. Bakker v. Welsh, 144 Mich. 632, 108 N.W. 94 (1906) (seventeen years); Gulf & Ship Island R.R. v. Sullivan, 155 Miss. 1, 119 So. 501 (1928) (seventeen years); Lacey v. Laird, 166 Ohio St. 12, 139 N.E.2d 25 (1956) (over eighteen years); Bishop v. Shurly, 237 Mich. 76, 211 N.W. 75 (1926) (nineteen years); Younts v. St. Francis Hosp., 205 Kan. 292, 469 P.2d 330 (1970) (seventeen

years); Smith v. Seibly, 72 Wash. 2d 16, 431 P.2d 719 (1967) (eighteen years); Sullivan v. Montgomery, 155 Misc. 448, 279 N.Y.S. 575 (City Ct. 1935) (twenty years).

13. Younts v. St. Francis Hosp. 205 Kan. 292, 300–01, 469 P.2d 330, 337–38 (1970); cf. Bishop v. Shurly, 237 Mich. 76, 211 N.W. 75 (1926); Smith v. Seibly, 72 Wash. 2d 16, 431 P.2d 719 (1967); Gulf & Ship Island R.R. v. Sullivan, 155 Miss. 1, 119 So. 501 (1928) (interpreting statute); Bonner v. Moran, 126 F.2d 121 (D.C. Cir. 1941).

14. Younts v. St. Francis Hosp., 205 Kan. 292, 295–300, 469 P.2d 330, 333–36 (1970) (parents unavailable, slight danger, good medical practice); Bakker v. Welsh, 144 Mich. 632, 635–36, 108 N.W. 94, 96 (1906) (father likely to have consented if asked); Smith v. Seibly, 72 Wash. 2d 16, 20–22, 431 P.2d. 719, 723 (1967) (emancipation); cf. Lacey v. Laird, 166 Ohio St. 12, 193 N.E.2d 25 (1956), a per curiam decision with concurring opinions where the court's syllabus appears to rely on the eighteen-year-old's maturity but does so in such conclusory language that the rationale is difficult to follow.

15. See Smith v. Seibly, 72 Wash. 2d 16, 431 P.2d 719 (1967).

16. Bonner v. Moran, 126 F.2d 121, 123 (D.C. Cir. 1941).

17. Younts v. St. Francis Hosp., 205 Kan. 292, 469 P.2d 330 (1970).

18. Younts v. St. Francis Hosp., 205 Kan. 292, 301, 469 P.2d 330, 338, (1970).

19. Luka v. Lowrie 171 Mich. 122, 135, 136 N.W. 1106, 1110–11 (1912). One early court rejected a suggested test of what was in the "paramount interest of the child." Moss v. Rishworth, 222 S.W. 225, 227, (Tex. Comm'n App. 1920).

20. Younts v. St. Francis Hosp., 205 Kan. 292, 301, 469 P.2d 330, 338 (1970); Wells v. McGehee, 39 So. 2d 196, 202 (La. App. 1949); Yackovach v. Yocum, 212 Iowa 914, 923–24, 237 N.W. 444, 449 (1931).

21. Younts v. St. Francis Hosp., 205 Kan 292, 301, 469 P.2d 330, 338 (1970); Bakker v. Welsh, 144 Mich 632, 635–36, 108 N.W. 94, 96 (1906); Luka v. Lowrie, 171 Mich 122, 134, 136 N.W. 1106, 1110 (1912).

22. Bakker v. Welsh, 144 Mich. 632, 635–36, 108 N.W. 94, 96 (1906). But see Bonner v. Moran, 126 F.2d 121 (D.C. Cir. 1941); Moss v. Rishworth, 222 S.W. 225 (Tex Comm'n App. 1920).

23. Younts v. St. Francis Hosp., 205 Kan. 292, 301, 469 P.2d 330, 338 (1970); Luka v. Lowrie, 171 Mich. 122, 134, 136 N.W. 1106, 1110 (1912).

24. Bishop v. Shurly, 237 Mich. 76, 85, 211 N.W. 75, 78 (1926). See also Lacey v. Laird, 166 Ohio St. 12, 26, 139 N.E.2d, 24, 34 (1956) (Taft, J., concurring).

25. 126 F.2d 121 (D.C. Cir. 1941).

26. Id. at 123.

27. Id.

28. E.g., N.M. Stat. Ann §13–13–1 (Supp. 1975); Tenn. Code Ann. §1–313 (Cum. Supp. 1975). Alaska and Nebraska have chosen nineteen as the age of majority. Alaska Stat. §25, 20.020 (1962); Neb. Rev. Stat §38–101 (1974).

29. Wash. Rev. Code Ann. §§26.28.010, 26.28.015 (Supp. 1974).

30. E.g., Ala. Code tit. 22, §104 (15) (Cum. Supp. 1973); Ore. Rev. Stat. §109.650 (1973).

31. E.g., Ill. Ann. Stat. ch. 91, §18.3 (Smith-Hurd Cum. Supp. 1975); N.C. Gen. Stat. §90–21.5 (Rep. Vol. 1975); Pa. Stat. Ann. tit. 35, §10104 (Cum. Supp. 1975).

32. E.g., Cal. Civ. Code §25.7 (West Supp. 1975); Ill. Ann. Stat. ch. 91, §§18.1, 18.2 (Smith-Hurd Cum. Supp. 1975); Md. Ann. Code art. 43, §135 (a) (Cum. Supp. 1975); Pa. Stat. Ann. tit. 35, §§10101–02 (Cum. Supp. 1975).

33. E.g., Minn. Stat. Ann. §144.341 (Cum. Supp. 1976).

34. Cal. Civ. Code §34.6 (West Supp. 1975); Colo. Rev. Stat. Ann. §13–22–103 (1973).

35. Miss. Code Ann. §41:41–3(h) (1972).

36. Id. §41–41–3.

37. Pa. Stat. Ann. tit. 35, §10105 (Cum. Supp. 1975).

38. E.g., N.C. Gen. Stat. §90–21.5 (b) (Rep. Vol. 1975) (no age limit), Ill. Ann. Stat. ch. 91, §18.4 (Smith-Hurd Cum. Supp. 1975) (limited to minors "12 years of age or older").

39. E.g., Ill. Ann. Stat. ch. 91, §18.7 (b) (Smith-Hurd Cum. Supp. 1975).

40. E.g., Id. §18.4.

41. Minn. Stat. Ann. §144.343 (Cum. Supp. 1975).

42. E.g., Ind. Ann. Stat. §16–8–2–1 (Cum. Supp. 1975) (seventeen or over).

43. See Jacobson v. Massachusetts, 197 U.S. 11 (1905).

44. See Zucht v. King, 260 U.S. 174 (1922); Sadlock v. Board of Educ., 137 N.J. 85, 58 A.2d 218 (1948); Board of Educ. v. Mass. 56 N.J. Super. 245, 152 A.2d 394 (1959), aff'd 31 N.J. 537, 158 A.2d 330, *cert. denied*, 363 U.S. 843 (1960); cf. Jacobson v. Massachusetts, 197 U.S. 11, 32 (1905).

45. Many states require at least one of these innoculations or tests prior to school entry: Cal. Health & Safety Code §3380, 3400, 3481 (West Supp. 1975) (polio, rubeola, diphtheria, pertussis, tetanus [the last three will hereinafter be abbreviated "dpt"]); Conn. Gen. Stat. Ann. 10–204, –204a, –204b (Supp. 1975) (measles, polio, rubella); Ind. Ann. Stat. §20–8.1–7–10, –12 (1975); (TB required; immunization history, but not immunization itself, required for smallpox [hereinafter "smlpx"] dpt., German Measles, measles, polio); Kan. Stat. Ann. §72–5209 (1972) (polio, smlpx, dpt., measles, rubella, TB test); La. Rev. Stat. Ann. §17.170 (Cum. Supp. 1976) (dpt. polio, measles); Mass. Ann. Laws ch. 76, §15 (Supp. 1974) (dpt., measles, polio); Mich. Stat. Ann. §§14.378(1), 14.379 (21) (1969), §15.3376 (Supp. 1975) (polio, dpt., smlpx., TB test); Mo. Ann. Stat. §167.181 (Cum. Supp. 1976) (polio, rubella, rubeola, dpt.); Neb. Rev. Stat. §79–444.01 (Cum. Supp. 1974) (measles, rubella, polio, dpt.); Nev. Rev. Stat. §392.435 (1973) (dpt., polio, rubella, rubeola); N.H. Rev. Stat. Ann. §200.38 (Supp. 1973) (innoculations designated by the state public health agency, TB test required); N.Y. Pub. Health Law §2164.2 (McKinney Cum. Supp. 1975) (polio, measles, dpt., rubella); N.C. Gen. Stat. §130.87 (Cum. Supp. 1975); Ohio Rev. Code Ann. §3313.671 (Baldwin 1971) (polio, smlpx., rubella, dpt., rubeola); Okla. Stat. Ann. tit. 70. §1210.191 (1972) (dpt., rubella, rubeola, polio, smlpx., TB test); S.D. Compiled Laws Ann. §13–28–7.1 (1975) (polio, diphtheria, measles, tetanus, TB test); W. Va. Code Ann. §§16–3–4, 16–3–4a (Cum. Supp. 1975) (dpt., polio, rubeola). Some states, including several that require specific immunizations, delegate enforcement of the requirement to state

officials or local boards of health or education: Alaska Stat. § 14.30.125 (1975); Ariz. Rev. Stat. Ann. § 36–629 (1974); Colo. Rev. Stat. Ann. § 25–4–905 (1973); Ga. Code Ann. § 32–911 (Cum. Supp. 1975); Hawaii Rev. Stat. § 321–11 (22) (1968); Ill. Ann. Stat. ch. 122, § 27–8 (Smith-Hurd Cum. Supp. 1975); Mass. Gen. Laws Ann. ch. 76, § 15 (Cum. Supp. 1975); Miss. Code Ann. § 37:7–301 (i) (1972); Mont. Rev. Codes Ann. § 75–5933 (19) (Cum. Supp. 1975); Nev. Rev. Stat. § 392.433 (1973); N.H. Rev. Stat. Ann. § 200:38 (Supp. 1973); N.M. Stat. Ann. § 12–3–4.1 (1953); N.C. Gen. Stat. § 130–87 (Cum. Supp. 1975); Ore. Rev. Stat. § 433.267 (Repl. Pt. 1974); R.I. Gen. Laws Ann. § 16–38–2 (Supp. 1975); Tenn. Code Ann. § 49–1765 (Cum. Supp. 1975).

In several other states, local power to require immunization is upheld without statutory authority. See, e.g., Auten v. School Board, 83 Ark. 431, 104 S.W. 130 (1907). At least two states that make no statutory provision seem to allow local authorities to require immunization. Idaho gives each school district the power to protect the health and morals of its pupils. Idaho Code § 33–512.4 (Cum. Supp. 1975). Texas stipulates that no local authority may require immunizations where they are medically contraindicated, thus by implication anticipating such local rules. Tex. Rev. Civ. Stat. art. 4447b (1966).

Finally, several states, while requiring certain kinds of immunizations, do not make those immunizations a prerequisite to entering school. See Ala. Code tit. 22, § 84 (1) (1958); Ky. Rev. Stat. § 214.034 (1975); S.C. Code Ann. § 32–574 (Cum. Supp. 1975); Tex. Rev. Civ. Stat. art. 4477–12 (1966); Va. Code Ann. § 32–57.1 (1973); Wyo. Stat. Ann. § 35–171 (1957).

46. Conn. Gen. Stat. Ann. § 10–204(b) (Supp. 1975); Mo. Ann. Stat. § 167.181 (Cum. Supp. 1976); Neb. Rev. Stat. § 79–444.01 (Cum. Supp. 1974); Ohio Rev. Code Ann. § 3313.671 (Baldwin 1971); Okla. Stat. Ann. tit. 70, § 1210.192 (1972). Apparently a school board in Ohio can still refuse to admit an unimmunized student. See State ex rel. Mack v. Board of Educ. 1 Ohio App. 2d 143 (1963).

47. Cal. Health & Safety Code § 3385, 3405, 3485 (West Supp. 1975); Colo. Rev. Stat. Ann. § 25–4–902 (1973); Ill. Ann. Stat. ch. 122, § 27–8 (Smith-Hurd Cum. Supp. 1975); Kan. Stat. Ann. § 72–5209 (1972); Ky. Rev. Stat. § 214.036 (1975); La. Rev. Stat. Ann. § 17:170E (Cum. Supp. 1976); Mass. Ann. Laws ch. 76, § 15 (Cum. Supp. 1975); Miss. Code Ann. § 37:7–301 (i) (1972); Mont. Rev. Codes Ann. § 75–5933(19) (Cum. Supp. 1975); N.H. Rev. Stat. Ann. § 200.38 (Supp. 1973); N.M. Stat. Ann. § 12–3–4.3 (1968); N.Y. Pub. Health Law § 2164.8 (McKinney Cum. Supp. 1975); N.C. Gen. Stat. § 130–91 (1974); Ohio Rev. Code Ann. § 3313.671 (Baldwin 1971); Okla. Stat. Ann. tit. 70, § 1210.192 (1972); Ore. Rev. Stat. § 433.267 (1973); R.I. Gen. Laws Ann. § 16–38–2 (Supp. 1975); S.D. Compiled Laws Ann. § 13–28–7.1 (1975); Tenn. Code Ann. § 49–1768 (Cum. Supp. 1975); Tex. Rev. Civ. Stat. art. 4447b (1966); Va. Code Ann. § 32–57.1 (1973); W. Va. Code Ann. § 16–3–4 (Cum. Supp. 1975).

48. Jacobson v. Massachusetts, 197 U.S. 11, 38–39 (1905).

49. Those doing so with only a requirement of a simple written invocation of the exception are: Cal. Health & Safety Code §§ 3384, 3404, 3486 (West. Supp. 1975); Colo. Rev. Stat. Ann. § 25–4–903 (1973); Ill. Ann. Stat. ch. 122, § 27–8

(Smith-Hurd Cum. Supp. 1975); Kan. Stat. Ann. §72–5209 (1972); La. Rev. Stat. Ann. §17:170E (Cum. Supp. 1976); Mass. Ann. Laws ch. 76, §15 (Supp. 1975); Mich. Stat. Ann. §14.379(21) (1969), §15.3376(b) (Supp. 1975); Nev. Rev. Stat. §392.437 (1973); N.H. Rev. Stat. Ann. §200:32 (Supp. 1973); Ore. Rev. Stat. §433.267 (1973); R.I. Gen. Laws Ann. §16–38–2 (Supp. 1975); S.D. Compiled Laws Ann. §13–28–7.1 (1975); Va. Code Ann. §32–57.1 (1973).

50. Ariz. Rev. Stat. Ann. §36–629 (1974).

51. Ala. Code tit. 52, §553 (Supp. 1973); Alaska Stat. §14.30.070 (1975); Ark. Stat. Ann. §80–1219 (1960); Cal. Educ. Code §§11823, 11823.1, 11824, 11825 (West 1975); Colo. Rev. Stat. Ann. §22–1–116 (1973); Conn. Gen. Stat. Ann. §10–206 (1967); Del. Code Ann. tit. 14, §122(b) (14) 1975; Fla. Stat. Ann. §232.291 (Cum. Supp. 1975); Ga. Code Ann. §32–445 (Cum. Supp. 1975); Hawaii Rev. Stat. §321–11(22) (1968); Ill. Ann. Stat. ch. 23, §233 et seq.; ch. 122, §27–8 (Smith-Hurd Cum. Supp. 1975); Ind. Ann. Stat. §§20–8.1–7–14 to 17 (1975); Kan. Stat. Ann. §§72–1205, 72–5201, 72–5205 (1972); La. Rev. Stat. Ann. §17:170B (Cum. Supp. 1976), Id. §17:2112 (1963); Me. Rev. Stat. Ann. tit. 20, §1135 (Cum. Supp. 1975); Md. Code Ann. art. 77, §85B (1975); Mass. Ann. Laws, ch. 71, §57 (Cum. Supp. 1975); Mich. Stat. Ann. §14.1241 (1969); 15.3376 (Supp. 1975); Minn. Stat. Ann. §126.02, (Supp. 1975) (by implication); Miss. Code Ann. §§37–9–5, 37–13–19 (1972); Mont. Rev. Codes Ann. §75–5934(3) (1971); Neb. Rev. Stat. §79–444(3) (Cum. Supp. 1974); Nev. Rev. Stat. §392.435 (1973); N.H. Rev. Stat. Ann. §200:32 (Supp. 1973); N.J. Rev. Stat. §18A:40–4 (Supp. 1975); N.M. Stat. Ann. §12–3–45 (Cum. Supp. 1975); N.Y. Educ. Law §§901 (McKinney 1969), 903, 904, 912, 912a (McKinney Supp. 1974); N.C. Gen. Stat. §115–204 (1975); N.D. Cent. Code §15–47–22 (1971); Ohio Rev. Code Ann. §§3113.69, 3113.73, 3709.22 (Baldwin 1971); Okla. Stat. Ann. tit. 70 §11–104 (1972); Ore. Rev. Stat. §336.375–400 (1973); Pa. Stat. Ann. tit. 24, §§14.1402, 1403 (Supp. 1975); R.I. Gen. Laws Ann. §16–21–9 (1970); S.D. Compiled Laws Ann. §34–4–8 (1972); Tenn. Code Ann. §§49–5115 (Cum. Supp. 1975); Utah Code Ann. §53–22–1, –4 (1970); Vt. Stat. Ann. tit. 16, §1422 (1974); Va. Code Ann. §22–220.1 (Cum. Supp. 1975); Wash. Rev. Code Ann. §28A31.030 (Supp. 1975); W. Va. Code Ann. §18–5–22 (1971); Wis. Stat. Ann. §118.25 (1973).

52. Cal. Educ. Code §§11823, 11823.1, 11824, 11825 (West 1975); Fla. Stat. Ann. §232.291 (Cum. Supp. 1975); La. Rev. Stat. Ann. §17:2112 (1963).

53. N.M. Stat. Ann. §12–3–45 (Cum. Supp. 1975); S.C. Code Ann. §32–562 (Cum. Supp. 1975).

54. Md. Code Ann. art. 77, §85B (1975); Mich. Stat. Ann. §14.1241 (1969), Id. §15.3376(2) (Supp. 1975); Wash. Rev. Code Ann. §28A31.030 (Supp. 1974).

55. Mass. Ann. Laws ch. 71, §57 (Supp. 1975).

56. Alabama, Alaska, Colorado, Delaware, Georgia, Hawaii, Iowa, Kansas, Mississippi, Montana, New Mexico, New York, North Carolina, North Dakota, Oklahoma, Rhode Island, South Dakota, Utah, Washington, W. Virginia, Wisconsin.

57. Ark. Stat. Ann. §80–1219 (1960); Cal. Educ. Code §11822 (West 1975); La. Rev. Stat. Ann. §17:156 (1963); Minn. Stat. Ann. §126.02 (Supp. 1975); Neb. Rev. Stat. §79–4, 133 (1971); Nev. Rev. Stat. §392.420 (1973); Ohio Rev. Code Ann. §3313.73 (Baldwin 1971); Vt. Stat. Ann. tit. 16, §1422 (1974). Florida honors any parental objection, and specifies that its intent is to offer a broad range of health services to school children, but only on a fully voluntary basis. Fla. Stat. Ann. §232.291 (Cum. Supp. 1975).

58. Conn. Gen. Stat. Ann. §10–208 (1967); Hawaii Rev. Stat. §321–11(22) (1968); Ill. Ann. Stat. ch. 23, §2336 (Smith-Hurd Cum. Supp. 1975); Ind. Ann. Stat. §20–8.1–7–2 (1975); Me. Rev. Stat. Ann. tit. 20, §1135 (Cum. Supp. 1975); Md. Ann. Code art. 77, §85(b) (1975); Mass. Ann. Laws ch. 71, §57, (Cum. Supp. 1975); Mich. Stat. Ann. §§14.379(1) (1969), Id. 15.3376(2) (1975); N.H. Rev. Stat. Ann. §200:32 (Supp. 1973); N.J. Stat. Ann. §18A:40–4 (Supp. 1975); Pa. Stat. Ann. tit. 23, §14–1419 (1962); Va. Code Ann. §22–220.1 (Cum. Supp. 1975).

59. Cal. Educ. Code §10921 (West 1975).

60. Ohio Rev. Code Ann. §3709.22 (Baldwin 1971).

61. N.H. Rev. Stat. Ann. §200:34 (Supp. 1973); N.Y. Educ. Laws §904 (McKinney Supp. 1974); R.I. Gen. Laws Ann. §16–21–12 (1969); W. Va. Code Ann. §18–5–23 (1971).

62. Ala. Code tit. 22, §58 (1958); Cal. Bus. & Prof. Code §551 (West 1974); Colo. Rev. Stat. Ann. §25–4–303 (1973); Conn. Gen. Stat. Ann. §19–92 (1969); D.C. Code Ann. §6–201 (1973); Fla. Stat. Ann. §383.04 (1975); Ga. Code Ann. §88–1605 (1971); Idaho Code §39–903 (1961); Ill. Rev. Stat. ch. 91, §106 (Smith-Hurd 1973); Iowa Code Ann. §140.13 (1972); Kan. Stat. Ann. §65–153b (Cum. Supp. 1975); Me. Rev. Stat. Ann. tit. 22, §1521 (1964); Md. Ann. Code art. 43 §90 (1971); Mass. Gen. Laws Ann. ch. 111, §109A (1971); Mich. Stat. Ann. §28.740 (1972); Miss. Code Ann. §41:35–9 (1972); Nev. Rev. Stat. §§442.040, 442.100 (1973); N.C. Gen. Stat. §130–108 (1974); Ohio Rev. Code Ann. §3701.55 (Baldwin 1971); Okla. Stat. Ann. tit. 63, §1–511 (1973); Tenn. Code Ann. §§53–621 to –622 (1966); Tex. Rev. Civ. Stat. art. 4441 (1966); Va. Code Ann. §32–107 (1973); W. Va. Code Ann. §§16–3–7 et seq. (1972); Wyo. Stat. Ann. §35–183 (1957). Cf. Minn. Stat. Ann. §144.12(8) (1970); S.D. Compiled Laws Ann. §34–24–8 (1972); Vt. Stat. Ann. tit. 18, §1010 (1968); Wis. Stat. Ann. §146.01 (1974).

63. Ind. Ann. Stat. §16–1–11–5 (1973); N.J. Stat. Ann. §§26:4–73 to –74, (1964); N.D. Cent. Code §23–07–10 (1971).

64. Kan. Stat. Ann. §65–153b (Cum. Supp. 1975); Minn. Stat. Ann. §144. 12(8) (1970); Okla. Stat. Ann. tit. 63, §1–511 (1973); S.D. Compiled Laws Ann. §34–24–8 (1972).

65. Colo. Rev. Stat. Ann. §25–4–304(2) (1973); Fla. Stat. Ann. §383.04 (1975); Iowa Code Ann. §140.13 (1972); Nev. Rev. Stat. §§442.050, 442.100 (1973); Wyo. Stat. Ann. §35–183 (1957).

66. Mich. Stat. Ann. §14.565(1) (1969) Mont. Rev. Codes Ann. §69–6911 (Cum. Supp. 1976); Neb. Rev. Stat. §71–604.01 (Supp. 1974); Ore. Rev. Stat. §433.285 (1974); Utah Code Ann. §26–17–21 (1969); W. Va. Code Ann. 16–22–1 to –3 (1972).

67. Alaska Stat. §18.15.200 (1974); Fla. Stat. Ann. §383.14 (1975); Nev. Rev. Stat. §442.115 (1973); N.M. Stat. Ann. §12–34–6 (Cum. Supp. 1975).

68. Ala. Code tit. 22, §58(1) (Cum. Supp. 1973); Ark. Stat. Ann. §§82–625, 82–627 (Cum. Supp. 1975); Cal. Health & Safety Code §309 (West Cum. Supp. 1975); Colo. Rev. Stat. Ann. §§25–4–801, 25–4–804 (1973); Conn. Gen. Stat. Ann. §19–21b (1969); Ga. Code Ann. §88–1201.1 (Cum. Supp. 1975); Hawaii Rev. Stat. §333–1 (1968); Idaho Code §39–909 (Cum. Supp. 1975); Ill. Rev. Stat. ch. 91. §§113f, 113h (Smith-Hurd 1973); Ind. Ann. Stat. §16–8–6–1 (1973); Kan. Stat. Ann. §65–182 (Cum. Supp. 1975); Ky. Rev. Stat. §214.155 (1972); Me. Rev. Stat. Ann. tit. 22, §1561 (Cum. Supp. 1975); Md. Ann. Code art. 43, §38A (1971); Mass. Ann. Laws ch. 111, §110A (1975); Minn. Stat. Ann. §144.125 (1970); N.J. Rev. Stat. §26:2–84 (Cum. Supp. 1975); N.Y. Pub. Health Law §2500a (McKinney Cum. Supp. 1975); N.D. Cent. Code §25–17–01 (1971); Okla. Rev. Code Ann. tit. 63, §§1–533, 1–534 (1973); R.I. Gen. Laws Ann. §23–13–12 (1968); S.D. Compiled Laws Ann. §§34–24–17 to –18 (Supp. 1975); Tenn. Code Ann. §§53–624, 53–631 (Cum. Supp. 1975); Va. Code Ann. §§32–112.1, 32–112.9 (1973); Wis. Stat. Ann. §146.02 (1974).

69. Kaul v. Chehalis, 45 Wash. 2d 616, 618, 277 P.2d 352, 353–4 (1954).

70. Conn. Gen. Stat. Ann. §19–13b (1969); Ohio Rev. Code §6111.13 (Baldwin 1974).

71. E.g., Cal. Pub. Util. Code §12814 (West 1965) provides that a water supply district may add fluorine to the water only after such action has been approved by residents of the district.

72. See, e.g., City Comm'n v. State ex rel Altenhoff, 143 So. 2d, 879 (Fla. App. 1962); Wilson v. Council Bluffs, 253 Iowa 162, 110 N.W.2d 569 (1961).

73. See, e.g., Chapman v. Shreveport, 225 La. 859, 74 So. 2d 142, *appeal dismissed*, 348 U.S. 892 (1954); Paduano v. New York, 45 Misc. 2d 718, 257 N.Y.S.2d 531 (Sup. Ct. 1965), *cert. denied*, 385 U.S. 1026 (1967); Kraus v. Cleveland, 121 N.E.2d 311 (Ohio App. 1954), *appeal dismissed*, 351 U.S. 935 (1956).

74. But cf. Illinois Pure Water Comm. v. Yoder, 6 Ill. App. 3d 659, 286 N.E. 2d 155 (1972).

75. See, e.g., Rogowski v. Detroit, 374 Mich. 408, 132 N.W.2d 16 (1965); Kaul v. Chehalis, 45 Wash. 2d 616, 277 P.2d 352 (1954); Kraus v. Cleveland, 116 N.E.2d 799 (C.P. 1953), *aff'd*, 131 N.E.2d 311 (Ohio App. 1954).

76. See, e.g., Graybeal v. McNevin, 439 S.W.2d 323 (Ky. 1969); Hall v. Bates, 247 S.C. 511, 148 S.E.2d 345 (1966); cf. Barsky v. Board of Regents, 347 U.S. 442, 449 (1954).

77. Chapman v. Shreveport, 225 La. 859, 74 So. 2d 142, *appeal dismissed*, 348 U.S. 892 (1954); Paduano v. New York, 45 Misc. 2d 718, 257 N.Y.S. 2d 531 (Sup. Ct. 1965), *cert. denied*, 385 U.S. 1026 (1967).

78. Chapman v. Shreveport, 225 La. 859, 74 So. 2d 142 *appeal dismissed*, 348 U.S. 892 (1954); Paduano v. New York, 45 Misc. 2d 718, 257 N.Y.S. 2d 531 (Sup. Ct. 1965), *cert. denied*, 385 U.S. 1026 (1967).

79. Schuringa v. Chicago, 30 Ill. 2d 504; 198 N.E.2d 326 (1964), *cert. denied*, 379 U.S. 964 (1965).

80. Id., Paduano v. New York, 45 Misc. 2d 718, 257 N.Y.S. 2d 531 (Sup. Ct. 1965), *cert. denied*, 385 U.S. 1026 (1967); Chapman v. Shreveport, 225 La. 859, 74 So. 2d 142, *appeal dismissed*, 348 U.S. 892 (1954): However, it seems to be acknowledged that dental fluorosis is an occasional harmful side effect. See Kraus v. Cleveland, 116 N.E.2d 799 (C.P. 1953), *aff'd*, 121 N.E.2d 311 (Ohio App. 1954).

81. Dowell v. Tulsa, 273 P.2d 859 (Okla. 1954), *cert. denied*, 348 U.S. 912 (1955); Paduano v. New York, 45 Misc. 2d 718, 257 N.Y.S. 2d 531 (Sup. Ct. 1965), *cert. denied*, 385 U.S. 1026 (1967).

82. E.g., Iowa Code Ann. §140.8 (1972) (VD); Mass. Ann. Laws ch. 111, §§94A, 95 (1975) (TB); Nev. Rev. Stat. §441.180 (1973) (VD); N.J. Stat. Ann. §26:4–36–37 (1964) (VD); N.C. Gen. Stat. §130–96 (1974) (VD), id. §26:4–71.1 (TB); Pa. Stat. Ann. tit. 35, §521.7, 521.11 (1964) (TB and VD).

83. Pa. Stat. Ann. tit. 11, §243 (5) (c) (1965). See also Ill. Rev. Stat. ch. 37, §702–4(1)(a) (Smith-Hurd 1972); N.Y. Soc. Serv. Law §371 (4–a) (i) (A) (McKinney Cum. Supp. 1975).

84. I will not specifically be dealing with the related problem of active abuse of children. However, the problem of distinguishing passive inattention from active abuse does complicate the search for realistic standards of intervention.

85. Cal. Welf. & Inst'ns Code §600 (West. 1972).

86. See In re Hudson, 13 Wash. 2d 673, 126 P.2d 765 (1942).

87. People ex rel Wallace v. Labrenz, 411 Ill. 618, 624, 104 N.E.2d 769, 773, *cert. denied*, 344 U.S. 824 (1952) (Schaefer, J.); See also In re Vasko, 238 App. Div. 128, 130, 263 N.Y.S. 552, 554 (1933).

88. See In re Clark, 21 Ohio Op. 2d 86, 185 N.E.2d 128 (C.P. 1962); State v. Perricone, 37 N.J. 463, 181 A.2d 751, *cert. denied*, 371 U.S. 890 (1962); In re Vasko, 238 App. Div. 128, 263 N.Y.S. 552 (1933); People ex rel. Wallace v. Labrenz, 411 Ill. 618, 104 N.E.2d 769, *cert. denied*, 344 U.S. 824 (1952); Hoener v. Bertinato, 67 N.J. Super. 517, 171 A.2d 140 (Juv. and Dom. Rel. Ct. 1961); Raleigh Fitkin-Paul Morgan Mem. Hosp. v. Anderson 42 N.J. 421, 201 A.2d 537, *cert. denied*, 377 U.S. 985 (1964). The only clear exceptions to the pattern are Mitchell v. Davis, 205 S.W.2d 812 (Tex. Civ. App. 1947), and In re Sampson, 65 Misc. 2d 658, 317 N.Y.S. 2d 641 (Fam. Ct. 1970), *aff'd*, 37 App. Div. 2d 668, 323 N.Y.S. 2d 253 (1971), *aff'd*, 29 N.Y.2d 900, 278 N.E.2d 918, 328 N.Y.S.2d 686 (1972).

89. See In re Carstairs, 115 N.Y.S. 2d 314 (Dom. Rel. Ct. 1952), *cert. denied*, 385 U.S. 949 (1966); In re Rotokowitz, 175 Misc. 948, 25 N.Y.S. 2d 624 (Dom. Rel. Ct. 1941).

90. See In re Karwath, 199 N.W.2d 147 (Iowa 1972); In re Weintraub, 166 Pa. Super. 342, 71 A.2d 823 (1950); In re Weberlist, 79 Misc. 2d 753, 360 N.Y.S. 2d 783 (1974); In re Comm'r of Soc. Serv., 72 Misc. 2d 428, 339 N.Y.S. 2d 89 (Fam. Ct. 1972).

91. In re Green, 448 Pa. 338, 292 A.2d 387 (1972).

92. In re Green, 452 Pa. 373, 307 A.2d 279 (1973).

93. In re Sieferth, 309 N.Y. 80, 127 N.E.2d 820 (1955).

94. Planned Parenthood v. Danforth, 96 Sup. Ct. 2831 (1976), *rev'g* 392 F. Supp. 1362 (E.D. Mo. 1975); Poe v. Gerstein, 517 F.2d 787 (5th Cir. 1975);

Foe v. Vanderhoff, 389 F. Supp. 947 (D. Colo. 1975); Baird v. Bellotti, 393 F. Supp. 847 (D. Mass. 1975); Wolfe v. Schroering, 388 F. Supp. 631 (W.D. Ky. 1974); Doe v. Rampton, 366 F. Supp. 189 (D. Utah 1973); State v. Koome 84 Wash. 2d 901, 530 P.2d 260 (1975); cf. Jones v. Smith, 278 So. 2d 339 (Fla. App. 1973).

95. Planned Parenthood v. Danforth, 96 Sup. Ct. 2831 (1976).

96. 84 Wash. 2d 901, 530 P.2d 260 (1975); see also Justice Steven's dissent in *Danforth*, 96 Sup. Ct. at 2856.

97. Id. at 903, 530 P.2d at 262.

98. See In re Hudson, 13 Wash. 2d 673, 126 P.2d 765 (1942).

99. 84 Wash. 2d at 906, 530 P.2d 264.

100. Id. at 906–07, 530 P.2d at 264.

101. Id. at 907, 530 P.2d at 264–65.

102. Id. at 908, 530 P.2d at 265.

103. Id.; cf. Poe v. Gerstein, 517 F.2d 787 (5th Cir. 1975).

104. 84 Wash. 2d at 910–11, 530 P.2d at 266.

105. Id. at 911, 530 P.2d at 267.

106. Id. The court noted further the physician's common law duty "subjectively [to] evaluate the capacity of a minor to give informed and meaningful consent to any type of medical care." 911–12, 530 P.2d at 267.

107. Id. at 912, 530 P.2d at 267.

108. Id. at 913, 530 P.2d at 268.

109. Id., quoting Roe v. Wade, 410 U.S. 113, 166 (1973).

110. Lacey v. Laird, 66 Ohio St. 12, 139 N.E.2d 25 (1956).

111. Exceptions for venereal disease and drug treatment are provided by the Ohio statutes. Ohio Rev. Code Ann. §§ 3709.241, 3719.012 (Baldwin Cum. Supp. 1974). The other exceptions are familiar from the common law.

112. The memorandum's only possible reference to the decision is tucked in at the end of a paragraph dealing with another subject: "In individual circumstances with approval of an administrative officer, exceptions are permitted under a concept of 'emancipated minor.'" "Emancipation" as we have seen is a concept largely unrelated to maturity, and it is difficult to believe that this mention represents the hospital's lawyers's reading of the *Lacey* decision.

113. 406 U.S. 205, 245 n.3 (1972) (dissenting opinion).

114. Cf. Tabor v. Scobee, 254 S.W. 2d 474 (Ky. 1951).

115. Roe v. Wade, 410 U.S. 113, 154 (1973).

116. See Poe v. Gerstein, 517 F.2d 787, 791 (5th Cir. 1975).

117. Compare Justice Stevens' dissent in Planned Parenthood v. Danforth, 96 Sup. Ct. 2831, 2856 (1976). I wish to join neither philosophical nor theological issue about whether an abortion decision or any other is irreversible. At this point my focus is on the individual patient, and hence it is his or her perception of irreversibility that matters. To the extent that irreversibility might become relevant to legal questions, a collective societal sense of irreversibility inevitably becomes the important one.

118. See Ginsberg v. New York, 390 U.S. 629, 639 (1968).

119. See generally White v. Osborne, 251 N.C. 56, 110 S.E.2d 449 (1959); State ex rel. Byrnes v. Goldman, 59 Misc. 2d 570, 302 N.Y.S.2d 926, (Sup. Ct. 1969).

120. There are also costs to the parent in time, effort, and perhaps foregone opportunities. The financial one, however, is the most tangible.

121. See, e.g., Hart v. Brown, 29 Conn. Supp. 368, 289 A.2d 386 (Super. Ct. 1972); In re Richardson, 284 So. 2d 185 (La. App. 1973).

122. See State v. Koome, 84 Wash. 2d 901, 530 P.2d 260 (1975); Poe v. Gerstein, 517 F.2d 787 (5th Cir. 1975).

123. See, e.g., In re Sampson, 29 N.Y.2d 900, 278 N.E.2d 918, 328 N.Y.S. 2d 686 (1972).

124. See Poe v. Gerstein, 517 F.2d 787 (5th Cir. 1975); Baird v. Bellotti, 393 F. Supp. 847 (D. Mass. 1975); State v. Koome, 84 Wash. 2d 901, 530 P.2d 260 (1975); cf. Foe v. Vanderhoff, 389 F. Supp. 947 (D. Colo. 1975).

125. See Commonwealth ex. rel. Thomas v. Gillard, 203 Pa. Super. 95, 198 A.2d 377 (1964).

126. See, e.g., Anguis v. Superior Court, 6 Ariz. App. 68, 429 P.2d 702 (1967); Gorusch v. Gorusch, 143 Neb. 578, 11 N.W.2d 456 (1943); Oversmith v. Lake, 295 Mich. 627, 295 N.W. 339 (1940).

127. In re Rinker, 180 Pa. Super. 143, 148, 117 A.2d 780, 783 (1955); see In re Adoption of Children by N, 96 N.J. Super. 415, 233 A.2d 188 (App. Div. 1967); but cf. Painter v. Bannister, 258 Iowa 1390, 140 N.W.2d 152 (1966).

128. See, e.g., Commonwealth ex rel. Lotz v. Lotz 188 Pa. Super. 241, 146 A.2d 362 (1958); Ex parte Travis, 126 N.Y.S.2d 130 (Sup. Ct. 1953). The much discussed book by J. Goldstein, A. Freud and A. Solnit, Beyond the Best Interest of the Child (1973), assumes that it is appropriate to search for what is best for the child quite apart from any parental interest in such custody disputes. For a criticism of this assumption, quite proper in my view, see Strauss & Strauss, Book Review, 74 Colum. L. Rev. 996, 1000–01 (1974).

129. 405 U.S. 645 (1972).

130. Id. at 652.

131. Id. at 657. *Stanley's* bearing on the question of parental interest is obscured somewhat because the Court treated the problem as one of discrimination between fathers of legitimate and of illegitimate children and employed the equal protection clause to reach its conclusion. It is thus possible to argue that the state could treat Stanley as it did if it treated all or a different group of fathers in the same way. The language and obvious import of the decision, however, fully supports the textual discussion.

132. Compare Goss v. Lopez, 419 U.S. 565 (1975), with Meyer v. Nebraska, 262 U.S. 390 (1923).

133. See, e.g., Application of Auster, 198 Misc. 1055, 100 N.Y.S.2d 60 (Sup. Ct. 1950), *aff'd sub nom.* Auster v. Weberman 278 App. Div. 784, 104 N.Y.S. 2d 65, *aff'd*, 302 N.Y. 855, 100 N.E.2d 47, *appeal dismissed*, 342 U.S. 884 (1951).

134. See, e.g., People v. DeCaro, 17 Ill. App. 3d 553, 308 N.E.2d 196 (1974).

135. See, e.g., Baker v. Owen, 395 F. Supp. 294 (M.D.N.C. 1975).

136. Hobbs v. Germany, 94 Miss. 469, 49 So. 515 (1909); Jones v. Day, 127 Miss. 136, 89 So. 906 (1921).

137. See, e.g., In re Green, 12 Crime and Del. 377 (Milw. Co. Wisc. 1966).

138. See, e.g., Meyer v. Nebraska, 262 U.S. 390, 401 (1923).
139. Roe v. Wade, 410 U.S. 113, 162–63 (1973).
140. See, e.g., United States v. George, 239 F. Supp. 752 (D. Conn. 1965); Luka v. Lowrie 171 Mich. 122, 136 N.W. 1106 (1912).
141. The reason usually given is that a person may not exercise his religious liberty so as to "jeopardize the life or health of another." See comment, 12 Wash. & Lee L. Rev. 239, 247 (1955).
142. This problem creates mischief even if a case never reaches trial, because it affects settlement discussions.
143. This is the conclusion reached by the United States Supreme Court on the abortion question, though Justice Steven's dissent on the point seems to me more sensitive to the complexities involved. See Planned Parenthood v. Danforth, 96 Sup. Ct. 2831, 2842–44, 2856–57 (1976).
144. See 42 U.S.C. §§ 1398b (g)(1)(e), 1395x (k) (Supp. IV 1974).
145. The delineation of "compelling personal" decisions would probably require governmental definition and might ultimately have to be made in constitutionally based court decisions.

REFERENCES

Areen, J. "Intervention between parent and child: a reappraisal of the state's role in child neglect and abuse cases," 63 Geo. L.J., 887 (1975).

Baron, C., et al. "Live organ and tissue transplants from minor donors in Massachusetts," 55 B. U. L. Rev. 159 (1975).

Clark, H.H. *Law of Domestic Relations in the United States.* St. Paul, Minn.: West Publishing Co. (Hornbook Series), 1968.

Comment, 12 Wash. & Lee L. Rev. 239 (1955).

Council of Judges. *Guides to the Judge in Medical Orders Affecting Children.* New York: National Council on Crime and Delinquency, 1968.

Davis, K.C. *Discretionary Justice, A Preliminary Inquiry.* Baton Rouge, La.: La. State U. Press, 1969.

Ellis, J.W. "Volunteering children: parental commitment of minors to mental institutions," 62 Calif. L. Rev. 840 (1974).

Family Planning. See U.S. Department of Health, Education and Welfare.

Foster, H.H., Jr. "Relational interests of the family," Univ. of Ill. Law Forum 493 (1962).

Foster, H.H., Jr., and Freed, D.J. "A Bill of rights for children," 6 Fam. L. Q. 343 (1972).

Havighurst, C.C., and Blumstein, J.F. "Coping with quality/cost trade-offs in medical care: the role of PSROS," 70 Nw. U. L. Rev. 6 (1975).

Hofman, A.D. "Consent, confidentiality, the law and adolescents," 45 Del. Med. J. 35 (1973).

Katz, S.N., Schroeder, W.A., and Sidman, L.R. "Emancipating our children: coming of legal age in America," 7 Fam. L. Q. 211 (1973).

Mnookin, R.H. "Foster case—in whose best interest?" 43 Harv. Educ. Rev. 599 (1973).

National Academy of Sciences. *Genetic Screening.* Washington, D.C.: National Academy of Sciences, 1975.

Note, "Parental consent requirements and privacy rights of minors: the contraceptive controversy," 88 Harv. L. Rev. 1001 (1975).

Note, "State intrusion into family affairs: justifications and limitations," 26 Stan. L. Rev. 1383 (1974).

Paulsen, M.G. "The legal framework of child protection," 66 Colum. L. Rev. 679 (1966).

Pilpel, H.F. "Minor's rights to medical care," 36 Alb. L. Rev. 462 (1972).

Pilpel, H.F., and Zuckerman, R.J. "Abortion and the rights of minors," 23 Case W. Res. L. Rev. 779 (1972).

Pound, R. "Individual interests in the domestic relations," 14 Mich. L. Rev. 177 (1916).

Prosser, W.L. *Law of Torts.* St. Paul, Minn.: West Publishing Co. (Hornbook series), 1971.

Restatement of Torts, vol. 1, American Law Institute, 1934.

Senate Committee on the Judiciary. *Juvenile Delinquency*, S. Rep. No. 93–1424, 93d Congress 2d Session (1974).

tenBroek, J. "California's dual system of family law: its origins, development, and present status (Part III)," 17 Stan. L. Rev. 614 (1965).

U.S. Department of Health, Education and Welfare. *Family Planning, Contraception, and Voluntary Sterilization: An Analysis of Laws and Policies in the United States.* USDHEW Pub. No. (HSA) 74–160001. Washington, D.C.: Government Printing Office, 1974.

Wald, M. "State intervention on behalf of 'neglected' children: a search for realistic standards," 27 Stan. L. Rev. 985 (1975).

Waltz, J.R., and Scheuneman, T.W. "Informed consent to therapy," 64 Nw. U. L. Rev. 628 (1969).